Literacy, Economy and Society

Results of the first International Adult Literacy Survey

ORGANISATION FOR ECONOMIC CO-OPERATION AND DEVELOPMENT

STATISTICS CANADA

ORGANISATION FOR ECONOMIC CO-OPERATION AND DEVELOPMENT

Pursuant to Article 1 of the Convention signed in Paris on 14th December 1960, and which came int 30th September 1961, the Organisation for Economic Co-operation and Development (OECD) shall prom designed:

- to achieve the highest sustainable economic growth and employment and a rising standard of living countries, while maintaining financial stability, and thus to contribute to the development of the worl
- to contribute to sound economic expansion in Member as well as non-member countries in the process development; and
- to contribute to the expansion of world trade on a multilateral, non-discriminatory basis in accor international obligations.

The original Member countries of the OECD are Austria, Belgium, Canada, Denmark, France, German Iceland, Ireland, Italy, Luxembourg, the Netherlands, Norway, Portugal, Spain, Sweden, Switzerland, T United Kingdom and the United States. The following countries became Members subsequently through acces dates indicated hereafter: Japan (28th April 1964), Finland (28th January 1969), Australia (7th June 1971), Ne (29th May 1973) and Mexico (18th May 1994). The Commission of the European Communities takes part in th the OECD (Article 13 of the OECD Convention).

STATISTICS CANADA

Statistics Canada, Canada's central statistical agency, has the mandate to "collect, compile, analyse, and pu statistical information relating to the commercial, industrial, financial, social, economic and general activities and c tion of the people of Canada." The organization, a federal government agency, is headed by the Chief Statisticia Canada and reports to Parliament through the Minister of Industry Canada.

Statistics Canada provides information to governments at every level and is the source of statistical information business, labour, academic and social institutions, professional associations, the international statistical community, an the general public. This information is produced at the national and provincial levels and, in somes cases, for majc population centres and other sub-provincial or "small" areas.

The Agency fosters relations not only within Canada but also throughout the world, by participating in a number c international meetings and professional exchanges.

Note of Appreciation

Canada owes the success of its statistical system to a long-standing co-operation involving Statistics Canada, the citizens of Canada, its businesses, governments and other institutions. Accurate and timely statistical information could not be produced without their continued co-operation and goodwill.

Publié en français sous le titre :
Littératie, Économie et Société
Résultats de la première Enquête internationale sur l'alphabétisation des adultes.

FOREWORD

ort presents data from a seven-country comparative study of adult literacy. We believe the report will
nal policy makers with valuable insights into a variety of pressing social and economic issues, particularly
f education, human resources development, and related labour market policies.

hout this report, the term ''literacy'' is used to refer to a particular mode of behaviour – namely the ability
d and employ printed information in daily activities, at home, at work and in the community – to achieve
, and to develop one's knowledge and potential. In denoting a broad set of information-processing
s, this conceptual approach points to the multiplicity of skills that constitute literacy in advanced industrial-
es. In contrast, a term such as illiteracy, which is still widely used in many countries, fails to alert the reader
rtant facts that all people are literate to a degree, and that no single standard of literacy can be set.

nternational Adult Literacy Survey was made possible through a unique collaboration involving national
offices, policy makers, testing experts, and international organizations. Our hope is that the study will
ute to the debate about the importance of literacy, education and human resource development in our societies,
t it will serve as a model to others.

Ivan P. Fellegi
Chief Statistician of Canada
Statistics Canada

Thomas J. Alexander
Director for Education,
Employment, Labour and Social Affairs
Organisation for Economic Co-operation
and Development

This report is dedicated to the memory of Brendan Hickey, the National Study Manager for Ireland. Brendan died tragically in January 1995 before he could see the fruits of his labour. His good humour and intelligence helped make the International Adult Literacy Survey a success.

Table of Contents

List of tables

List of figures

Appendix B tables

Appendix C tables

Introduction

Adult literacy is seen as crucial to economic performance...

In recent years, adult literacy has come to be seen as crucial to the economic performance of industrialized nations. Literacy is no longer defined merely in terms of a basic threshold of reading ability, mastered by almost all those growing up in developed countries. Rather, literacy is now seen as how adults use written information to function in society. Today, adults need a higher level of literacy to function well: society has become more complex and low-skill jobs are disappearing. Therefore, inadequate levels of literacy among a broad section of the population potentially threaten the strength of economies and the social cohesion of nations.

...therefore governments and international bodies want to understand more about shortfalls in literacy skill levels...

With these high stakes, governments have a growing interest in understanding the level and distribution of literacy among their adult populations, and what can be done to improve them. In particular, they have been trying for the first time to measure adult literacy directly. Pioneering studies (Educational Testing Service 1986; The Creative Research Group 1987; Statistics Canada 1991; U.S. Department of Labor 1992; National Center for Education Statistics 1993) published in North America in the early 1990s revealed that a significant proportion of people lacked the literacy skills they were likely to need in their everyday lives. In 1992, the Organisation for Economic Co-operation and Development (OECD) concluded that low literacy levels were a serious threat to economic performance and social cohesion (OECD 1992). But a broader understanding of literacy problems across industrialized countries, and of consequent policy lessons, was hindered by a lack of comparable international data.

...and have supported a major study of adult literacy in seven countries.

The International Adult Literacy Survey (IALS) was a collaborative effort by seven governments and three intergovernmental organizations[1] to begin filling that information gap. A large sample of adults (ranging from 1,500 to 8,000 per country) in Europe and North America were given the same wide-ranging test of their literacy skills during the autumn of 1994. This report presents the results. The data paint the most detailed portrait ever available on the condition of adult literacy and its relationship with a host of background and demographic characteristics of European and North American adults.

The IALS aimed to make valid comparisons of people of all abilities across countries.

The IALS venture started out with two underlying goals. First, the aim was to develop scales that permitted useful comparisons of literacy performance among people with a wide range of abilities. Second, if such an assessment could be produced, the aim was to describe and compare the demonstrated literacy skills of people from different countries. This second objective presented the challenge of comparing literacy across cultures and across languages.

It was co-ordinated by two agencies in partnership with the partici- pating countries.

The development and management of the IALS were co-ordinated by Statistics Canada, the statistical arm of the Canadian government, and by the Educational Testing Service, the leading private testing organization in the United States. These organizations were guided by national research teams from the participating countries, who helped draw up the definitions adopted and develop the survey design. The IALS preparation built on national surveys that have been carried out in the United States and Canada to assess adult literacy.[2] It also drew on recent research and methodological and technical advances in assessment and psychometrics.

---

[1]   The international organizations, government agencies and government-appointed research organizations who collaborated in the IALS are listed at the end of this introduction (also see Appendix A).

[2]   Canada's 1989 Survey of Literacy Skills Used in Daily Activities and the 1990 National Adult Literacy Survey conducted in the United States.

The remainder of this introduction summarizes how the survey defined and measured literacy, how it was conducted, and how the results are reported in this volume.

Defining and measuring literacy

The IALS did not set a single international literacy standard...

Many previous studies have treated literacy as a condition that adults either have or do not have, and hence tried to count the number of illiterates. These efforts tend to define literacy in terms of a number of completed years of schooling or a grade-level score on school-based reading tests. The IALS survey design team agreed that it would be undesirable to establish a single international standard for literacy. Such a standard would not only be arbitrary, but would fail to acknowledge the multifaceted nature of literacy and the complexity of the literacy problem. Instead, the participating countries agreed that, in common with recent North American and Australian surveys (The Commonwealth Department of Employment, Education and Training 1989), the IALS would define literacy in terms of a mode of adult behaviour, namely:

> Using printed and written information to function in society, to achieve one's goals, and to develop one's knowledge and potential.

...but defined literacy in terms of a broad set of skills...

This definition attempts to encompass a broad set of information-processing skills that adults may be called upon to use in performing many different types of tasks—at work, at home, or in their communities. Some other types of knowledge and skill (including teamwork, interpersonal and other communication skills) were recognized as important, but could not be measured with the resources available.

...that can be grouped into three domains.

Literacy can neither be narrowed down to a single skill suited for dealing with all types of text, nor defined as an infinite set of skills, each particular to a different type of material. Following the example of the North American studies referred to above, the IALS experts decided to define literacy in terms of three domains, each encompassing a common set of skills relevant for diverse tasks:

1. *Prose literacy* - the knowledge and skills needed to understand and use information from texts including editorials, news stories, poems and fiction;

2. *Document literacy* - the knowledge and skills required to locate and use information contained in various formats, including job applications, payroll forms, transportation schedules, maps, tables and graphics; and

3. *Quantitative literacy* - the knowledge and skills required to apply arithmetic operations, either alone or sequentially, to numbers embedded in printed materials, such as balancing a chequebook, figuring out a tip, completing an order form or determining the amount of interest on a loan from an advertisement.[3]

In each domain, proficiency was expressed on a scale of 0 to 500, subdivided into five levels...

In each of these three domains, rather than expressing a threshold for achieving literacy, a scale from 0 to 500 was constructed, upon which tasks of varying difficulty were placed. A person's literacy ability in each domain can be expressed by a score, defined as the point at which he or she has an 80% chance of successfully performing a given task. For analytical purposes and for designing remedial programs, it is useful to group people into five levels of literacy, corresponding to ranges of scores achieved (for example, Level 1 includes scores from 0 to 225). This measurement system is described in more detail in Chapter 2.

---

[3] Quantitative literacy as defined in the IALS is equivalent to the term "numeracy" used in Canada's 1989 Survey of Literacy Skills Used in Daily Activities.

The use of these three parallel literacy scales makes it possible to profile and compare the various types and levels of literacy demonstrated by adults in several countries, and by subgroups within those countries. In doing so, they help us to understand the broad and diverse nature of literacy. The aim is not to establish a single international literacy standard, but to improve understanding of literacy's meaning, extent and distribution by policy makers, business leaders, educators and others.

How the survey was conducted

Testing adult literacy directly necessitates going to people's homes to assess their abilities in a manner usually done in schools. Thus the IALS, like the two preceding national studies in North America[4] was unusual because it combined the techniques of household-based survey research with those of educational testing. (However, in contrast with most standardized tests, multiple-choice questions were avoided; it was thought that adults would be more interested in answering open-ended questions.) In each case, the test was accompanied by a background questionnaire to obtain detailed information on demographic and other characteristics of the respondent.

Each country was obliged to draw a probability sample from which results representative of the civilian, non-institutionalized population aged 16 to 65 could be derived.[5] Countries were free to sample older adults too, and several did so. In six countries, the survey was carried out in the national language; in Canada, respondents were given a choice of English or French; in Switzerland, samples drawn from French-speaking and German-speaking cantons were required to respond in those respective languages (Italian- and Rhaeto-Romanic-speaking regions were excluded). When respondents could not speak the designated language, attempts were made to complete the background questionnaire to allow estimates of their literacy level and to reduce the possibility of distorted results.

Table I.1

Survey coverage, language of test and sample yields of the International Adult Literacy Survey

Country	Population aged 16 to 65 covered by the study	Language of test	Sample yield
Canada	13,676,612	English	3,130
	4,773,648	French	1,370
Germany	53,826,289	German	2,062
Netherlands	10,460,359	Dutch	2,837
Poland	24,475,649	Polish	3,000
Sweden	5,361,942	Swedish	2,645
Switzerland	1,008,275	French	1,435
	3,144,912	German	1,393
United States	161,121,972	English	3,053

---

[4]   Op. cit.

[5]   All IALS samples excluded full-time members of the military and inmates of institutions such as prisons, hospitals and psychiatric facilities.

In testing literacy internationally, a number of special factors needed to be taken into account. Although the IALS team agreed to adopt the North American definition of the three literacy scales, it noted that a new set of literacy tasks would need to be constructed to account for the various languages and cultures. Study managers from each participating country were encouraged to submit materials that could be used in constructing such tasks. The goal was to build a new pool of literacy tasks that could be linked to established scales.

One way of trying to guard against cultural bias in the results was by constructing a large number of tasks—considerably more than would technically have been needed to obtain statistically valid estimates of each person's literacy level. This built in a cross-check on results. In all, some 175 literacy tasks were constructed for the field test. Of these, some 114 tasks that proved valid across cultures were selected for the main assessment. About half of these tasks were based on materials originating from outside North America.

About 20 minutes of the interview were devoted to obtaining background and demographic information from respondents. These data provide a means for exploring how literacy is connected to social, educational, economic and other variables and for exploring the extent to which these relationships are similar across cultures.

No individual could be expected to respond to the entire set of 114 literacy tasks. Accordingly, the survey was designed to give each participant a subset of tasks that were carefully selected from the total pool, while at the same time ensuring that each task was administered to nationally representative samples of adults. Literacy tasks were assigned to blocks. Each test booklet consisted of three blocks, and was designed for completion in about 45 minutes. During a personal interview, each survey participant was first asked to complete a core booklet of six tasks, designed to avoid the embarassment of giving the full test to adults with very low literacy skills. Only those able to answer at least two tasks correctly in the core booklet (some 93.1% of respondents) were given the full test.

Reporting the results

The IALS has yielded a rich array of data on the literacy skills of adults in seven advanced industrialized nations, data that have been demonstrated to be comparable across language and culture. From the scientific perspective, this empirical validation of the literacy models underlying the assessment is perhaps the most important finding of the study. As the first international survey to test adult abilities directly, its results have a wide interest and will be useful for many different kinds of analysis. Each participating country will be able to make its own extensive use of the data. The present report can do no more than report some of the main findings at the international level. It does so in four main ways.

In Chapter 2, Irwin Kirsch of the Educational Testing Service in Princeton, New Jersey, presents the framework for understanding and interpreting literacy levels on the three scales, alongside the proportion of people achieving each level in each participating country. This chapter helps readers understand the results in the context of the multifaceted nature of literacy, and uses examples to demonstrate what the levels mean in terms of tasks performed.

A more detailed analysis of the distribution of literacy appears in Chapter 3, by Stan Jones of Carleton University in Ottawa, Canada. This chapter analyzes the shape of the distribution across the national populations—which differs considerably from one country to another. It also looks at the distribution of literacy skills among different subgroups, defined by initial educational attainment, age, immigration status, sex, employment status, industry, occupation, income and participation in adult education and training.

...the importance of the way literacy skills are actually used, in Chapter 4...

...and conclusions for policy makers, in Chapter 5.

But first, Chapter 1 explains why governments consider it so important to understand literacy.

In Chapter 4, Stan Jones explores the relationship between an array of literacy practices—at work and in the community—and levels of literacy. He shows how the actual use of literacy skills in daily life is quite closely related to tested abilities. This analysis demonstrates that practice sustains and enhances performance in literacy. Together, Chapters 3 and 4 shed light on the complex historical, social and economic factors that have led to observed literacy distributions. They identify factors closely associated with higher or lower literacy levels, either because they play a role in sustaining or hindering literacy throughout adult life, or because they are influenced by a person's literacy level.

A concluding chapter, written by T. Scott Murray of Statistics Canada, pulls together the key findings identified in the preceding four chapters, and points to the importance of these findings for policy. Its aim, however, is not to summarize all that can be made of the IALS results, but to encourage national authorities to undertake their own in-depth national analyses, making clear the full implications of the study for national priorities, policies and programs.

To put the IALS findings in context, it is important to understand the significance of literacy in a world that is rapidly changing into an "information society." To set the scene for the results reported here in chapter 1, Albert Tuijnman of the OECD Secretariat discusses why governments are taking a new interest in literacy. This chapter reviews the social and economic forces that created the impetus for IALS, and which render its findings so important.

Throughout this report, graphs have been used to communicate study results to a broad, non-technical audience, as well as to provide a source of informative displays that policy makers and others may use for their own purposes. To satisfy the more technical reader, detailed data tables are included in Appendices B and C at the end of the report.

The International Adult Literacy Survey is the product of a unique collaboration between governments and international organizations, which came together to provide the resources, the know-how, the political will and the hard work needed to bring the project to fruition. The following organizations were most directly involved in this collaboration[6]:

International organizations

OECD	Organisation for Economic Co-operation and Development, Directorate for Education, Employment, Labour and Social Affairs
European Union	Task Force for Human Resources, Education, Training and Youth, Commission of the European Union
	Statistical Office of the European Communities (EUROSTAT)
UNESCO	Institute for Education, Hamburg

National agencies and research organizations

CANADA	Human Resources Development Canada
	National Literacy Secretariat
	Statistics Canada
GERMANY	Federal Ministry of Education, Science, Research and Technology
	University of Hamburg
IRELAND	Educational Research Centre, St. Patrick's College[7]
NETHERLANDS	Max Goote Expert Center for Vocational and Continuing Education and Training
POLAND	Centre for Science Policy and Higher Education, Warsaw University
SWEDEN	National Agency for Education
	TEMO AB
SWITZERLAND	Swiss National Science Foundation, National Research Programme 33
	University of Zurich
UNITED STATES	National Center for Education Statistics
	Bureau of the Census
	National Institute for Literacy
	Office of Vocational and Adult Education, Department of Education
	Educational Testing Service

---

[6] Full details of the institutions and individuals who supported and conducted the study are given in Appendix A.

[7] Due to the untimely death of their National Study Manager it was not possible to include the Irish data in this volume. The IALS data for Ireland will be published by the Educational Research Centre in the spring of 1996.

Note to readers

Statistical error

Multiple sources of uncertainty and error are a fact of life in social science research. Given the comparative nature of the International Adult Literacy Survey (IALS), those responsible for the study's design and implementation went to extraordinary lengths to control and quantify such error and to establish the validity and reliability of the measures across languages and cultures. Yet error remains, error that must be taken into account in interpreting the statistical significance of observed differences in national means or proportions. A summary of the key sources of error present in the IALS study are presented below.

Firstly, the IALS data are based on samples of individuals and are therefore subject to sampling error. Given the small size of the IALS sample in some countries, many small differences observed between countries are not statistically significant.

Secondly, the IALS data are based on different combinations of test items being administered to sampled individuals, a fact that introduces a degree of imprecision into the estimation of ability. This source of error must also be taken into account in determining if observed differences are statistically significant.

The Educational Testing Service (ETS) has computed standard errors that capture the error associated with each estimate in the report. Interested readers may contact the publishers to obtain a diskette including these data.

Finally, subtle differences in design and implementation and in the pattern of non-response across countries may have introduced additional error. Such non-sampling error usually has a direction. Thus, if present, it can lead one to overestimate or underestimate the true size of differences between populations.

Statistics Canada, the ETS and the national study teams have performed extensive analyses to understand the nature and extent of error associated with the differences in design and implementation and have yet to find evidence of serious problems. The IALS has also been the subject of an independent quality review; the reviewers unanimously recommended publication of this report. Interested readers may obtain a copy of the quality review report and related technical documentation by contacting the publishers. Where analyses have uncovered idiosyncratic aspects of each country's study design, these are noted in the text.

References

Kirsch, Irwin S. and Ann Jungeblut. *Literacy: Profiles of America's Young Adults.* Princeton, N.J.: Educational Testing Service, 1986.

Kirsch, Irwin S., Ann Jungeblut and Anne Campbell. *Beyond the School Doors: The Literacy Needs of Job Seekers Served by the U.S. Department of Labor.* U.S. Department of Labor, 1992.

Kirsch, Irwin S., Jenkins, Lynn, Jungeblut, Ann and Kolstad, Andrew, *Adult Literacy in America: A First Look at the Results of the National Adult Literacy Survey.* Washington, D.C.: National Center for Education Statistics, U.S. Department of Education, 1993.

Montigny, Gilles, Karen Kelly and Stan Jones. *Adult Literacy in Canada: Results of a National Study.* Ottawa: Minister of Industry, Science and Technology (Statistics Canada, Catalogue no. 89-525E), 1991.

Organisation for Economic Co-operation and Development, *Adult Illiteracy and Economic Performance*, Paris, 1992.

The Creative Research Group. *Literacy in Canada: a research report* (Prepared for Southam News, Ottawa). Toronto, 1987.

Wickert, Rosie. *No Single Measure: A Survey of Australian Adult Literacy.* Canberra, Australia: The Commonwealth Department of Employment, Education, and Training, 1989.

Chapter 1

The importance of literacy in OECD societies

Albert Tuijnman, Education and Training Division, Organisation for Economic Co-operation and Development, Paris, France

Literacy has moved to centre stage on the policy agenda...

This opening chapter briefly explores why a group of major industrialized countries undertook—for the first time ever—a common survey and assessment of the literacy profiles of their adult populations. It reviews the major contextual changes that suggest OECD societies are in transition; specifically, countries face the challenge of managing a fundamental shift towards learning economies and societies. The trends and developments also explain why literacy has once again moved to the centre stage of policy agendas. The sea changes that have already occurred in society and the economy have changed skill requirements; notions of literacy have evolved concomitantly, broadening their relevance for policy. Against such a background, this chapter examines how the significant advances over many years—in the quality of schooling, participation rates, and the overall level of educational attainment—have not diminished, but have reinforced, the OECD countries' concern with literacy.

...because of a new phase of globalization...

In recent years, several factors have opened up the world to new global impulses. Accords such as the North American Free Trade Agreement and the Maastricht Treaty, which established the European Union, have eliminated certain barriers to cross-national trade. The deregulation of markets and financial services followed, along with the widespread diffusion of information and communication technologies and exploitation of increasingly efficient means of transportation. Globalization is not new; the factors that steer developments in this direction have been building for a long time. What is new, on the eve of the 21st century, however, is the specific nature and pace of the transformation. Until now, shifts in the relative comparative advantage of nations have occurred slowly and gradually. As a result, governments have been able to anticipate and adapt to the changes at an equally slow pace. In today's world, however, major shifts that influence the competitiveness of nations can occur quickly.

...bringing uncertainty and opportunities in terms of the use of labour...

The emerging global economy is characterized by greatly increased flows of information and financial capital, which both tend to decrease the traditional hold of governments and social partners over certain policy domains. In addition, the reintegration of the Central and Eastern European countries into the world economy, and the continuing rapid advance of industrialized countries in Asia and Latin America, have upset the economic status quo. OECD economies now face the reality of a large, well-educated and relatively low-wage labour force on their doorsteps. While new forms of co-operation across borders have emerged, competition for investment capital has also intensified. New opportunities—as well as uncertainties and risks—are inherent in this situation. Certain countries, firms and individuals are well positioned to compete successfully in global markets; others may have difficulty taking advantage of the opportunities. A massive reallocation of labour is expected to occur as OECD countries try to adapt and maintain their economic positions.

High-technology industries are often at the centre of policy discussions about the competitiveness of countries, because they are export-driven and because they generate the new technologies subsequently used throughout the economy. Over all OECD countries, from 1970 to 1991, low-technology, low-skill and low-wage industries saw their share of total employment decrease, while that of high-technology, high-skill and high-wage manufacturing expanded (OECD 1994a). Data show that the share of value added by high technology industries has increased since 1970, much more so in some countries than in others.

Long-established patterns of job entry and career progression are increasingly called into question as the knowledge content of jobs evolves and low-skill production is displaced or reallocated. Occupational projections for a number of countries suggest a continuing demand for moderately and highly skilled professional, technical and administrative workers, and a weakening demand for low-skilled workers (OECD 1995a). At the same time, literacy requirements have increased dramatically. Even though the citizens of OECD countries receive more education and their environments are richer in written materials than ever before, a large and increasing number of adults often find their skills are deficient in everyday situations.

As firms and labour markets change, some jobs become obsolete and new ones are created. The new jobs require literate workers. In a flexible economy that is well positioned to take advantage of change, people will need to change jobs—perhaps many times. Hence, workers need to continuously acquire new skills and qualifications. As the skill required for certain jobs increases, the pressure on poorly trained workers likewise increases. Whereas occupational change opens up new opportunities for literate and skilled individuals, this is not true for those who lack the appropriate skills, many of whom are at risk of long-term unemployment. Poorly trained adults who cannot adapt to new conditions and labour market demands face increased risks of social alienation and economic exclusion. This, in turn, poses the acute problem of how to upgrade the skills of the adult population.

Lifelong learning is an important means of acquiring new competencies and qualifications. Securing continued participation in the worlds of lifelong learning and employment depends first and foremost on adequate foundation skills. But governments can no longer rely on a policy of gradually expanding school enrolments and improving the quality of education over time to meet the demands for new and high-level competencies generated by the economy. The current rate of structural adjustment is producing serious mismatches between the supply of skills and demand for them. Because literacy has an effect on the ability of workers to learn efficiently and to be flexible in learning, it also has an effect on the rate at which a culture of lifelong learning can be realized. For some it is the *sine qua non* of workplace learning. Therefore, literacy will also have distributional effects.

The current demographic structures of labour markets throughout the industrialized world are such that whatever barriers to productivity and innovation are implied in the literacy and competency profiles of national populations, they are likely to persist over the next decades. As such, they assume a strategic importance of considerable magnitude. Literacy is also seen as a critical element in designing policies to lessen the economic burden associated with increasing dependency ratios. Literate senior citizens will also be far better equipped to maintain their independence and quality of life, thus lessening the need for social services. People who are literate by today's standards are much more likely to participate actively in the political processes that shape civil societies.

...as growth industries require high skills...

...which changes the relationship between skills and job prospects...

...and implies a growth in demand for literacy.

But there is a mismatch between this demand and the present supply of skills...

...exacerbated by the aging of the population...

The best way of exploiting the new economic environment is to strengthen the capacity of firms and labour markets to adjust to change, improve their productivity and capitalize on innovation (OECD 1994a). But this capacity depends first and foremost on the knowledge and skills of the population. People are the key resource and their level of literacy is a powerful determinant of a country's innovative and adaptive capacity. The distribution of literacy in a population is, moreover, a good predictor of the magnitude of differences between social groups. Literacy is therefore an essential element in any strategy for promoting social cohesion. An instrumental view of literacy, focussed on economic objectives only, is therefore untenable.

...as people need literacy more than ever before to organize the information that is accessible to them.

The emerging information economy changes both the expectations and demands on the population. In this new context information is abundant. Those lacking the skills and opportunities to access, organize and use this information in novel ways are at a disadvantage. More than ever, people need the literacy and analytical skills to search for and select the information they need, and to put it into perspective. A literate and educated population is the key to unlocking the benefits of globalization, including the diffusion of information technologies and structural adjustment, while safeguarding cherished values. But evidence from Canada and the United States suggests that literacy is not sufficiently developed (Montigny, Kelly and Jones1991; Kirsch, Jenkins, Jungeblut and Kolstad 1993). The challenges therefore call attention to the level and distribution of literacy in society, and to education, training and learning as means of acquiring and developing literacy. The central importance of the human factor in securing an adequate foundation for economic growth, personal development and social and cultural revitalization underscores the imperative of cultivating a highly literate population.

Why did this lead countries to participate in this international study?

So the case for the increased importance of the human factor in learning economies and societies is clear. But what does this have to do with a large-scale, international effort to measure various literacy dimensions, estimate the levels of literacy in entire populations, and profile these levels by classification variables such as age, sex, initial educational attainment, employment, occupational status, industry, and participation in adult education and continuing vocational training?

First, because policies to improve literacy need to draw on a strong knowledge base...

Cultivating and developing literacy should be an important element in every country's long-term policy strategies. Systematic knowledge about the dimensions and levels of literacy and sound information about its distribution in the population are prerequisites for formulating good policy (OECD 1995c). However, there are a number of questions. What are the conditions of literacy in OECD countries? What are the characteristics of effective policy? And is literacy susceptible to policy intervention? These questions were addressed, albeit in different ways and with varying success, in three comparative studies conducted during the early 1990s. These studies investigated the reading literacy and computer literacy of school-based populations in several countries (Postlethwaite and Ross 1992; Pelgrum and Plomp 1993; Elley 1994). Until now, however, information on literacy in the labour force—with the exceptions of Australia, Canada and the United States—was limited. Most public discussion and practical action was based on indirectly obtained information, or on data relevant to limited subpopulations.

...and existing knowledge of educational attainment across countries is deficient...

The OECD-INES (Indicators of National Education Systems) project on developing education indicators provided data on the levels of formal schooling and initial educational attainment in member countries (OECD 1994b; OECD 1995b). However useful such indicators may be in profiling qualification levels, a drawback is that the methodology is not always applied consistently across countries. The qualification profiles are based on the percentage of the population that has reached a certain level defined in accordance with the International Standard Classification of Education (ISCED), but the definition of the contents constituting such levels differ across countries, and there is large variation in

...in particular in terms of measures of adults' performance rather than just their qualifications.

Second, to identify differences between groups, to help target policy interventions.

Literacy is a relative concept that must be set in the context of economic and social demands...

performance within the ISCED levels. Hence, such statistics provide only indirect and quite poor measures of the skills and competencies of each group.

Because people learn on the job and develop their adult roles in community and work, relying on an indirect measure such as initial schooling is certain to misrepresent the actual stock of knowledge and skills available for the labour market. Some skills, if not used in the post-education years, deteriorate rapidly while others do not; other skills are acquired, by and large, independent of formal education and training. The findings reported in this volume make it possible, for the first time, to compare the performance levels associated with the educational qualifications awarded in the participating countries. Moreover, in so far as human capital investment decisions require information concerning skill appreciation and depreciation, the IALS results point to important conclusions about the framework conditions for policy.

A second reason for undertaking the IALS was to increase our understanding of the literacy conditions and profiles of specific subpopulations. Much has been written about the need for improving the efficiency of the labour market in assessing and pricing competence, and overcoming the problems of under-investment in the skill development of certain subpopulations. The data collected in the IALS suggest that literacy is a recognized and rewarded skill. This finding might contradict the idea that knowledge and skill are mostly tacit and difficult to evaluate. If employers reward quantifiable skills then the debate on income distributions should be focussed on securing sufficient high-quality educational access and learning opportunities relevant to the conditions and needs of disadvantaged groups. Market failures, which are prevalent in education and training (Berryman, in press), generally point to a need for government intervention. But devising sound and effective policy to offset the biases inherent in education and training markets requires information not only about the levels of literacy, but especially about the distribution across a large number of classification variables. Then, intervention programs may be better targeted towards those who need them most. The IALS was undertaken with the explicit aim of supplying such information, and to validate the results and facilitate their interpretation in an international and comparative context.

Until recently, the level of literacy was often inferred from data about the percentage of the population that had attended four to six years of primary schooling. Serious deficiencies beset such an approach. It is based on the notion that literacy can be expressed as a dichotomy: either you have it or you do not. But because literacy involves a complex and multidimensional set of traits, dispositions and competencies, thinking in terms of a single literacy cut-off— you are literate when you can read simple prose or if you have received at least four years of schooling, and illiterate when you cannot and have not— is neither appropriate nor conducive to formulating sound policy strategies. Although useful in helping governments gauge the magnitude of the literacy "problem," the use of a discrete dichotomy has limited the discourse in a number of ways. Firstly, illiteracy has come to be treated as a pathological condition, as a "disease" that afflicts an unfortunate few. A second unfortunate consequence of the literacy dichotomy has been the suppressed debate about the adequacy of the skills of those judged to be literate. Literacy is, in effect, a relative concept that can be given meaning only in relation to the demands of the economy and society. Adults who are highly literate in terms of being able to understand and act upon complex messages contained in a text may be completely at a loss when other domains of literacy are considered. At a time when societal demands are growing, even those judged to be literate may need remedial education or skills upgrading. An additional objective of the IALS survey was, therefore, to assess literacy performance along three continuous scales—prose, document and quantitative. This reporting framework recognizes that everyone has some level of proficiency, which may or may not be sufficient given the skills demanded.

...and the IALS is based on a powerful theory of what factors underlie difficulty in adult reading...

...which is enriched by an international perspective...

...and provides a unique database for research on effective literacy instruction.

The IALS builds on the seminal work of Kirsch and Mosenthal (1990) with respect to adult reading. The IALS exploits their theoretical framework, which explains the factors that underlie difficulty in adult reading. Previously, empirical work on adult literacy employed theories and models that offered little predictive value and virtually no differentiation between levels of ability. This new theoretical framework has opened the way to the efficient assessment of adult literacy proficiencies. Its cognitive roots offer educators insight into designing more efficient and effective initial and remedial education curricula.

Conditions and attributes of literacy are not static, neither over time nor across countries, an argument in favour of comparative assessment. Unless it is possible to use the results obtained in an assessment of literacy profiles in a population as a benchmark to measure results from different contexts and in different countries, validating and interpreting the results will be difficult, and the formulation of policy conclusions may be misguided. A strong point about the IALS survey is that the findings are classified by a range of background variables, so that increased understanding is facilitated, while the comparative analysis strengthens the reliability and validity parameters.

A further reason for measuring the distribution of literacy in the adult population is that little information is currently available about the cause-and-effect relationships that can explain the intertwined processes of skill acquisition and obsolescence. Why is it that some adults with little former education perform at a higher level than that predicted by background variables, while others with a more privileged educational career and adequate opportunities to learn fail to develop their skills? Understanding these processes is crucial to the design of successful adult literacy instruction. Increased knowledge of the factors that influence acquisition processes and outcomes is essential if effective instructional practices for different skill domains and different categories of adults are to be identified. The information collected in the survey will permit the building of statistical models, providing an important impetus for the research field and, in the longer run, for the development of good practice.

References

Berryman, Sue B. "The contribution of literacy to the wealth of individuals and nations." In *Adult Basic Skills: Advances in Measurement and Policy Analysis.* Edited by Albert Tuijnman, Irwin Kirsch and Daniel A. Wagner. New York: Hampton Press, in press.

Elley, Warwick B., ed. *The International Association for the Evaluation of Educational Achievement (IEA) Study of Reading Literacy: Achievement and Instruction in Thirty-two School Systems.* Oxford: Pergamon Press, 1994.

Kirsch, Irwin S., et al. *Adult Literacy in America: A First Look at the Results of the National Adult Literacy Survey.* Washington, D.C.: National Center for Education Statistics, U.S. Department of Education, 1993.

Kirsch, Irwin S. and Peter Mosenthal. "Exploring Document Literacy: Variables Underlying the Performance of Young Adults, " *in Reading Research Quarterly*, (25, 1990): 5-30.

Montigny, Gilles, Karen Kelly and Stan Jones. *Adult Literacy in Canada: Results of a National Study.* Ottawa: Minister of Industry, Science and Technology (Statistics Canada, Catalogue no. 89-525E), 1991.

Organisation for Economic Co-operation and Development. *The Jobs Study*, Vols. I-II. Paris, 1994a.

Organisation for Economic Co-operation and Development. *Making Education Count: Developing and Using Education Indicators.* Paris, 1994b.

Organisation for Economic Co-operation and Development. *Employment Outlook.* Paris, 1995a.

Organisation for Economic Co-operation and Development. *Education at a Glance*, 1995 Edition. Paris, 1995b.

Organisation for Economic Co-operation and Development. *Educational Research and Development: Trends and Issues.* Paris, 1995c.

Pelgrum, Willem J. and Tjeerd Plomp, eds. *The IEA Study of Computers in Education: Implementation and Innovation in 21 Education Systems.* Oxford: Pergamon Press, 1993.

Postlethwaite, T. Neville and Kenneth N. Ross. *Effective Schools in Reading: Implications for Educational Planners.* The Hague: IEA, 1992.

Chapter 2

Literacy performance on three scales: definitions and results

Irwin S. Kirsch, Educational Testing Service, Princeton, New Jersey, United States

This chapter explains how to read the results of performance on the three literacy scales...

The performance results for the 1994 International Adult Literacy Survey (IALS) are reported on three scales — prose, document and quantitative — rather than on a single scale. Each scale ranges from 0 to 500. Scale scores have, in turn, been grouped into five empirically determined literacy levels. As illustrated on page 29, each of these levels implies an ability to cope with a particular subset of reading tasks. The balance of this chapter reports the proficiency achieved on each scale by adults in each participating country, and explains how to interpret this data by describing the scales and the kinds of tasks that were used in the test and the literacy levels that have been adopted.

...which have no intrinsic meaning...

While the literacy scales make it possible to compare the prose, document and quantitative skills of different populations and to study the relationships between literacy skills and various factors, the scale scores by themselves carry little or no meaning. In other words, whereas most people have a practical understanding of what it means when the temperature outside reaches 10°C, it is not intuitively clear what it means when a particular group is at 287 on the prose scale, or 250 on the document scale, or in Level 2 on the quantitative scale.

...but relate to tasks and the skills needed to perform them.

One way to gain some understanding about what it means to perform at various points along a literacy scale is to identify a set of variables that can be shown to underlie performance on these tasks. Collectively, these variables provide a framework for understanding what is being measured in a particular assessment and what skills and knowledge are being demonstrated by various levels of proficiency.

The chapter defines the scales and levels, gives examples of tasks and gives country results at each level.

Toward this end, the chapter begins by describing how the literacy scale scores were defined. A detailed description of the prose, document and quantitative literacy scales is then provided, including a definition of each of the five levels and the percentages of adults in each of the participating countries demonstrating proficiency in each level. Sample tasks are presented to illustrate the types of materials and task demands that characterize the five levels on each scale.

Defining the literacy levels

The scales were set up by looking at how people actually perform on various tasks...

The item response theory (IRT) scaling procedures that were used in the IALS provide a statistical solution for establishing one or more scales for a set of tasks in which the ordering of difficulty is essentially the same for everyone. First, the difficulty of tasks is ranked on the scale according to how well respondents actually perform them. Next, individuals are assigned scores according to how well they do on a variety of tasks at different levels.

...and defining proficiency as having an 80% chance of completing a task at a particular level...

...just as a high jumper is proficient at a height that she or he can usually clear.

The tasks on each scale are ordered according to the skills needed to complete them...

...which can be grouped into five levels requiring successively higher orders of skill...

...which will now be described.

The scale point assigned to each task is the point at which individuals with that proficiency score have a given probability of responding correctly. In this survey, an 80% probability of correct response was the criterion used. This means that individuals estimated to have a particular scale score will consistently perform tasks — with an 80% probability — like those at that point on the scale. It also means they will have a greater than 80% chance of performing tasks that are lower than their estimated proficiency on the scale. It does not mean, however, that individuals with low proficiency can never succeed at more difficult tasks — that is, on tasks with difficulty values higher than their proficiencies. They may do so some of the time. Thus, it means that their probability of success is relatively low. In other words, the more difficult the task relative to their proficiency, the lower the likelihood of a correct response.

An analogy might help clarify this point. The relationship between task difficulty and individual proficiency is much like the high jump event in track and field, in which an athlete tries to jump over a bar that is placed at increasing heights. Each high jumper has a height at which he or she is proficient. That is, the jumper can clear the bar at that height with a high probability of success, and can clear the bar at lower heights almost every time. When the bar is higher than the athlete's level of proficiency, however, it is expected that the athlete will be unable to clear the bar consistently.

Once the literacy tasks are placed along each of the scales using the criterion of 80%, it is possible to see how well the interactions among various task characteristics explain the placement of tasks along the scales. Analyses of the interactions between the materials being read and the tasks based on these materials reveal that an ordered set of information-processing skills appears to be called into play to successfully perform the various tasks displayed along each scale (Kirsch and Mosenthal 1994).

To capture this order, each scale is divided into five levels reflecting the empirically determined progression of information-processing skills and strategies:

- Level 1 (0 to 225)
- Level 2 (226 to 275)
- Level 3 (276 to 325)
- Level 4 (326 to 375)
- Level 5 (376 to 500).

It is worth noting that, while some of the tasks were at the low end of a scale and some at the very high end, most had values in the 200-to-400 range. It is also important to recognize that these levels were selected not as a result of any statistical property of the scales, but rather as the result of shifts in the skills and strategies required to succeed on various tasks along the scales, ranging from simple to complex.

The remainder of this report describes each scale in terms of the nature of task demands at each of the five levels, and reports the proportion of respondents proficient at each level in each country. For each scale, sample tasks at each level are presented, and the factors contributing to their difficulty are discussed. The aim of this chapter is to provide meaning to the scales and to facilitate interpretation of the overall results as well as the breakdowns given in the subsequent chapters.

	Prose	Document	Quantitative
Level 1 (0 to 225)	Most of the tasks at this level require the reader to locate one piece of information in the text that is identical or synonymous to the information given in the directive. If a plausible incorrect answer is present in the text, it tends not to be near the correct information.	Most of the tasks at this level require the reader to locate a piece of information based on a literal match. Distracting information, if present, is typically located away from the correct answer. Some tasks may direct the reader to enter personal information onto a form.	Although no quantitative tasks used in the IALS fall below the score value of 225, experience suggests that such tasks would require the reader to perform a single, relatively simple operation (usually addition) for which either the numbers are already entered onto the given document and the operation is stipulated, or the numbers are provided and the operation does not require the reader to borrow.
Level 2 (226 to 275)	Tasks at this level tend to require the reader to locate one or more pieces of information in the text, but several distractors may be present, or low-level inferences may be required. Tasks at this level also begin to ask readers to integrate two or more pieces of information, or to compare and contrast information.	Document tasks at this level are a bit more varied. While some still require the reader to match on a single feature, more distracting information may be present or the match may require a low-level inference. Some tasks at this level may require the reader to enter information onto a form or to cycle through information in a document.	Tasks in this level typically require readers to perform a single arithmetic operation (frequently addition or subtraction) using numbers that are easily located in the text or document. The operation to be performed may be easily inferred from the wording of the question or the format of the material (for example, a bank deposit form or an order form).
Level 3 (276 to 325)	Tasks at this level tend to direct readers to search texts to match information that require low-level inferences or that meet specified conditions. Sometimes the reader is required to identify several pieces of information that are located in different sentences or paragraphs rather than in a single sentence. Readers may also be asked to integrate or to compare and contrast information across paragraphs or sections of text.	Tasks at this level appear to be most varied. Some require the reader to make literal or synonymous matches, but usually the matches require the reader to take conditional information into account or to match on multiple features of information. Some tasks at this level require the reader to integrate information from one or more displays of information. Other tasks ask the reader to cycle through a document to provide multiple responses.	Tasks found in this level typically require the reader to perform a single operation. However, the operations become more varied—some multiplication and division tasks are found in this level. Sometimes two or more numbers are needed to solve the problem and the numbers are frequently embedded in more complex displays. While semantic relation terms such as "how many" or "calculate the difference" are often used, some of the tasks require the reader to make higher order inferences to determine the appropriate operation.
Level 4 (326 to 375)	These tasks require readers to perform multiple-feature matching or to provide several responses where the requested information must be identified through text-based inferences. Tasks at this level may also require the reader to integrate or contrast pieces of information, sometimes presented in relatively lengthy texts. Typically, these texts contain more distracting information and the information that is requested is more abstract.	Tasks at this level, like those in the previous levels, ask the reader to match on multiple features of information, to cycle through documents, and to integrate information; frequently however, these tasks require the reader to make higher order inferences to arrive at the correct answer. Sometimes, conditional information is present in the document, which must be taken into account by the reader.	With one exception, the tasks at this level require the reader to perform a single arithmetic operation where typically either the quantities or the operation are not easily determined. That is, for most of the tasks at this level, the question or directive does not provide a semantic relation term such as "how many" or "calculate the difference" to help the reader.
Level 5 (376 to 500)	Some tasks at this level require the reader to search for information in dense text that contains a number of plausible distractors. Some require readers to make high-level inferences or use specialized knowledge.	Tasks at this level require the reader to search through complex displays of information that contain multiple distractors, to make high-level inferences, process conditional information, or use specialized knowledge.	These tasks require readers to perform multiple operations sequentially, and they must disembed the features of the problem from the material provided or rely on background knowledge to determine the quantities or operations needed.

Interpreting the literacy levels

Prose literacy

Prose literacy is measured using various types of textual material...

The ability to understand and use information contained in various kinds of textual material is an important aspect of literacy. The International Adult Literacy Survey therefore included an array of prose selections, including text from newspapers, magazines and brochures. The material varied in length, density, content, and use of structural or organizational aids such as headings, bullets and special typefaces. All prose samples were reprinted in their entirety with the original layout and typography intact.

...and asking the reader to perform tasks requiring information-processing skills...

Each prose selection was accompanied by one or more questions or directives asking the reader to perform specific tasks. These tasks represent three major aspects of information-processing: ***locating***, ***integrating*** and ***generating***. Locating tasks require the reader to find information in the text based on conditions or features specified in the question or directive. The match may be literal or synonymous, or the reader may need to make an inference in order to perform successfully. Integrating tasks ask the reader to pull together two or more pieces of information in the text. In some cases the information can be found in a single paragraph, while in others it appears in different paragraphs or sections. In the generating tasks, readers must produce a written response by processing information from the text and also by making text-based inferences or drawing on their own background knowledge.

...with 34 tasks of varying difficulty being included in the IALS.

In all, the prose literacy scale includes 34 tasks with difficulty values ranging from 188 to 377. These tasks are distributed by level as follows: Level 1 (5 tasks); Level 2 (9 tasks); Level 3 (14 tasks); Level 4 (5 tasks); and Level 5 (1 task). It is important to remember that the tasks requiring the reader to locate, integrate and generate information extend over a range of difficulty as a result of interactions with other variables including:

- the number of categories or features of information the reader must process

- the extent to which information given in the question or directive is obviously related to the information contained in the text

- the amount and location of information in the text that shares some of the features with the information being requested and thus, seems plausible but does not fully answer the question; these are called "distractors"

- the length and density of the text.

The five levels of prose literacy are defined on the following pages.

Percentage of adults by country performing at Level 1:

Canada	16.6
Germany	14.4
Netherlands	10.5
Poland	42.6
Sweden	7.5
Switzerland (French)	17.6
Switzerland (German)	19.3
United States	20.7

Prose Level 1   **Score range: 0 to 225**

Most of the tasks at this level require the reader to locate one piece of information in the text that is identical or synonymous to the information given in the directive. If a plausible incorrect answer is present in the text, it tends not to be near the correct information.

Tasks at this level require the reader to locate and match a single piece of information in the text. Typically the match between the task and the text is literal, although sometimes a low-level inference may be necessary. The text is usually brief or has organizational aids such as paragraph headings or italics that suggest where in the text the reader should search for the specified information. Generally, the target word or phrase appears only once in the text.

The easiest task in Level 1 (difficulty value of 188) directs respondents to look at a medicine label to determine the "maximum number of days you should take this medicine." The label contains only one reference to number of days and this information is located under the heading "DOSAGE." The reader must go to this part of the label and locate the phrase "not longer than 7 days."

MEDCO ASPIRIN   *500*

INDICATIONS: Headaches, muscle pains, rheumatic pains, toothaches, earaches. RELIEVES COMMON COLD SYMPTOMS.

DOSAGE: ORAL. 1 or 2 tablets every 6 hours, preferably accompanied by food, for not longer than 7 days. Store in a cool, dry place.

CAUTION: Do not use for gastritis or peptic ulcer. Do not use if taking anticoagulant drugs. Do not use for serious liver illness or bronchial asthma. If taken in large doses and for an extended period, may cause harm to kidneys. Before using this medication for chicken pox or influenza in children, consult with a doctor about Reyes Syndrome, a rare but serious illness. During lactation and pregnancy, consult with a doctor before using this product, especially in the last trimester of pregnancy. If symptoms persist, or in case of an accidental overdose, consult a doctor. Keep out of reach of children.

INGREDIENTS: Each tablet contains 500 mg acetylsalicylic acid.
Excipient c.b.p.   1 tablet.
Reg. No. 88246

Made in Canada by STERLING PRODUCTS, INC.
1600 Industrial Blvd., Montreal, Quebec H9J 3P1

0 67736 11079

Reprinted by permission

Percentage of adults by country performing at Level 2:

Canada	25.6
Germany	34.2
Netherlands	30.1
Poland	34.5
Sweden	20.3
Switzerland (French)	33.7
Switzerland (German)	35.7
United States	25.9

Prose Level 2   Score range: 226 to 275

Tasks at this level tend to require the reader to locate one or more pieces of information in the text, but several distractors may be present, or low-level inferences may be required. Tasks at this level also begin to ask readers to integrate two or more pieces of information, or to compare and contrast information.

Like the tasks at Level 1, most of the tasks at Level 2 ask the reader to locate information. However, more varied demands are placed on the reader in terms of the number of responses the question requires, or in terms of the distracting information that may be present. For example, a task based on an article about the impatiens plant asks the reader to determine what happens when the plant is exposed to temperatures of 14°C or lower. A sentence under the section "**General care**" states that "When the plant is exposed to temperatures of 12-14°C, it loses its leaves and won't bloom anymore." This task received a difficulty value of 230, just in the Level 2 range. What made this task somewhat harder than those identified at Level 1 is that the previous sentence in the text contains information about the requirements of the impatiens plant in various temperatures. This information could have distracted some readers, making the task slightly more difficult.

IMPATIENS

Like many other cultured plants, impatiens plants have a long history behind them. One of the older varieties was sure to be found on grandmother's windowsill. Nowadays, the hybrids are used in many ways in the house and garden.

Origin: The ancestors of the impatiens, *Impatiens sultani* and *Impatiens holstii*, are probably still to be found in the mountain forests of tropical East Africa and on the islands off the coast, mainly Zanzibar. The cultivated European plant received the name *Impatiens walleriana.*

Appearance: It is a herbaceous bushy plant with a height of 30 to 40 cm. The thick, fleshy stems are branched and very juicy, which means, because of the tropical origin, that the plant is sensitive to cold. The light green or white speckled leaves are pointed, elliptical, and slightly indented on the edges. The smooth leaf surfaces and the stems indicate a great need of water.

Bloom: The flowers, which come in all shades of red, appear plentifully all year long, except for the darkest months. They grow from "suckers" (in the stem's "armpit").

Assortment: Some are compact and low-growing types, about 20 to 25 cm. high, suitable for growing in pots. A variety of hybrids can be grown in pots, window boxes, or flower beds. Older varieties with taller stems add dramatic colour to flower beds.

General care: In summer, a place in the shade without direct sunlight is best; in fall and spring, half-shade is best. When placed in a bright spot during winter, the plant requires temperatures of at least 20°C; in a darker spot, a temperature of 15°C will do. When the plant is exposed to temperatures of 12-14°C, it loses its leaves and won't bloom anymore. In wet ground, the stems will rot.

Watering: The warmer and lighter the plant's location, the more water it needs. Always use water without a lot of minerals. It is not known for sure whether or not the plant needs humid air. In any case, do not spray water directly onto the leaves, which causes stains.

Feeding: Feed weekly during the growing period from March to September.

Repotting: If necessary, repot in the spring or in the summer in light soil with humus (prepacked potting soil). It is better to throw the old plants away and start cultivating new ones.

Propagating: Slip or use seeds. Seeds will germinate in ten days.

Diseases: In summer, too much sun makes the plant woody. If the air is too dry, small white flies or aphids may appear.

A similar task involving the same text asks the reader to identify "what the smooth leaf and stem suggest about the plant." The second paragraph of the article is labelled "**Appearance**" and contains a sentence that states, ". . . stems are branched and very juicy, which means, because of the tropical origin, that the plant is sensitive to cold." This sentence distracted some readers from the last sentence in the paragraph: "The smooth leaf surfaces and the stems indicate a great need of water." This task received a difficulty value of 254, placing it in the middle of Level 2.

Percentage of adults by country performing at Level 3:

Canada	35.1
Germany	38.0
Netherlands	44.1
Poland	19.8
Sweden	39.7
Switzerland (French)	38.6
Switzerland (German)	36.1
United States	32.4

Prose Level 3	Score range: 276 to 325

Tasks at this level tend to direct readers to search texts to match information that require low-level inferences or that meet specified conditions. Sometimes the reader is required to identify several pieces of information that are located in different sentences or paragraphs rather than in a single sentence. Readers may also be asked to integrate or to compare and contrast information across paragraphs or sections of text.

Tasks at Level 3 on the prose scale tend to require the reader to search for information that requires low-level inferences or that meet conditions stated in the question. Sometimes the reader needs to identify several pieces of information that are located in different sentences or paragraphs rather than in a single sentence. Readers may also be asked to integrate or to compare and contrast information across paragraphs or sections of text.

A task at this level (with a difficulty value of 281) refers the reader to a page from a bicycle owner's manual to determine how to check to make sure the seat is in the proper position. The reader must locate the section labelled "**Fitting the Bicycle**." Then readers must identify and summarize the correct information in writing, making sure the conditions stated are contained in their summary.

PROPER FRAME FIT

RIDER MUST BE ABLE TO STRADDLE BICYCLE WITH AT LEAST 2 cm CLEARANCE ABOVE THE HORIZONTAL BAR WHEN STANDING.

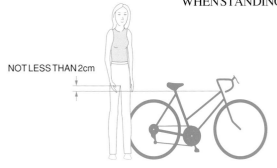

NOT LESS THAN 2cm

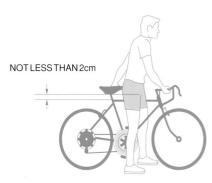

NOT LESS THAN 2cm

NOTE: Measurement for a female should be determined using a men's model as a basis.

PROPER SIZE OF BICYCLE	
FRAME SIZE	LEG LENGTH OF RIDER
430mm	660mm-760mm
460mm	690mm-790mm
480mm	710mm-790mm
530mm	760mm-840mm
560mm	790mm-860mm
580mm	810mm-890mm
635mm	860mm-940mm

OWNER'S RESPONSIBILITY

1. **Bicycle Selection and Purchase:** Make sure this bicycle fits the intended rider. Bicycles come in a variety of sizes. Personal adjustment of seat and handlebars is necessary to assure maximum safety and comfort. Bicycles come with a wide variety of equipment and accessories . . . make sure the rider can operate them.

2. **Assembly:** Carefully follow all assembly instructions. Make sure that all nuts, bolts and screws are securely tightened.

3. **Fitting the Bicycle:** To ride safely and comfortably, the bicycle must fit the rider. Check the seat position, adjusting it up or down so that with the sole of rider's foot on the pedal in its lowest position the rider's knee is slightly bent.

Note: Specific charts illustrated at left detail the proper method of deter-mining the correct frame size.

The manufacturer is not responsible for failure, injury, or damage caused by improper completion of assembly or improper maintenance after shipment.

A second Level 3 task, receiving a difficulty value of 310, directs the reader to look at a set of four movie reviews to determine which review was least favourable. Unlike some reviews that rate movies by points or some graphic such as stars, these reviews contain no such indicators. The reader needs to glance at the text of each review to compare what the reviewer said in order to judge which movie received the worst rating.

Another Level 3 question involved an article about cotton diapers. Here readers were asked to write three reasons why the author prefers to use cotton diapers over disposable diapers. This task was relatively difficult (318) because of several variables. First, the reader has to provide several answers requiring text-based inferences. Nowhere in the text does the author say, "I prefer cotton diapers because . . . ." These inferences are made somewhat more difficult because the type of information being requested is a "reason" rather than something more concrete such as a date or person. And finally, the text contains information that may distract the reader.

Percentage of adults by country performing at Level 4:	
Canada	20.0
Germany	12.3
Netherlands	14.6
Poland	2.9
Sweden	26.1
Switzerland (French)	9.5
Switzerland (German)	8.7
United States	17.3

Prose Level 4   **Score range: 326 to 375**

These tasks require readers to perform multiple-feature matching or to provide several responses where the requested information must be identified through text-based inferences. Tasks at this level may also require the reader to integrate or contrast pieces of information, sometimes presented in relatively lengthy texts. Typically, these texts contain more distracting information and the information that is requested is more abstract.

One task falling in the middle of Level 4 with a difficulty value of 338 directs readers to use the information from a pamphlet about a hiring interview to "write in your own words one difference between the panel interview and the group interview." Here readers needed to read the brief descriptions about each type of interview. And, rather than merely locating a fact about each or identifying a similarity, they need to integrate what was being presented to infer a characteristic on which the two types of interviews differ. Experience from other large-scale assessments reveals that tasks in which readers are asked to contrast information are more difficult, on average, than tasks in which they are asked to compare information to find similarities.

The Hiring Interview

Preinterview

Try to learn more about the business. What products does it manufacture or services does it provide? What methods or procedures does it use? This information can be found in trade directories, chamber of commerce or industrial directories, or at your local employment office.

Find out more about the position. Would you replace someone or is the position newly created? In which departments or shops would you work? Collective agreements describing various standardized positions and duties are available at most local employment offices. You can also contact the appropriate trade union.

The Interview

Ask questions about the position and the business. Answer clearly and accurately all questions put to you. Bring along a note pad as well as your work and training documents.

The Most Common Types of Interview

One-on-one: Self explanatory.

Panel: A number of people ask you questions and then compare notes on your application.

Group: After hearing a presentation with other applicants on the position and duties, you take part in a group discussion.

Postinterview

Note the key points discussed. Compare questions that caused you difficulty with those that allowed you to highlight your strong points. Such a review will help you prepare for future interviews. If you wish, you can talk about it with the placement officer or career counsellor at your local employment office.

Canada	2.7
Germany	1.1
Netherlands	0.7
Poland	0.1
Sweden	6.4
Switzerland (French)	0.5
Switzerland (German)	0.3
United States	3.8

Document literacy refers to success in processing everyday documents...

...with 34 tasks of varying difficulty being included in the IALS...

Prose Level 5   **Score range: 376 to 500**

Some tasks at this level require the reader to search for information in dense text that contains a number of plausible distractors. Some require readers to make high-level inferences or use specialized knowledge.

Two tasks used in this assessment fell in Level 5. One of these tasks, receiving a difficulty value of 377, requires the reader to look at an announcement from a personnel department and "list two ways in which CIEM helps people who will lose their jobs because of a departmental reorganization." The correct response requires readers to search through this text to locate the embedded sentence "CIEM acts as a mediator for employees who are threatened with dismissal resulting from reorganization, and assists with finding new positions when necessary." This task is difficult because the announcement is organized around information that is different from what is being requested in the question. Thus, while the correct information is located in a single sentence, this information is embedded under a list of headings describing CIEM's activities for employees looking for other work. This list of headings serves as an excellent set of distractors for the reader who does not search for or locate the phrase containing the conditional information stated in the directive; that is, those who lose their jobs because of a departmental reorganization.

Document literacy

Adults often encounter materials such as tables, schedules, charts, graphs, maps and forms at home, at work, or when travelling in their communities. The knowledge and skills needed to process information contained in these documents is therefore an important aspect of being literate in a modern society. Success in processing documents appears to depend at least in part on the ability to locate information in a variety of displays, and to use this information in various ways. Sometimes procedural knowledge may be required to transfer information from one source to another, as is necessary in completing applications or order forms.

The IALS document literacy scale contains 34 tasks that are ordered along the scale from 182 to 408 as the result of responses of adults from each of the participating countries. These tasks are distributed as follows: Level 1 (6 tasks); Level 2 (12 tasks); Level 3 (14 tasks); Level 4 (1 task); and Level 5 (1 task). By examining tasks associated with these proficiency levels, characteristics that are likely to make particular document tasks more or less difficult can be identified. Questions or directives associated with the various document tasks are basically of four types: *locating, cycling, integrating* and *generating*. Locating tasks require the reader to match one or more features of information stated in the question to either identical or synonymous information given in the document. Cycling tasks require the reader to locate and match one or more features of information, but differ from locating tasks because they require the reader to engage in a series of feature matches to satisfy conditions given in the question. The integrating tasks typically require the reader to compare and contrast information in adjacent parts of the document. In the generating tasks, readers must produce a written response by processing information found in the document and by making text-based inferences or drawing on their own background knowledge.

CANCO

Centre on Internal and External Mobility

What is CIEM?

CIEM stands for Centre on Internal and External Mobility, an initiative of the personnel department. A number of workers of this department work in CIEM, together with members from other departments and outside career consultants.

CIEM is available to help employees in their search for another job inside or outside the Canco Manufacturing Company.

What does CIEM do?

CIEM supports employees who are seriously considering other work through the following activities:
- **Job Data Bank**
After an interview with the employee, information is entered into a data bank that tracks job seekers and job openings at Canco and at other manufacturing companies.
- **Guidance**
The employee's potential is explored through career counselling discussions.
- **Courses**
Courses are being organized (in collaboration with the department for information and training) that will deal with job search and career planning.
- **Career Change Projects**
CIEM supports and coordinates projects to help employees prepare for new careers and new perspectives.
- **Mediation**
CIEM acts as a mediator for employees who are threatened with dismissal resulting from reorganization, and assists with finding new positions when necessary.

How much does CIEM cost?

Payment is determined in consultation with the department where you work. A number of services of CIEM are free. You may also be asked to pay, either in money or in time.

How does CIEM work?

CIEM assists employees who are seriously considering another job within or outside the company.

That process begins by submitting an application. A discussion with a personnel counsellor can also be useful. It is obvious that you should talk with the counsellor first about your wishes and the internal possibilities regarding your career. The counsellor is familiar with your abilities and with developments within your unit.

Contact with CIEM in any case is made via the personnel counsellor. He or she handles the application for you, after which you are invited to a discussion with a CIEM representative.

For more information

The personnel department can give you more information.

...each of which had elements ranging in difficulty.

Here are some examples, together with country results, at each of the five levels.

Percentage of adults by country performing at Level 1:

Canada	18.2
Germany	9.0
Netherlands	10.1
Poland	45.4
Sweden	6.2
Switzerland (French)	16.2
Switzerland (German)	18.1
United States	23.7

As with the prose tasks, each type of question or directive associated with a document task extends over a range of difficulty as a result of interactions among several other characteristics:

- the number of categories or features of information in the question the reader must process or match

- the number of categories or features of information in the document that seem plausible or correct because they share some but not all of the information with the correct answer

- the extent to which the information asked for in the question is obviously related to the information stated in the document

- the structure and content of the document.

A more detailed discussion of the five levels of document literacy follows.

Document Level 1   **Score range: 0 to 225**

Most of the tasks at this level require the reader to locate a piece of information based on a literal match. Distracting information, if present, is typically located away from the correct answer. Some tasks may direct the reader to enter personal information onto a form.

Tasks at this level require the reader to make a literal match on the basis of a single piece of information. Information that could distract the reader, if present, is typically located away from the correct answer. One document task meeting this description (188) directs the reader to identify from a chart the percentage of teachers from Greece who are women. The chart displays the percentages of women teachers from various countries. Only one number appears on the chart for each country.

FEW DUTCH WOMEN AT THE BLACKBOARD

There is a low percentage of women teachers in the Netherlands compared to other countries. In most of the other countries, the majority of teachers are women. However, if we include the figures for inspectors and school principals, the proportion shrinks considerably and women are in a minority everywhere.

Luxembourg	Italy	France	Ireland	United Kingdom	Spain	Belgium	Greece	Denmark	Netherlands
74.8	72.0	63.1	61.6	58.8	58.5	57.4	51.2	41.2	38.1

Percentage of women teachers (kindergarten, elementary, and secondary).

A very similar task involves a chart displayed in a newspaper showing the expected amounts of radioactive waste by country. This task, which has a difficulty value of 218, directs the reader to identify the country that is projected to have the smallest amount of waste by the year 2000. Again, there is only one percentage associated with each country. In this task, however, the reader must first identify the percentage associated with the smallest amount of waste and then match it to the country.

Percentage of adults by country performing at Level 2:	
Canada	24.7
Germany	32.7
Netherlands	25.7
Poland	30.7
Sweden	18.9
Switzerland (French)	28.8
Switzerland (German)	29.1
United States	25.9

Document Level 2　　　　　　　　　　**Score range: 226 to 275**

Document tasks at this level are a bit more varied. While some still require the reader to match on a single feature, more distracting information may be present or the match may require a low-level inference. Some tasks at this level may require the reader to enter information onto a form or to cycle through information in a document.

One Level 2 task on the document scale (242) seems very similar to one described above for Level 1. This task directs the reader to use a chart to identify the year in which the fewest people in the Netherlands were injured by fireworks. Part of what may have made this task somewhat more difficult is that two charts were presented instead of just one. One, labelled "Fireworks in the Netherlands," depicts years and numbers representing funds spent in millions of U.S. dollars, while the other, "Victims of fireworks," uses a line to show numbers of people treated in hospitals. Another contributing factor may have been that neither graph contains the label "number injured by fireworks." The reader needs to make a low inference that victims or number treated equates to injuries.

Several other tasks falling within Level 2 direct the reader to use information given to complete a form. In one case they are asked to fill out an order form to purchase tickets to see a play on a particular day, at a particular time. In another, readers are asked to complete the availability section of an employment application based on information provided that included: total number of hours they are willing to work, hours they are available, how they heard about the job, and availability of transportation.

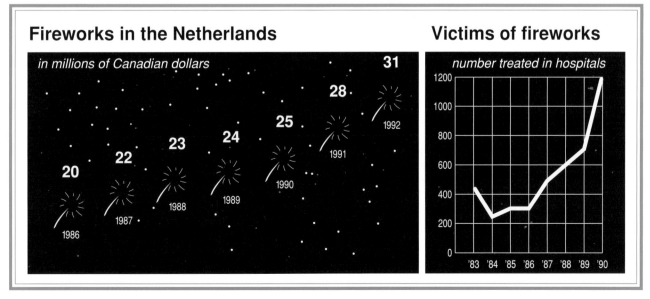

Percentage of adults by country performing at Level 3:

Canada	32.1
Germany	39.5
Netherlands	44.2
Poland	18.0
Sweden	39.4
Switzerland (French)	38.9
Switzerland (German)	36.6
United States	31.4

Document Level 3　　　　　　　　**Score range: 276 to 325**

Tasks at this level appear to be most varied. Some require the reader to make literal or synonymous matches, but usually the matches require the reader to take conditional information into account or to match on multiple features of information. Some tasks at this level require the reader to integrate information from one or more displays of information. Other tasks ask the reader to cycle through a document to provide multiple responses.

One task falling around the middle of Level 3 in difficulty involves the fireworks charts shown earlier (see page 39). This task directs the reader to write a brief description of the relationship between sales and injuries based on the information shown in the two graphs. This task received a difficulty value of 295. A second task, receiving a similar difficulty value, directs readers to a bus schedule. They are asked to identify the time of the last bus they could take from a particular location on a Saturday night. Here the reader must match several pieces of information — the last time, a particular location, on Saturday, in the evening — to arrive at a correct answer. This task received a difficulty value of 297.

QUICK COPY Printing Requisition

FILL IN ALL INFORMATION REQUESTED

GUIDELINES: This requisition may be used to order materials to be printed BLACK INK only, and in the quantities that are listed at the right.

■ SINGLE SHEET PRINTED 1 OR 2 SIDES — 2000 copies maximum
■ MORE THAN ONE SHEET UP TO 100 PAGES — 400 copies maximum
　　　　　　　　　　　　　　　　OVER 100 PAGES — 200 copies maximum

1. PROJECT TO BE CHARGED

2. TODAY'S DATE

3. TITLE OR DESCRIPTION

4. DATE DELIVERY REQUIRED

5. DO NOT MARK IN SHADED BOXES

X

NUMBER OF ORIGINALS

=

NUMBER OF COPIES TO BE PRINTED

TOTAL NUMBER OF IMPRESSIONS

6. NUMBER OF SIDES TO BE PRINTED (Check one box.)　　1 ☐ One side　　2 ☐ BOTH sides

7. COLOR OF PAPER (Fill in only if NOT white.) _____

8. SIZE OF PAPER (Fill in only if NOT $8^1/_2$ x 11) _____

9. Check any that apply:
☐ COLLATE

BINDING: ☐ One staple at upper left
☐ Two staples in left margin
☐ BIND-FAST: ☐ Black
　　　　　　☐ Brown
☐ 3-hole punch

☐ Other instructions _____

AUTHORIZATION AND DELIVERY

10. Project Director (print name) _____

11. Requisitioner (print your own name and phone no.) _____
extension

12. Check one:
☐ Requisitioner will PICK UP completed job.
☐ Mail completed job to: _____
Print name, room number, and mail stop

MAIL STOP

ROOM NO.

13. **KEEP PINK COPY at least 3 months.** When requesting information, you must refer to the requisition number printed here.

140468
QUICK COPY REGISTRATION NUMBER

D1320-03116 • 000000 • 000000

A third task, falling at high end of Level 3 (321), involves the use of a quick copy printing requisition form that might be found in the workplace. The task asks the reader to explain whether or not the quick copy centre would make 300 copies of a statement that is 105 pages long. In responding to this directive, the reader must determine whether conditions stated in the question meet those provided in the guidelines to this document.

Percentage of adults by country performing at Level 4:	
Canada	19.6
Germany	17.0
Netherlands	18.5
Poland	5.5
Sweden	27.8
Switzerland (French)	14.2
Switzerland (German)	14.2
United States	15.3

Document Level 4 **Score range: 326 to 375**

Tasks at this level, like those in the previous levels, ask the reader to match on multiple features of information, to cycle through documents, and to integrate information; frequently however, these tasks require the reader to make higher order inferences to arrive at the correct answer. Sometimes, conditional information is present in the document, which must be taken into account by the reader.

The only task falling at this level (341) asks the reader to look at two pie charts showing oil use for 1970 and 1989. The question directs the reader to summarize how the percentages of oil used for different purposes changed over the period specified. Here the reader must cycle through the two charts, comparing and contrasting the percentages for each of the four stated purposes. Then the reader must generate a statement that captures these changes.

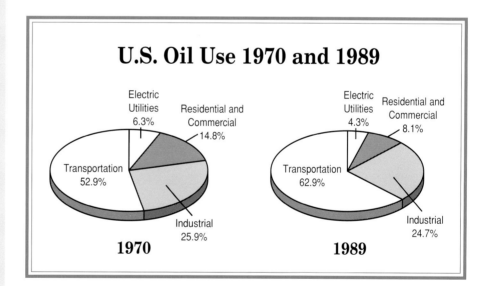

Document Level 5 **Score range: 376 to 500**

Tasks at this level require the reader to search through complex displays of information that contain multiple distractors, to make high-level inferences, process conditional information, or use specialized knowledge.

Percentage of adults by country performing at Level 5:	
Canada	5.4
Germany	1.9
Netherlands	1.4
Poland	0.4
Sweden	7.7
Switzerland (French)	1.9
Switzerland (German)	1.9
United States	3.7

The only Level 5 task in this international assessment involved a page taken from a consumer magazine rating clock radios. The most difficult task (408) involving this document asked the reader for the average advertised price for the basic clock radio receiving the highest overall score. As can be seen on page 43, this task required readers to process two types of conditional information. First, they needed to identify the radio receiving the highest overall score while distinguishing among the three types of clock radios reviewed: full-featured, basic and those with a cassette player. Second, they needed to locate a price. In making this final match, they needed to notice that two prices were given; the first, the suggested retail and the second, the average advertised price.

A second and considerably easier task involving this document and falling at the high end of Level 2 (321) asks the reader "which full-featured radio is rated the highest on performance." Again, readers needed to find the correct category of clock radio. Yet, they needed to process fewer conditions. Here they only needed to distinguish between the rating for "Overall Score" and "Performance." It is possible that some adults identified the full-featured radio as receiving the highest "Overall Score" rather than the one rated highest in "Performance" as specified in the question. As such, "Overall Score" would be considered a plausible distractor. Another factor that likely contributed to this task's difficulty is that "Overall Score" is given a numerical value while the other features are rated by a symbol. It may be that some adults found the correct category ("Performance"), but selected the first radio listed, assuming it performed best. The text accompanying this table indicates the radios are rated within a category by overall score. It is easy to imagine that some people may have equated overall score with overall performance.

Quantitative literacy

Since adults are frequently required to perform arithmetic operations in everyday life, the ability to perform quantitative literacy tasks is another important aspect of literacy. These skills may seem, at first glance, to be fundamentally different from the types of knowledge and skill associated with prose and document literacy and therefore, to extend the concept of literacy beyond its traditional limits. However, experience in North America with large-scale assessments of adults indicates that the processing of printed information plays an important role in affecting the difficulty of tasks along the scale (Kirsch et al. 1993; Montigny et al. 1991).

In general, it appears that many individuals can perform single arithmetic operations when both the numbers and operations are made explicit. However, when the numbers to be used must be located in and extracted from different types of documents that contain similar but irrelevant information, when the operations to be used must be inferred from printed directions, and when multiple operations must be performed, the tasks become increasingly difficult.

The IALS quantitative literacy scale contains 33 tasks ranging from 225 to 408 in difficulty. These tasks are distributed as follows: Level 1 (1 task); Level 2 (9 tasks); Level 3 (15 tasks); Level 4 (6 tasks); and Level 5 (2 tasks). The difficulty of these tasks and, therefore, their placement along the scale, appears to be a function of several factors including:

- the particular arithmetic operation required to complete the task
- the number of operations needed to perform the task successfully
- the extent to which the numbers are embedded in printed materials
- the extent to which an inference must be made to identify the type of operation to be performed.

Quantitative literacy also requires the processing of printed information...

...which make arithmetic skills inadequate on their own.

There were 33 quantitative literacy tasks in the IALS...

RATINGS

● ◐ ○ ◗ ●
Better ←――――――――→ Worse

Listed by types; within types, listed in order of overall score. Differences in score of 4 points or less were not deemed significant.

1 Brand and model. If you can't find a model, call the company. Phone numbers are listed on page 736.

2 Price. The manufacturer's suggested or approximate retail price, followed by the average advertised price.

3 Dimensions. To the nearest centimetre.

4 Overall score. A composite, encompassing all our tests and judgments. A "perfect" radio would have earned 100 points.

5 Convenience. This composite judgment reflects such things as the legibility of the display, the ease of tuning the radio and setting the alarm, and the presence or absence of useful features.

6 Performance. An overall judgment reflecting performance in our tests of: sensitivity and selectivity; tuning ease; capture ratio, the ability to bring in the stronger of two stations on the same frequency; image rejection, the ability to ignore signals from just above the band, resistance to interference from signals bouncing off aircraft and such.

7 Sensitivity. How well each radio received a station with little interference.

8 Selectivity. How well each radio received clearly a weak station next to a strong one on the dial.

9 Tone quality. Based mainly on computer analysis of the speaker's output and on listening tests, using music from CDs. No model produced high-fidelity sound.

10 Reversible time-setting. This useful feature makes setting clock and alarm times easy. If you overshoot the desired setting, you simply back up.

11 Dual alarm. Lets you set two separate wake-up times.

Brand and model	Price	Dimensions, HxWxD, cm.	Overall Score	Convenience	Performance	Sensitivity	Selectivity	Tone quality	Reversible time setting	Dual alarm	Warranty, months	Advantages	Disadvantages	Comments
Full-featured clock radios														
RCA RP-3690	$50/$40	8x25x18	86	●	◐	◐	◗	●	✓	✓	12	A,B,D,H,J,L,O,T,U		A
Sony ICF-C303	50/45	5x20x15	84	●	◐	●	○	◐	✓	✓	12	C,E,F,I,N,T		C
Panasonic RC-X220	50/45	10x28x13	82	◐	◐	◐	◐	○	✓	✓	12	A,G,K,M,O,S,T,U	b,c	A
Realistic 272	50/30	5x28x15	79	◐	○	◐	◐	◐	✓	✓	3	A,G,H,K,O,T		D
Magnavox AJ3900	65/—	15x38x13	78	○	●	◐	●	◐	—	✓	3	D,G,K,M,O,R,T	b,g	B
Emerson AK2745	39/20	8x28x15	70	○	◐	◐	◐	○	✓	✓	3	G,O	g	K
Soundesign 3753	20/20	8x23x13	62	○	◐	●	○	○	✓	✓	3	J,Q	d,h	J
Basic clock radios														
Realistic 263	28/18	10x20x10	74	○	◐	◐	○	◐	—	—	3	A,D,H,O,P,U	h	—
Soundesign 3622	12/10	5x20x13	68	◐	◐	●	◐	◐	—	—	3	U	d	L
Panasonic RC-6064	18/15	5x20x13	67	◐	◐	●	○	○	—	—	12	—	b,c	—
General Electric 7-4612	13/10	5x20x13	66	◐	◐	●	○	◐	—	—	12	A,D	a,g	—
Lloyds CR001	20/15	5x18x13	64	◐	◐	●	○	◐	—	—	3	U	—	—
Sony ICF-C240	15/13	5x18x15	63	◐	○	●	◐	◐	—	—	12	—	f,g	—
Emerson AK2720	19/10	5x20x13	61	◐	○	◐	●	○	—	—	3	O,T	e	K
Gran Prix D507	15/10	5x18x10	54	◐	●	○	●	●	—	—	3	—	d	—
Clock radios with cassette player														
General Electric 7-4965	60/50	10x30x15	85	◐	◐	◐	◐	◐	✓	✓	12	A,D,G,H,K,O,S,T	—	B,E
Pansonic RC-X250	[1]	10x33x13	76	◐	◐	○	◐	◐	✓	✓	12	A,G,K,O,R,U	b,c	A,H
Sony ICF-CS650	75/65	15x28x15	74	○	◐	●	○	◐	✓	✓	12	G,R,T,U	c,f,i	A,F,H
Soundesign 3844MGY	40/30	13x30x13	62	○	●	●	●	◐	—	—	3	G,K,J,S,U		F,G,I,M

[1] *Discontinued. Replaced by* **RC-X260,** *$79 list and $60 average advertised sale price.*

Features in Common

All: • Permit snooze time of about 8 min. • Retain time settings during short power failures.
Except as noted, all have: • Battery backup for clock and alarm memory. • Red display digits 1 cm. high. • Sleep-time radio play for up to 60 min. before automatic shutoff. • Switch to reset alarm.

Keys to Advantages

A–Alarm works despite power failure.
B–Shows actual time plus up to 2 alarm times.
C–Twin alarms settable for 2 different stations.
D–Tone alarm has adjustable volume control.
E–Memory needs no battery.
F–Digital tuner with presettable stations.
G–Tuner can receive in stereo.
H–Battery-strength indicator.
I–Illuminated tuning dial.
J–Illuminated tuning pointer.

K–Earphone jack.
L–Nap timer.
M–Audio input for tape deck or CD player.
N–Display can show date and time.
O–Display has high/low brightness switch.
P–Display has larger digits than most.
Q–Night light—adjusts for room light.
R–Bass-boost tone control.
S–Treble-cut tone control.
T–Better than most in tuning ease.
U–Better than most in image rejection.

Key to Disadvantages

a–Possible to reset time by accident.
b–Controls for time-setting or dimmer inconveniently located on radio's bottom or rear.
c–Display dimmer than most in brightly lit room.
d–Radio volume must be turned completely down for alarm buzzer to sound.

e–Lacks alarm buzzer; radio is sole alarm.
f–Lacks indication alarm is set.
g–Lacks alarm-reset button.
h–Time-setting lacks fast reverse.
i–No slow forward, fast reverse for time setting.

Key to Comments

A–Display shows green digits.
B–Display shows blue digits.
C–Display uses LCD (liquid crystal) digits.
D–Terminals for external antenna.
E–3-position graphic equalizer.
F–Cassette player lacks Record function.
G–Cassette player lacks Rewind function.
H–Model permits wake-up to cassette play.
I–Cassette-deck flutter worse than most.
J–Warranty repairs cost $3 for handling.
K–Warranty repairs cost $3.50 for handling.
L–Warranty repairs cost $6 for handling.
M–Warranty repairs cost $10 for handling.

A detailed discussion of the five levels of quantitative literacy follows.

Percentage of adults by country performing at Level 1:	
Canada	16.9
Germany	6.7
Netherlands	10.3
Poland	39.1
Sweden	6.6
Switzerland (French)	12.9
Switzerland (German)	14.2
United States	21.0

Quantitative Level 1   **Score range: 0 to 225**

Although no quantitative tasks used in the IALS fall below the score value of 225, experience suggests that such tasks would require the reader to perform a single, relatively simple operation (usually addition) for which either the numbers are already entered onto the given document and the operation is stipulated, or the numbers are provided and the operation does not require the reader to borrow.

The easiest quantitative task in the IALS (225) directs the reader to complete an order form. The last line on this form says "Total with Handling." The line above it says "Handling Charge $2.00." The reader simply had to add the $2.00 to the $50.00 they had entered on a previous line to indicate the cost of the tickets. In this task, one of the numbers was stipulated, the operation was easily identified from the word "total" and the operation did not require the reader to borrow. Moreover, the format of the form set the problem up in a simple column format, further facilitating the task for the reader.

Percentage of adults by country performing at Level 2:	
Canada	26.1
Germany	26.6
Netherlands	25.5
Poland	30.1
Sweden	18.6
Switzerland (French)	24.5
Switzerland (German)	26.2
United States	25.3

Quantitative Level 2   **Score range: 226 to 275**

Tasks in this level typically require readers to perform a single arithmetic operation (frequently addition or subtraction) using numbers that are easily located in the text or document. The operation to be performed may be easily inferred from the wording of the question or the format of the material (for example, a bank deposit form or an order form).

A typical Level 2 task on the quantitative scale directs the reader to use a weather chart in a newspaper to determine how many degrees warmer today's high temperature is expected to be in Bangkok than in Seoul. Here the reader had to cycle through the table to locate the two temperatures and then subtract them to determine the difference. This task received a difficulty value of 255.

WEATHER

Europe

	Today			Tomorrow		
	High C	Low C	W	High C	Low C	W
Algarve	19	7	s	21	9	s
Amsterdam	11	6	pc	12	7	pc
Ankara	17	7	pc	19	8	pc
Athens	22	15	pc	23	14	pc
Barcelona	16	8	s	14	9	s
Belgrade	14	6	pc	10	1	c
Berlin	8	2	c	6	1	c
Brussels	11	6	pc	14	7	pc
Budapest	9	1	pc	9	2	c
Copenhagen	7	1	r	6	2	c
Costa del Sol	21	8	s	21	10	s
Dublin	10	6	pc	13	8	pc
Edinburgh	10	6	c	10	6	c
Florence	11	5	s	14	6	s
Frankfurt	12	6	pc	13	4	pc
Geneva	9	2	s	12	4	s
Helsinki	-1	-7	sf	-3	-10	c
Istanbul	17	10	pc	15	9	sh
Las Palmas	26	18	pc	27	18	pc
Lisbon	19	9	s	19	10	s
London	12	5	pc	13	7	pc
Madrid	17	3	s	18	4	s
Milan	9	3	s	13	6	s
Moscow	1	-3	r	-3	-11	sf
Munich	11	3	pc	12	6	pc
Nice	14	7	s	15	8	s
Oslo	4	-4	c	5	-2	c
Paris	12	6	pc	13	6	pc
Prague	11	1	pc	8	2	c
Reykjavik	4	2	r	6	-1	c
Rome	20	12	s	20	10	s
St. Petersburg	-1	-7	sf	-4	-12	pc
Stockholm	1	-5	sn	-2	-7	c
Strasbourg	12	5	pc	15	7	pc
Tallinn	-1	-7	sf	-4	-10	pc
Venice	10	3	s	11	4	s
Vienna	9	-1	pc	10	2	c
Warsaw	8	2	sh	6	1	c
Zurich	8	0	s	9	1	pc

Oceania

Auckland	20	14	s	17	11	sh
Sydney	27	17	pc	25	16	pc

Forecast for Friday through Sunday

Jetstream · Unseasonably Cold · Unseasonably Hot · Heavy Rain · Heavy Snow

North America
Cold weather will engulf the Mid-western and Northeastern United States Friday and over the weekend. Although it will be cold in Chicago, Toronto and New York City, the weather is expected to be dry. Los Angeles will have some sunshine and seasonable temperatures each day.

Europe
Western and central Europe will have a spell of mild weather Friday into the weekend. London and Paris will have dry weather with some sunshine Friday into Sunday. Rain will continue to soak south-western Norway. Snow will blanket the area from Minsk to Moscow.

Asia
Typhoon Elsie will probably stay to the east of the Philippines and south of Japan Friday and the weekend. Some rain is apt to fall in Seoul and there could even be a little ice or snow. Cold air will pour into Beijing and snow is a possibility. Hong Kong will start the weekend warm.

Middle East

	Today			Tomorrow		
	High C	Low C	W	High C	Low C	w
Beirut	28	19	pc	29	20	s
Cairo	29	20	pc	28	19	pc
Damascus	24	12	s	26	14	s
Jerusalem	27	15	s	26	14	s
Riyadh	34	13	s	32	13	s

Latin America

	Today			Tomorrow		
	High C	Low C	W	High C	Low C	W
Buenos Aires	23	11	pc	26	13	s
Caracas	29	20	s	31	18	s
Lima	23	17	c	23	16	c
Mexico City	23	11	sh	23	12	pc
Rio de Janiero	32	22	s	28	21	sh
Santiago	24	4	s	22	6	pc

Legend: s-sunny, pc-partly cloudy, c-cloudy, sh-showers, t-thunderstorms, r-rain, sf-snow flurries, sn-snow, i-ice, W-Weather. **All maps, forecasts and data provided by Accu-Weather, Inc. © 1992**

Asia

	Today			Tomorrow		
	High C	Low C	W	High C	Low C	W
Bangkok	32	22	pc	30	23	s
Beijing	11	0	s	8	2	pc
Hong Kong	30	23	s	29	22	pc
Manila	31	25	s	31	25	sh
New Delhi	31	13	s	32	16	s
Seoul	14	6	pc	14	4	pc
Shanghai	22	10	pc	24	12	s
Singapore	31	24	pc	28	23	sh
Taipei	26	21	pc	26	19	pc
Tokyo	18	9	pc	17	7	pc

Africa

Algiers	27	14	s	26	13	s
Cape Town	20	11	sh	18	11	pc
Casablanca	20	14	c	21	11	pc
Harare	34	17	s	32	18	pc
Lagos	30	24	pc	29	24	pc
Nairobi	27	12	pc	26	13	pc
Tunis	27	17	pc	17	14	pc

North

Anchorage	0	-2	c	3	0	sh
Atlanta	14	4	pc	8	2	pc
Boston	15	4	c	8	-1	pc
Chicago	2	-5	c	-2	-8	pc
Denver	8	-3	pc	4	-6	sn
Detroit	4	-2	c	4	-5	pc
Honolulu	31	20	s	31	21	pc
Houston	15	3	pc	12	6	pc
Los Angeles	28	14	s	24	13	s
Miami	30	22	pc	29	21	pc
Minneapolis	-1	-8	c	1	-7	pc
Montreal	7	-2	sf	4	-3	c
Nassau	31	22	pc	28	21	sh
New York	14	4	r	10	2	pc
Phoenix	23	11	pc	22	8	s
San Fran.	20	11	pc	21	8	s
Seattle	11	6	pc	13	7	r
Toronto	6	-3	c	3	-3	c
Washington	14	6	r	11	4	pc

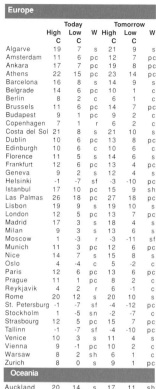

Percentage of adults by country performing at Level 3:

Canada	34.8
Germany	43.2
Netherlands	44.3
Poland	23.9
Sweden	39.0
Switzerland (French)	42.2
Switzerland (German)	40.7
United States	31.3

A similar but slightly more difficult task (268) requires the reader to use the chart about women in the teaching profession in Europe that is displayed in Level 1 for the document scale (see page 38). This task directs the reader to calculate the percentage of men in the teaching profession in Italy. Both this task and the one just mentioned involved calculating the difference between two numbers. Part of what distinguishes these two tasks is that in the former, both temperatures could be identified in the table from the newspaper. For the task involving men teachers in Italy, the reader needed to make the inference that the percentage of men teachers is equal to 100% minus the percentage of women teachers.

Quantitative Level 3　　　　　　　　　**Score range: 276 to 325**

Tasks found in this level typically require the reader to perform a single operation. However, the operations become more varied — some multiplication and division tasks are found in this level. Sometimes two or more numbers are needed to solve the problem and the numbers are frequently embedded in more complex displays. While semantic relation terms such as "how many" or "calculate the difference" are often used, some of the tasks require the reader to make higher order inferences to determine the appropriate operation.

Tasks falling around 300 on the quantitative scale still require the reader to perform single arithmetic operations, but the operations become more varied. Part of what distinguishes tasks at this level from those seen at lower levels is that the displays of information become more complex and the reader must identify two or more numbers from various places in the document. For example, one task located at 302 on the quantitative scale directs the reader to look at two graphs containing information about consumers and producers of primary energy. In one question, they are asked to calculate how much more energy Canada produces than it consumes. Here the operation is not facilitated by the format of the document and the reader must locate the information using both bar graphs. In another question using this document, the reader is directed to calculate the total amount of energy in quadrillion (10^{15}) Btu consumed by Canada, Mexico and the United States. This task falls at 300 on the scale. It requires the reader to add three numbers. Presenting two graphs likely contributed to the difficulty of this task. Some respondents may have performed the appropriate calculation for the three countries specified using the producer energy chart rather than the consumer energy chart.

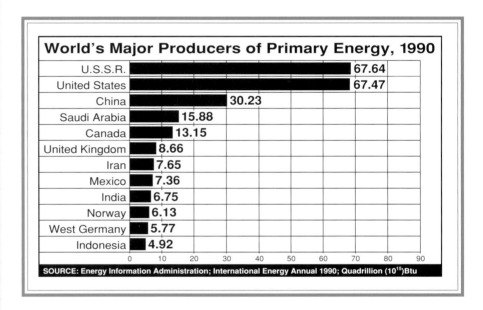

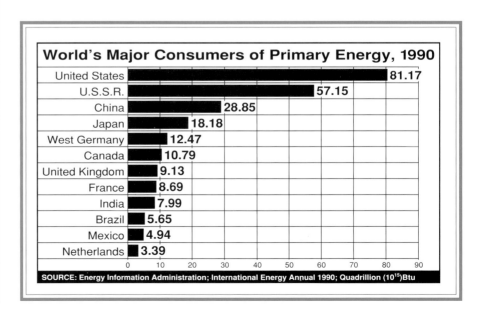

Another task at this level involves the fireworks chart shown earlier for the document scale (see page 39). This quantitative task asks the reader to calculate how many more people were injured in 1989 than in 1988. What contributes to this task receiving a difficulty value of 293 is that one of the numbers was not given in the line graph. The reader needed to interpolate the number from information provided along the vertical axis.

In a more difficult task (located at 317 on the scale), readers are asked to look at a recipe for scrambled eggs with tomatoes. The recipe gives the ingredients for four servings: 3 tablespoons of oil, 1 garlic clove, 1 teaspoon of sugar, 500 grams of fresh red tomatoes and 6 eggs. The question asks them to determine the number of eggs they will need if they are using the recipe for six people. Here they must know how to calculate or determine the ratio needed. This task is somewhat easier than might be expected, given other tasks at this level. This may be because people are familiar with recipes and with manipulating them to fit a particular situation.

This appears to be true for another question using this recipe. It asks the reader to determine the amount of oil that would be needed if the recipe were being used for two people. This task received a value of 253 on the scale. A larger percentage of respondents found it easier to halve an ingredient than to increase one by 50%. It is not clear why this is so. It may be that some of the respondents have an algorithm for responding to certain familiar tasks that does not require them to apply general arithmetic principles for solving the problem.

Percentage of adults by country performing at Level 4:	
Canada	17.5
Germany	20.7
Netherlands	17.8
Poland	6.1
Sweden	27.4
Switzerland (French)	19.2
Switzerland (German)	17.1
United States	17.5

Quantitative Level 4 Score range: 326 to 375

With one exception, the tasks at this level require the reader to perform a single arithmetic operation where typically either the quantities or the operation are not easily determined. That is, for most of the tasks at this level, the question or directive does not provide a semantic relation term such as "how many" or "calculate the difference" to help the reader.

Tasks around 350 on the quantitative scale tend to require the application of a single operation where either the quantities or the operation are not easily determined. One such task involves a compound interest table. It directs the reader to "calculate the total amount of money you will have if you invest $100 at a rate of 6% for 10 years." This task received a difficulty value of 348, in part because many people treated this as a document rather than a quantitative task and simply looked up the amount of interest that would be earned. They likely forgot to add the interest to their $100 investment.

Compound Interest
Compounded Annually

Principal	Period	4%	5%	6%	7%	8%	9%	10%	12%	14%	16%
$100	1 day	0.011	0.014	0.016	0.019	0.022	0.025	0.027	0.033	0.038	0.044
	1 week	0.077	0.096	0.115	0.134	0.153	0.173	0.192	0.230	0.268	0.307
	6 mos	2.00	2.50	3.00	3.50	4.00	4.50	5.00	6.00	7.00	8.00
	1 year	4.00	5.00	6.00	7.00	8.00	9.00	10.00	12.00	14.00	16.00
	2 years	8.16	10.25	12.36	14.49	16.64	18.81	21.00	25.44	29.96	34.56
	3 years	12.49	15.76	19.10	22.50	25.97	29.50	33.10	40.49	48.15	56.09
	4 years	16.99	21.55	26.25	31.08	36.05	41.16	46.41	57.35	68.90	81.06
	5 years	21.67	27.63	33.82	40.26	46.93	53.86	61.05	76.23	92.54	110.03
	6 years	26.53	34.01	41.85	50.07	58.69	67.71	77.16	97.38	119.50	143.64
	7 years	31.59	40.71	50.36	60.58	71.38	82.80	94.87	121.07	150.23	182.62
	8 years	36.86	47.75	59.38	71.82	85.09	99.26	114.36	147.60	185.26	227.84
	9 years	42.33	55.13	68.95	83.85	99.90	117.19	135.79	177.31	225.19	280.30
	10 years	48.02	62.89	79.08	96.72	115.89	136.74	159.37	210.58	270.72	341.14
	12 years	60.10	79.59	101.22	125.22	151.82	181.27	213.84	289.60	381.79	493.60
	15 years	80.09	107.89	139.66	175.90	217.22	264.25	317.72	447.36	613.79	826.55
	20 years	119.11	165.33	220.71	286.97	366.10	460.44	572.75	864.63	1,274.35	1,846.08

Another task at this level requires respondents to read a newspaper article describing a research finding linking allergies to a particular genetic mutation. The question directs the reader to calculate the number of people studied who were found to have the mutant gene. To answer the question correctly, readers must know how to convert the phrase "64 percent" to a decimal number and then multiply it by the number of patients studied (400). The text provides no clues on how to set up this problem.

A third task involves the distance chart shown on the next page. Readers were asked to "calculate the total number of kilometres travelled in a trip from Guadalajara to Tecoman and then to Zamora." Here a semantic relation term was provided, but the quantities were not easily identified. As a result, this task received a difficulty value of 335. Making the inference that the trip was from Guadalajara to Tecoman and then from Tecoman to Zamora was difficult for some respondents. In a different task, respondents were asked to determine how much less the distance from Guadalajara to Tecoman is than the distance from Guadalajara to Puerto Vallarta. In this Level 3 task (308), the quantities were relatively easy to locate.

TABLE OF APPROXIMATE DISTANCES (in kilometres)

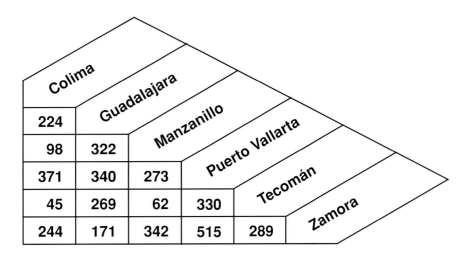

A person's score indicates the probability of being able to perform a task at various levels.

Quantitative Level 5   **Score range: 376 to 500**

These tasks require readers to perform multiple operations sequentially, and they must disembed the features of the problem from the material provided or rely on background knowledge to determine the quantities or operations needed.

One of the most difficult tasks on the quantitative scale (381) requires readers to look at a table providing nutritional analysis of food and then, using the information given, determine the percentage of calories in a Big Mac® that comes from total fat. To answer this question, readers must first recognize that the information about total fat provided is given in grams. In the question, they are told that a gram of fat has 9 calories. Therefore, they must convert the number of fat grams to calories. Then, they need to calculate this number of calories as a percentage of the total calories given for a Big Mac®. Only one other item on this scale received a higher score.

Estimating literacy performance across the levels

The literacy levels not only provide a means for exploring the progression of information-processing demands across each of the scales, but they also can be used to help explain how the proficiencies individuals demonstrate reflect the likelihood they will respond correctly to the broad range of tasks used in this assessment as well as to similar tasks that were not included. In practical terms, this means that individuals performing at 250 on each scale are expected to be able to perform the average Level 1 and 2 tasks with a high degree of proficiency. That is, they will be able to perform these kinds of tasks with an average probability of 80% or higher. It does not mean that they will not be able to perform tasks in Levels 3 or higher. They will do so some of the time, but not consistently.

Nutritional Analysis

	Serving Size	Calories	Protein (g)	Carbohydrates (g)	Total Fat (g)	Saturated Fat (g)	Monounsaturated Fat (g)	Polyunsaturated Fat (g)	Cholesterol (mg)	Sodium (mg)
Sandwiches										
Hamburger	102 g	255	12	30	9	5	1	3	37	490
Cheeseburger	116 g	305	15	30	13	7	1	5	50	725
Quarter Pounder®	166 g	410	23	34	20	11	1	8	85	645
Quarter Pounder® w/Cheese	194 g	510	28	34	28	16	1	11	115	1110
McLean Deluxe™	206 g	320	22	35	10	5	1	4	60	670
McLean Deluxe™ w/Cheese	219 g	370	24	35	14	8	1	5	75	890
Big Mac®	215 g	500	25	42	26	16	1	9	100	890
Filet-O-Fish®	141 g	370	14	38	18	8	6	4	50	730
McChicken®	187 g	415	19	39	19	9	7	4	50	830
French Fries										
Small French Fries	68 g	220	3	26	12	8	1	2.5	0	110
Medium French Fries	97 g	320	4	36	17	12	1.5	3.5	0	150
Large French Fries	122 g	400	6	46	22	15	2	5	0	200
Salads										
Chef Salad	265 g	170	17	8	9	4	1	4	111	400
Garden Salad	189 g	50	4	6	2	1	0.4	0.6	65	70
Chunky Chicken Salad	255 g	150	25	7	4	2	1	1	78	230
Side Salad	106 g	30	2	4	1	0.5	0.2	0.3	33	35
Croutons	11 g	50	1	7	2	1.3	0.1	0.5	0	140
Bacon Bits	3 g	15	1	0	1	0.3	0.2	0.5	1	95

Soft Drinks

	Coca-Cola Classic®				diet Coke®				Sprite®			
	Small	Medium	Large	Jumbo	Small	Medium	Large	Jumbo	Small	Medium	Large	Jumbo
Calories	140	190	260	380	1	1	2	3	140	190	260	380
Carbohydrates (g)	38	50	70	101	0.3	0.4	0.5	0.6	36	48	66	96
Sodium (mg)	15	20	25	40	30	40	60	80	15	20	25	40

These probabilities are shown in Tables 2.1a to 2.1c, and are explained here.

The three charts given in Table 2.1a to 2.1c display the probability that individuals performing at selected points on each of the scales will give a correct response to tasks of varying difficulty. For example, a reader whose prose proficiency is 150 has less than a 50% chance of giving a correct response to the Level 1 tasks. Individuals whose proficiency score is 200, in contrast, have about an 80% probability of responding correctly to these Level 1 tasks.

In terms of task demands, it can be inferred that adults performing at 200 on the prose scale are likely to be able to locate a single piece of information in a brief text when there is no distracting information, or if plausible but incorrect information is present but located away from the correct answer. However, these individuals are likely to demonstrate far more difficulty with tasks in Levels 2 through 5. For example, they would have only about a 40% chance of performing the average Level 2 task correctly and an 18% chance of success with tasks in Level 3 and no more than a 7% chance with tasks in Levels 4 and 5.

Tables 2.1a to 2.1c

Average probabilities of successful performance by individuals with selected proficiency scores on tasks in each literacy level of the prose, document and quantitative scales

Tables 2.1a

Prose scale

	Selected proficiency scores				
Prose level	**150**	**200**	**250**	**300**	**350**
			%		
1	48	81	95	99	100
2	14	40	76	94	99
3	6	18	46	78	93
4	2	7	21	50	80
5 *	2	6	18	40	68

Table 2.1b

Document scale

	Selected proficiency scores				
Document level	**150**	**200**	**250**	**300**	**350**
			%		
1	40	72	94	99	100
2	19	50	82	95	99
3	7	20	49	79	94
4 *	4	12	31	60	83
5 *	<1	1	3	13	41

Table 2.1c

Quantitative scale

	Selected proficiency scores				
Quantitative level	**150**	**200**	**250**	**300**	**350**
			%		
1 *	34	67	89	97	99
2	20	45	75	92	98
3	7	20	48	78	93
4	1	6	22	58	87
5	1	2	7	20	53

*Probabilities in this row are based on one task.

In contrast, respondents demonstrating a proficiency of 300 on the prose scale have about an 80% chance or higher of succeeding on tasks in Levels 1, 2 and 3. This means that they demonstrate success with tasks that require them to make low-level inferences and with tasks that require them to take some conditional information into account. They can also integrate or compare and contrast information that is easily identified in the text. On the other hand, they are likely to demonstrate some difficulty with tasks where they must make high text-based inferences or where they need to process more abstract types of information. These more difficult tasks may also require them to draw on less familiar or more specialized types of knowledge beyond that given in the text. On average, they have about a 50% probability of performing Level 4 tasks correctly; with Level 5 tasks, their likelihood of responding correctly decreases to 40%.

Similar kinds of interpretations can be made using the information presented for the document and quantitative literacy scales. For example, someone who is at 200 on the quantitative scale has, on average, a 67% chance of responding correctly to Level 1 tasks. His or her likelihood of responding correctly decreases to 45% for Level 2 tasks, 20% for Level 3 tasks, 6% for Level 4 tasks and only 2% for Level 5 tasks. Similarly, readers with a proficiency of 300 on the quantitative scale would have a probability of 95% or higher of responding correctly to tasks in Levels 1 and 2. Their average probability would decrease to 78% for Level 3 tasks, 58% for Level 4 and 20% for Level 5.

Conclusion

One of the goals of large-scale surveys is to provide a set of information that can inform policy makers and help them during the decision-making process. Presenting information in a way that will enhance understanding of what has been measured and what conclusions may be drawn from the data is important to reaching this goal. This chapter has presented a framework for understanding the consistency of task responses demonstrated by adults from a number of countries. This framework identifies a set of variables shown to underlie successful performance on a broad array of literacy tasks. Collectively, these variables provide a means for moving away from interpreting survey results in terms of discrete tasks or a single number and towards identifying levels of performance that have generalizability and validity across assessments and groups.

The knowledge and understanding such a framework provides contribute to the evolving concept of test design as more than merely assigning a numerical value (or position) to an individual based on his or her responses to a set of tasks, but rather, to assigning meaning and interpretability to this number. As concern ceases to centre on discrete behaviours or isolated observations and concentrates more on providing a meaningful score, a higher level of measurement is reached (Messick 1989).

References

Kirsch, Irwin S. and Peter Mosenthal. "Interpreting the IEA Reading/Literacy Scales." In *Methodological Issues in Comparative Educational Studies: The Case of the IEA Reading Literacy Study*. Edited by M. Binkley, K. Rust and M. Winglee. Washington, D.C.: National Center for Education Statistics, U.S. Department of Education, 1993.

Kirsch, Irwin S., et al. *Adult Literacy in America: A First Look at the Results of the National Adult Literacy Survey*. Washington, D.C.: National Center for Education Statistics, U.S. Department of Education, 1993.

Montigny, Gilles, Karen Kelly and Stan Jones. *Adult Literacy in Canada: Results of a National Study*. Ottawa: Minister of Industry, Science and Technology (Statistics Canada, Catalogue no. 89-525E), 1991.

Messick, S. "Validity." In *Educational Measurement*, 3rd ed. Edited by R. Linn. New York: Macmillan, 1989.

Chapter 3

The distribution of literacy

Stan Jones, Centre for the Study of Adult Literacy, Carleton University, Ottawa, Canada

This chapter is concerned with factors that lead to and follow from literacy...
...among adults aged 16 to 65.

The purpose of IALS was to focus on differences in skill distribution...

The central goal of the International Adult Literacy Survey (IALS) was to investigate and compare factors related to literacy skills in a variety of countries. These factors include those that lead to literacy, such as educational experience; those that might be thought of as consequences of literacy, such as income and occupation; and, an important group of factors that sustain literacy, such as reading at work.

This chapter is primarily concerned with the first and the second set of factors. The third group of factors that sustain literacy are the subject of the next chapter.

In some, but not all, IALS countries the study population included adults over 65 years old.[1] This chapter and the next report only on the population aged 16 to 65, which allows appropriate comparisons across all countries.[2]

It was not the purpose of the IALS to rank countries on any measures of literacy skill. These countries differ in demographic makeup, in how they organize education, and in employment opportunities. Still, the populations of the countries do differ, in interesting ways, on the literacy measures. This is apparent in Tables 3.1a to 3.1c which present the estimated proportion of each country's[3] population at each level[4] on each of the three scales (prose, document and quantitative). Figure 3.1 shows these differences in distribution.

---

[1] The literacy levels of those over age 65 are lower than those under age 65 in all the countries that included them in the sample.

[2] Information on background and demographic factors, such as age, occupation, and reports on literacy practices, were collected in a background questionnaire. In a few cases one or two of the countries did not include a particular question; these are noted as appropriate. More importantly, not all individuals answered every question. In some cases they simply did not know the information; for example, information on parents' education. In others, individuals chose not to answer, as in questions about income. When large numbers did not answer a question, this is noted in the discussion.

The background questionnaire contained a wide range of questions. No attempt has been made to exhaustively report on all of them in these two chapters. Each of the participating countries is planning one or more further reports specific to their own country and it is expected that there will be other international reports on particular topics.

[3] The decision to combine the data from the two language groups in Canada (English and French) follows from the practice in Statistics Canada's 1989 Survey of Literacy Skills Used in Daily Activities in which the results were reported for the country as a whole.

[4] Because the proportion at Level 5 is under 5% in most countries, Levels 4 and 5 have been combined in the analyses presented in this chapter and in Chapter 4. For many of the analyses, then, a reliable estimate could not be made for the subgroup proportions at this level. Rather than simply leave blank cells in tables, Level 5 was combined with Level 4. As well, there seems to be no compelling policy interest in the relative proportions at Levels 4 and 5. As the data presented here show, even the difference between Level 3 and Level 4/5 is of minor interest. Given the large numbers at Levels 1 and 2 for which lack of literacy skill has a large impact, the pressing policy concern is how to increase Level 3 relative to Levels 1 and 2.

Figure 3.1

Estimated distribution of population by literacy level, all scales

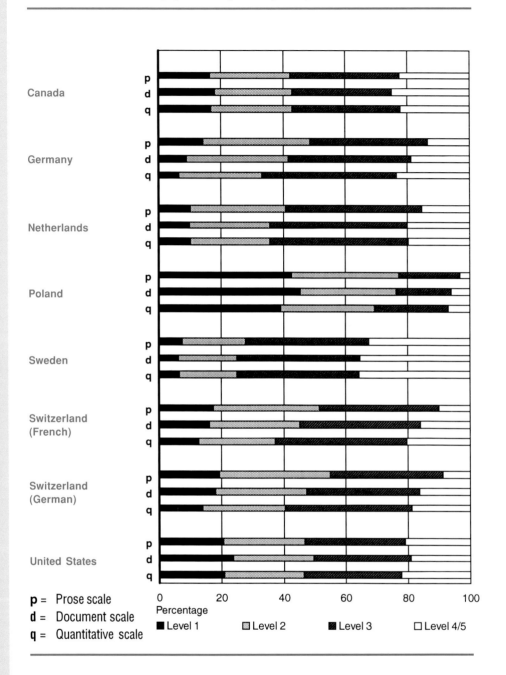

p = Prose scale
d = Document scale
q = Quantitative scale

It is particularly interesting to note that:

- Canada and the United States have quite similar distribution patterns, though there is a slightly larger proportion at Level 1 in the United States. What distinguishes both countries is that both have relatively large numbers at Level 1 and at Level 4/5. In both countries there are larger numbers at Level 1 on the document scale than at this level on the other two scales. In Canada there are also larger numbers at Level 4/5 on the document scale than on the prose and quantitative scales; in the United States there are smaller numbers at Level 4/5 on the document scale than on the other two scales.

Table 3.1a

Distribution of population in each country, prose scale

	Level 1	Level 2	Level 3	Level 4/5
	Percentage			
Canada	16.6	25.6	35.1	22.7
Germany	14.4	34.2	38.0	13.4
Netherlands	10.5	30.1	44.1	15.3
Poland	42.6	34.5	19.8	3.1
Sweden	7.5	20.3	39.7	32.4
Switzerland (French)	17.6	33.7	38.6	10.0
Switzerland (German)	19.3	35.7	36.1	8.9
United States	20.7	25.9	32.4	21.1

These tables demonstrate country differences in the distribution of literacy. Some, such as Germany and the Netherlands, have large proportions at Levels 2 and 3 and smaller proportions at Levels 1 and 4/5

Table 3.1b

Distribution of the population in each country, document scale

	Level 1	Level 2	Level 3	Level 4/5
	Percentage			
Canada	18.2	24.7	32.1	25.1
Germany	9.0	32.7	39.5	18.9
Netherlands	10.1	25.7	44.2	20.0
Poland	45.4	30.7	18.0	5.8
Sweden	6.2	18.9	39.4	35.5
Switzerland (French)	16.2	28.8	38.9	16.0
Switzerland (German)	18.1	29.1	36.6	16.1
United States	23.7	25.9	31.4	19.0

Table 3.1c

Distribution of the population in each country, quantitative scale

	Level 1	Level 2	Level 3	Level 4/5
	Percentage			
Canada	16.9	26.1	34.8	22.2
Germany	6.7	26.6	43.2	23.5
Netherlands	10.3	25.5	44.3	19.9
Poland	39.1	30.1	23.9	6.8
Sweden	6.6	18.6	39.0	35.8
Switzerland (French)	12.9	24.5	42.2	20.4
Switzerland (German)	14.2	26.2	40.7	19.0
United States	21.0	25.3	31.3	22.5

- Germany demonstrates considerable variation across scales, particularly when the proportion at Level 4/5 on the prose scale is compared with Level 4/5 in the quantitative scale.

- The Netherlands shows great internal consistency across scales with an especially large number at Level 3 on all three scales. As in Germany, the number at Level 4/5 on the prose scale is smaller than the number at this level on the other two scales.

- Poland's results point to interesting differences across the scales and the dimensions of literacy they measure. There are larger proportions at the two higher levels on the prose and quantitative scales. The smaller proportions on the document and prose scales may reflect the changing economic situation there, as these scales represent a type of literacy likely to be more common in a fully market-oriented society.

- Sweden is characterized by substantial numbers at all the higher levels on all three scales. When literacy practices are discussed in the next chapter, it will be seen that Sweden is equally high on those variables that capture the actual use of literacy in daily life.

...and this chapter suggests some reasons for these differences.

- The two language groups in Switzerland (French and German) show few differences. There are substantial numbers at Level 3 and there are more at higher levels on the quantitative scale. In this way, Switzerland is similar to the Netherlands and Germany.

This chapter also explores the underlying factors that shape these national distributions and suggests some reasons for the differences. It begins with a discussion of the direct economic consequences of differences in literacy skill, such as differences in employment and in income. These differences in skill are then linked to particular occupations and industries, showing how changes in employment patterns favour more highly skilled individuals. An examination of how education and other policies, such as immigration, shape the literacy profile of a country follows.

Some consequences of literacy skill

Literacy has broad economic effects...

If literacy had no consequences it would be of only minor interest, but literacy has broad consequences—particularly economic. Other consequences, ones that might be thought of as related more to citizenship and social participation, are related to literacy practices and are discussed in the next chapter.

Employment

...people in jobs are more likely to be literate...

The IALS collected data on a number of factors related to employment: the most central is employment status. In all countries (Figures 3.2a to 3.2d)[5] employment is positively related to literacy, in that those who are employed (or who are in school) are more likely to be at higher literacy skill levels than those who are unemployed or who are outside the work force.

...conversely, high-level literates are less likely to be unemployed.

Table 3.2 summarizes the data, by literacy level, on those who reported being unemployed. Except in the United States, the proportion of unemployed by level decreases as the level increases (the actual proportion varies from country to country because the unemployment rate differs), though the decrease between Level 1 and Level 2 is small in some cases. In all countries, very few individuals at Levels 3 and 4/5 find themselves unemployed, while many of those at Level 1 are without work. The proportion at Level 1 who are unemployed is comparatively large in Germany, Sweden and Poland. Clearly, literacy and employment are strongly linked.

Table 3.2

Proportion of population at each literacy level who are unemployed, document scale

This table shows that when compared with other levels, more of those at Level 1 are unemployed and fewer of those at Level 4 are unemployed. Skill seems to make the greatest impact on employment in Germany, Poland and Sweden.

	Level 1	Level 2	Level 3	Level 4/5
	Percentage			
Canada	9.3	4.1	3.2	2.6
Germany	20.1	11.0	9.1	2.5
Netherlands	7.6	7.5	2.7	0.9
Poland	25.8	13.9	6.5	3.8
Sweden	23.1	12.4	4.9	1.8
Switzerland (French)	8.5	4.5	3.9	1.6
Switzerland (German)	3.4	3.0	2.9	0.7
United States	6.1	8.3	3.9	1.4

---

[5]   Tables that support the graphs can be found in Appendix B. In some cases only portions of a table are included in the text. In these cases, too, the complete table can be found in Appendix B.

Figures 3.2 a, b, c and d

Literacy and employment, document scale

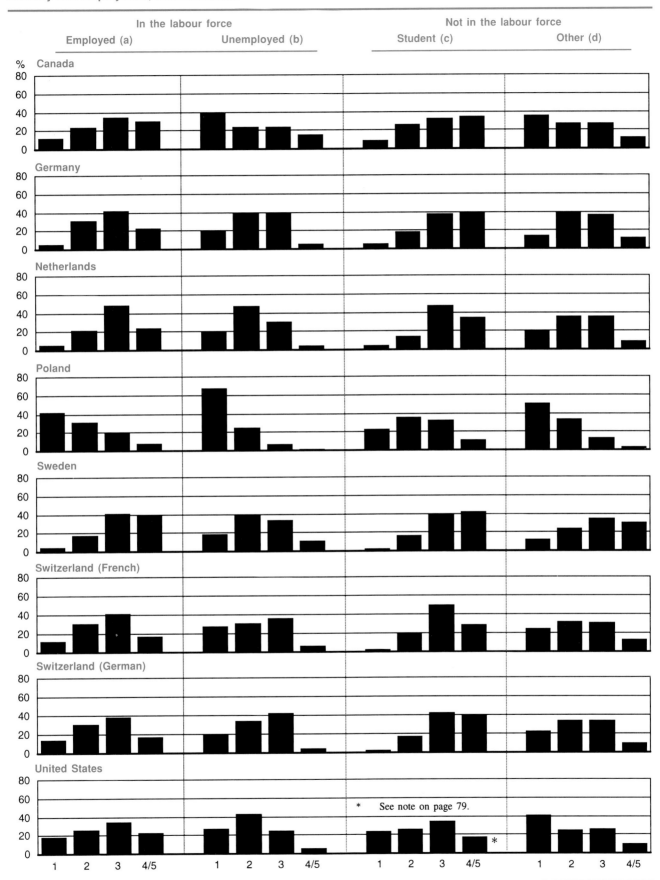

Literacy is strongly related to income...

...particularly in the case of the low-level literates...

Income

Because literacy is connected to employment, it follows that it is related to income. As Figure 3.3 and Table 3.3 show, there appears to be a strong bivariate relationship. The income groups in this table represent wage income quintiles specific to each country. That is, the income range covered by each quintile includes 20% of the income earners in that country. This means that quintile 1 in the Netherlands does not represent the same range of income as quintile 1 in Poland; the comparisons across countries are, therefore, relative to the distribution of income within a country. If the income range in a country is small, then it will be more difficult to detect a literacy effect than in a country with a larger income range.

In all the countries there is a clear direct effect of literacy on wage income. In all cases,[6] individuals at Level 1 are much more likely to have no income than those at other skill levels. At the same time, in all cases those at Level 4/5 are more likely to be in the top income quintile. But it is also important to point out that individuals performing at Level 3 are also likely to have relatively high incomes. In some countries, the Netherlands and Sweden in particular, the difference between the percentage of Level 3 at quintile 5 and the percentage of Level 4/5 at that quintile is small.

Figure 3.3

Percentage of population within each country with low incomes* by literacy level

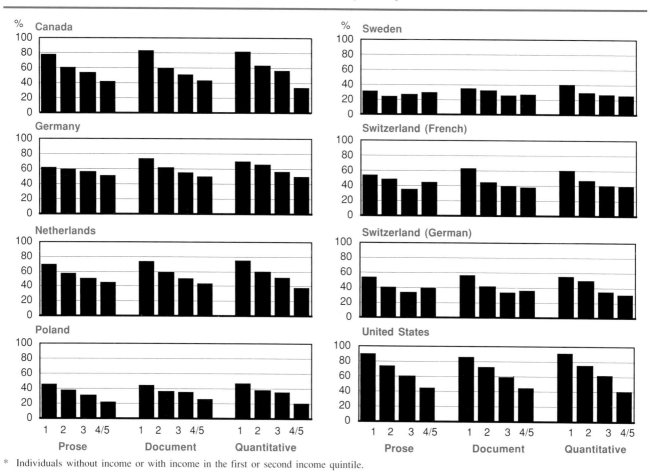

* Individuals without income or with income in the first or second income quintile.

---

6 In the Switzerland data, individuals with no income were given the same coding as those in quintile 1; hence, there are no Swiss respondents reported as having no income. While this makes it more difficult to see that low literacy is closely connected to low income in Switzerland, there can be no doubt that the data show a relation between high literacy and high income.

Table 3.3

Proportion of population at each literacy level whose ~~income~~ is within a particular quintile, document scale

		Level 1	Level 2	Level 3	Level 4/5
			Percentage		
Canada	No income	51.7	27.7	20.3	11.9
	Quintile 1	12.1	17.6	16.5	17.2
	Quintile 2	18.8	13.6	13.9	13.6
	Quintile 3	7.4	15.1	17.8	11.9
	Quintile 4	5.0	13.1	18.8	18.9
	Quintile 5	5.0	12.8	12.7	26.5
Germany	No income	42.2	34.6	33.5	27.7
	Quintile 1	5.6	9.9	8.0	8.4
	Quintile 2	25.8	17.5	13.6	13.3
	Quintile 3	11.8	17.7	13.2	13.2
	Quintile 4	10.6	12.0	16.4	14.7
	Quintile 5	4.1	8.3	15.2	22.7
Netherlands	No income	58.0	41.2	25.7	22.0
	Quintile 1	8.2	8.4	12.2	10.9
	Quintile 2	6.1	8.8	12.7	9.7
	Quintile 3	20.1	20.2	20.5	21.8
	Quintile 4	6.2	12.5	13.3	14.2
	Quintile 5	1.4	8.8	15.6	21.5
Poland	No income	0.0	0.0	0.0	1.0
	Quintile 1	24.4	16.4	18.8	11.1
	Quintile 2	20.0	20.1	15.8	13.1
	Quintile 3	20.1	24.4	24.0	23.4
	Quintile 4	16.7	22.7	17.1	22.4
	Quintile 5	18.9	16.4	24.2	29.0
Sweden	No income	3.5	0.0	0.3	0.2
	Quintile 1	5.0	13.2	12.9	17.2
	Quintile 2	26.3	18.7	11.8	9.2
	Quintile 3	27.7	21.0	20.1	15.1
	Quintile 4	24.4	27.2	23.7	18.7
	Quintile 5	13.0	20.0	31.3	39.6
Switzerland (French)	No income	N/A	N/A	N/A	N/A
	Quintile 1	33.4	22.4	20.1	23.5
	Quintile 2	28.8	21.1	19.2	13.9
	Quintile 3	19.3	22.6	19.2	20.0
	Quintile 4	13.5	21.3	21.8	22.2
	Quintile 5	5.0	12.6	19.7	20.3
Switzerland (German)	No income	N/A	N/A	N/A	N/A
	Quintile 1	33.2	26.6	23.8	26.7
	Quintile 2	22.3	14.9	9.7	9.3
	Quintile 3	22.0	20.9	22.3	22.4
	Quintile 4	18.3	17.7	21.5	16.5
	Quintile 5	4.1	20.0	22.7	25.1
United States	No income	44.2	30.5	19.2	11.4
	Quintile 1	25.9	20.2	21.5	14.6
	Quintile 2	15.9	21.8	18.1	17.7
	Quintile 3	10.4	16.3	19.6	22.9
	Quintile 4	2.9	9.0	15.9	21.7
	Quintile 5	0.7	2.0	5.7	11.8

This table shows that individuals at Level 4/5 are more likely to have high incomes (in quintiles 4 and 5), while those at Level 1 are more likely to have no income or be in a lower income quintile. The quintiles are specific to each country and cannot be compared across countries.

...since higher literacy levels protect against very low income.

It is also useful to consider what proportion of each level has income below each quintile; this will help us understand how income increases with higher literacy skill. Table 3.4 presents these data for Canada as an example. It is clear that the higher the literacy level, the smaller the proportion of the population with incomes below a given quintile. The other countries show similar patterns.

Table 3.4

Proportion of Canadian population at each literacy level whose income is below a particular quintile, document scale

	Level 1	Level 2	Level 3	Level 4/5
	Percentage			
Below quintile 2	63.8	45.3	36.8	29.1
Below quintile 3	82.6	58.9	50.7	42.3
Below quintile 4	90.0	74.0	68.5	54.2
Below quintile 5	95.0	87.1	87.3	73.1

Occupation

Literacy is linked to occupation, but varies for each of the three literacy dimensions...

Occupations differ in the skills they require. Indeed, most classifications of occupations, whether national schemes or the International Standard Classification of Occupations (ISCO-88) used in the IALS, group them by some measure of skill, often educational attainment. As Figure 3.4 shows, there is a consistent and expected relationship between literacy and occupation, and there are also some interesting differences across the scales for particular occupations.

...across clusters of occupations.

It is useful to consider each occupation separately:

- Manager/Professional (ISCO 1 and 2) is predominately a high-skill occupation group with 60% to 75% at Levels 3 and 4/5. There are also usually larger proportions at Level 4/5 on the quantitative and document scales, when compared with the prose scale.

- Technician (ISCO 3) is also a high-skill occupation group, though there are more technicians at Level 2 than managers/professionals and fewer technicians at Level 4/5.

- Clerks (ISCO 4) regularly deal with documents and it would be expected that high literacy skills are required. Compared with other occupations with similar education qualifications, such as sales, service, skilled craft workers and machine operators, clerks do have higher skills. It must be noted, though, that the largest numbers of clerks are at Levels 2 and 3, not at Level 4/5, suggesting that the highest level of literacy skill is not required for the kind of tasks clerks regularly perform with text. From the descriptions of the levels found in the previous chapter, it is apparent that the task descriptions for Levels 2 and 3 (locate and identify information in complex texts) match closely with typical clerical tasks. That is not to say that there are no clerks at Level 4/5; indeed there are, and there are always more clerks at this level than craft and machine workers.

- Sales and service workers (ISCO 5) are the most difficult occupational group to relate to particular literacy levels. There are usually some of these workers at each literacy level; in many countries, such as Canada and Sweden, there are even quite significant proportions at Level 4/5. The literacy data suggest that this occupational group is the least homogeneous. When industry and literacy are examined below it will be seen that the literacy skills of service workers in finance are different from those in personal service industries.

- Skilled craft workers (ISCO 7) differ noticeably from country to country. In the United States and Canada, between 25% and 30% of the craft workers are at Level 1 (document scale), but in Germany only 7% are at this level. Similar large differences between the Level 1 proportions of these three countries can be found on the other scales. This reflects the fact that entry into craft occupations in North America is relatively easy and often unregulated, in contrast to Europe where these occupations are usually subject to more rigorous entry requirements and/or certification based on demonstrated skill.

Figure 3.4
Literacy by occupation, document scale

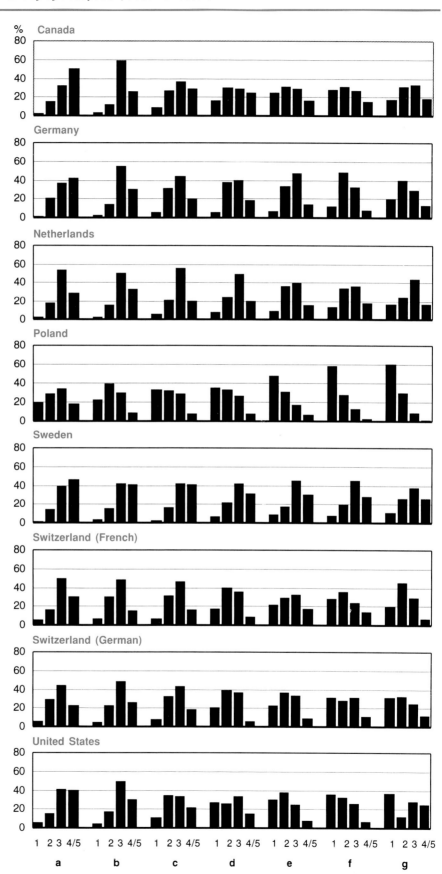

- Machine operators (ISCO 8) have skill levels similar to those of skilled craft workers when the latter are relatively low skilled (as in North America). However, they have lower skill levels when craft work is subject to certification (as in Germany). In particular, machine operators tend to have lower skills on the quantitative and document scales.

- Agricultural (ISCO 6) and primary occupations (ISCO 9) have the lowest demonstrated literacy skills. This is particularly noticeable in countries with larger agricultural sectors, such as Poland.

Different skills are needed in particular occupations in different countries...

While Germany and the United States have similar proportions at each of the literacy levels for the Manager/Professional occupations on the quantitative and document scales, there is a larger proportion in the United States at Level 4/5 on the prose scale. At the same time, in the traditional blue-collar occupations (ISCO 7 and 8) there are larger proportions at higher literacy levels in Germany on all three scales. This suggests that comparisons of occupations across countries must be made with care, because there are quite real differences in the basic skills required. It is also surely worth further study to understand why this occurs and how this affects the organization of work in otherwise similar occupations in different countries.[7]

...so it is misleading to link skill only to educational attainment.

It is also important to note that the traditional assignment of skill to occupations through educational attainment is misleading. Clerks, sales workers, service workers, skilled craft workers, and machine operators are all identified with the same level of education (some secondary education) in the ISCO classification system. The IALS data demonstrate that there are quite significant literacy skill differences across these occupations; therefore, analyses that treat them as equivalent in skill will be misleading.

Industry

Growth sectors have the most literate workers...

As Figures 3.5a and 3.5b show, there is an interesting and important relation between changes in employment by industry and literacy.[8] Those industries, such as financial and personal services, that have grown in all countries in the last 20 years are those where the incumbents have the highest average scores. At the same time, industries in decline, especially agriculture, are characterized by workers with the lowest average literacy skill. Much commentary and forecasting has emphasized the growth in skill demand in the changing industrial economies; the IALS data provide concrete evidence of that change.[9]

---

[7] It is also worth noting that the organization of work may affect literacy skills. If jobs are designed for workers with low literacy skills, then everyday practice will not encourage the retention or development of higher skills. This possibility is discussed in more detail in the next chapter.

[8] Germany and Canada were selected for analysis because they represent countries with small and large agricultural sectors. Similar patterns were found in all countries (data on similar industrial change in Poland are not available).

[9] It might be thought that the increased literacy of the growing industries is due simply to an age difference: growing industries might be thought to have a younger workforce than the declining ones. This is not systematically the case. In the IALS sample in Canada, for example, 35% of the workers in personal services were over 45, but only 23% of those working in agriculture were this age and only 19% of those in manufacturing; 45% of those in financial services are under 35, but 60% of the workers in sales were this age. The agricultural work force is older in Germany, where 43% are over 45, but here, too, the personal service industry has an equal number in this age group, 42%. The differences among industries cannot be attributed primarily to a simple difference in age composition.

Figure 3.5a

Employment growth and literacy patterns, Germany

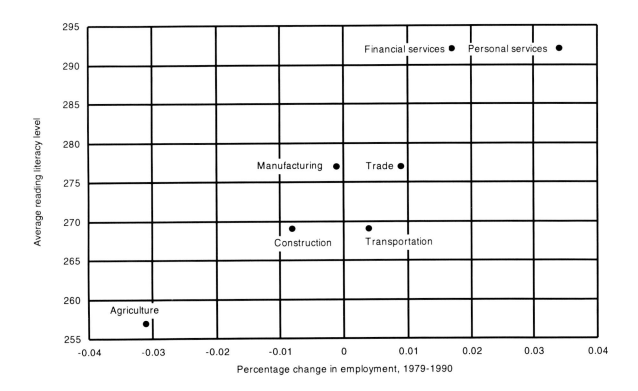

Figure 3.5b

Employment growth and literacy patterns, Canada

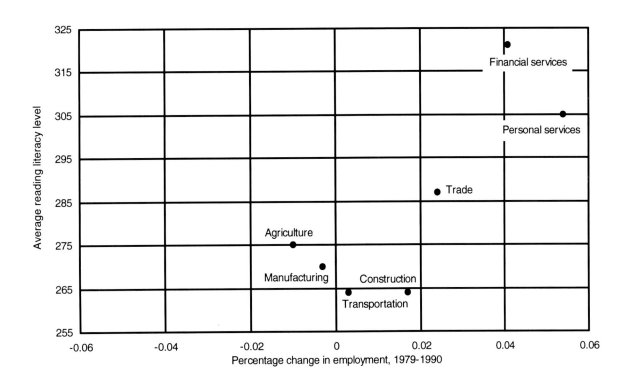

Table 3.5

Proportion of workers in each industry who are at a particular literacy level, document scale

		Level 1	Level 2	Level 3	Level 4/5
			Percentage		
Canada	Agriculture/Mining	16.9	27.6	32.8	22.7
	Manufacturing	21.6	24.0	31.3	23.2
	Construction/Transport	19.6	32.4	26.7	21.3
	Trade/Hospitality	13.9	29.0	32.4	24.7
	Financial services	3.3	15.7	33.7	47.4
	Personal services	7.9	19.7	40.4	32.0
Germany	Agriculture/Mining	8.5	49.1	18.8	23.5
	Manufacturing	5.6	29.3	43.5	21.5
	Construction/Transport	7.7	40.5	33.1	18.7
	Trade/Hospitality	6.7	33.2	39.2	21.0
	Financial services	5.6	19.7	52.7	21.9
	Personal services	5.1	23.5	44.5	27.0
Netherlands	Agriculture/Mining	9.8	19.8	48.3	22.1
	Manufacturing	6.5	28.3	43.7	21.5
	Construction/Transport	10.5	28.5	42.6	18.4
	Trade/Hospitality	5.7	24.5	52.3	17.5
	Financial services	4.7	13.5	50.7	31.1
	Personal services	4.6	18.4	49.3	27.7
Poland	Agriculture/Mining	60.5	26.4	10.8	2.3
	Manufacturing	49.8	28.6	15.0	6.7
	Construction/Transport	38.8	38.1	18.2	4.9
	Trade/Hospitality	30.3	38.4	24.7	6.7
	Financial services	27.3	25.5	29.4	17.9
	Personal services	33.1	30.9	26.9	9.1
Sweden	Agriculture/Mining	6.9	21.0	44.3	27.8
	Manufacturing	5.6	16.1	39.7	38.6
	Construction/Transport	4.0	14.4	42.4	39.1
	Trade/Hospitality	5.8	18.9	44.3	31.0
	Financial services	2.3	11.0	34.4	52.3
	Personal services	4.2	18.4	41.4	36.1
Switzerland (French)	Agriculture/Mining	5.2	58.0	26.1	10.7
	Manufacturing	16.3	34.1	38.6	11.0
	Construction/Transport	22.3	22.7	37.3	17.8
	Trade/Hospitality	11.8	39.2	39.2	9.8
	Financial services	2.9	22.0	52.6	22.4
	Personal services	8.9	25.6	43.6	22.0
Switzerland (German)	Agriculture/Mining	17.2	43.4	31.5	7.9
	Manufacturing	13.3	35.0	32.3	19.3
	Construction/Transport	17.5	26.6	42.2	13.7
	Trade/Hospitality	16.4	33.8	37.5	12.3
	Financial services	5.3	21.6	50.9	22.2
	Personal services	10.6	28.3	40.7	20.4
United States	Agriculture/Mining	22.1	19.9	26.1	32.0
	Manufacturing	25.0	28.3	30.6	16.2
	Construction/Transport	19.8	30.3	30.9	19.0
	Trade/Hospitality	22.5	28.0	32.0	17.5
	Financial services	12.4	24.7	35.5	27.4
	Personal services	14.2	20.8	38.2	26.8

Different industries make different literacy demands. The service industries have the largest numbers at the higher literacy levels and agriculture, manufacturing and construction have smaller numbers.

...and the declining agricultural sector has the least literate workers.

The connection between industrial sectors and skill is set out for all the countries in Table 3.5, using proportions in each level of the document scale (similar patterns are found on the prose and quantitative scales). Agriculture, the industry in greatest decline, has high proportions at Level 1 and low proportions at Level 4/5. The growth sectors, finance and personal service, are marked by large proportions at Level 4/5.

Reserve labour force

If the pattern demonstrated in Figures 3.5a and 3.5b is characteristic of all modern economies, then for an economy to grow there should be a source of skilled workers to fill the jobs in the growth industries. One source is students leaving school and Figure 3.2c suggests that in all countries this is a relatively highly skilled group. The unemployed, Figure 3.2b, as just noted, are not typically highly skilled. Another source are those who are out of the labour force, but not in school, who might be attracted into the work force.

As Figure 3.2d indicates, it is not always the case that this reserve pool is very skilled. In every country, on all scales, large numbers of this group are at Level 1 and in many countries, the number at Level 4/5 is about the same as the number of unemployed at that level: Sweden is a notable exception. Certain countries do have a large proportion outside the labour force at Level 3 (Germany and the German-speaking group in Switzerland have over 40% at this level), suggesting that they do have a resource that might be available if conditions were appropriate. Canada, the United States and Poland would seem to have the smallest reserve resource; in all three countries over 30% of this group is at Level 1.

Full-time versus part-time work

Another potential source of skilled workers are those working only part time. But this is a source only if part-time workers are not less skilled than full-time workers. Overall, there is no systematic relation between literacy skill and whether an individual has full- or part-time employment, as Figure 3.6 portrays. On some scales, in some countries, full-time workers have slightly larger proportions at the higher skill levels; on other scales, often in the same country, there are also large proportions of part-time workers at the upper skill levels. For example, in Switzerland, among the French-speaking population, there are almost twice as many part-time workers at Level 4/5 on the prose scale (part-time, 18%; full-time, 9%), but on the quantitative scale there are virtually the same numbers at this level (part-time, 21.7%; full-time, 21.5%). Among the German-speaking population in Switzerland, more full- than part-time workers are at Level 4/5 on the quantitative scale (23% vs. 12% part-time), but the numbers are approximately the same on the prose scale (part-time, 8.5%; full-time, 9.4%).

One reason that part-time workers demonstrate high skills may be that much part-time work is carried out by students. In the United States and Canada about one-third of the part-time workers said they were students and over 20% of the part-time workers in the Netherlands were also in school. This explanation does not exist for all countries with highly skilled part-time workers. In some, only a small number were in school; in Germany and Switzerland, for example, only about 10% were also going to school.

A second frequently reported reason for part-time work was that the individual had child care or other family responsibilities that limited working hours. In Switzerland, Germany and the Netherlands, over 30% of the part-time workers gave this reason. This suggests that factors other than skill and competitiveness drive much part-time employment. In still other countries, those working part time said they could not find full-time work; in Canada this represents 30% of the responses.

Figure 3.6

Estimated distribution by literacy level of the full-time employed and part-time employed populations

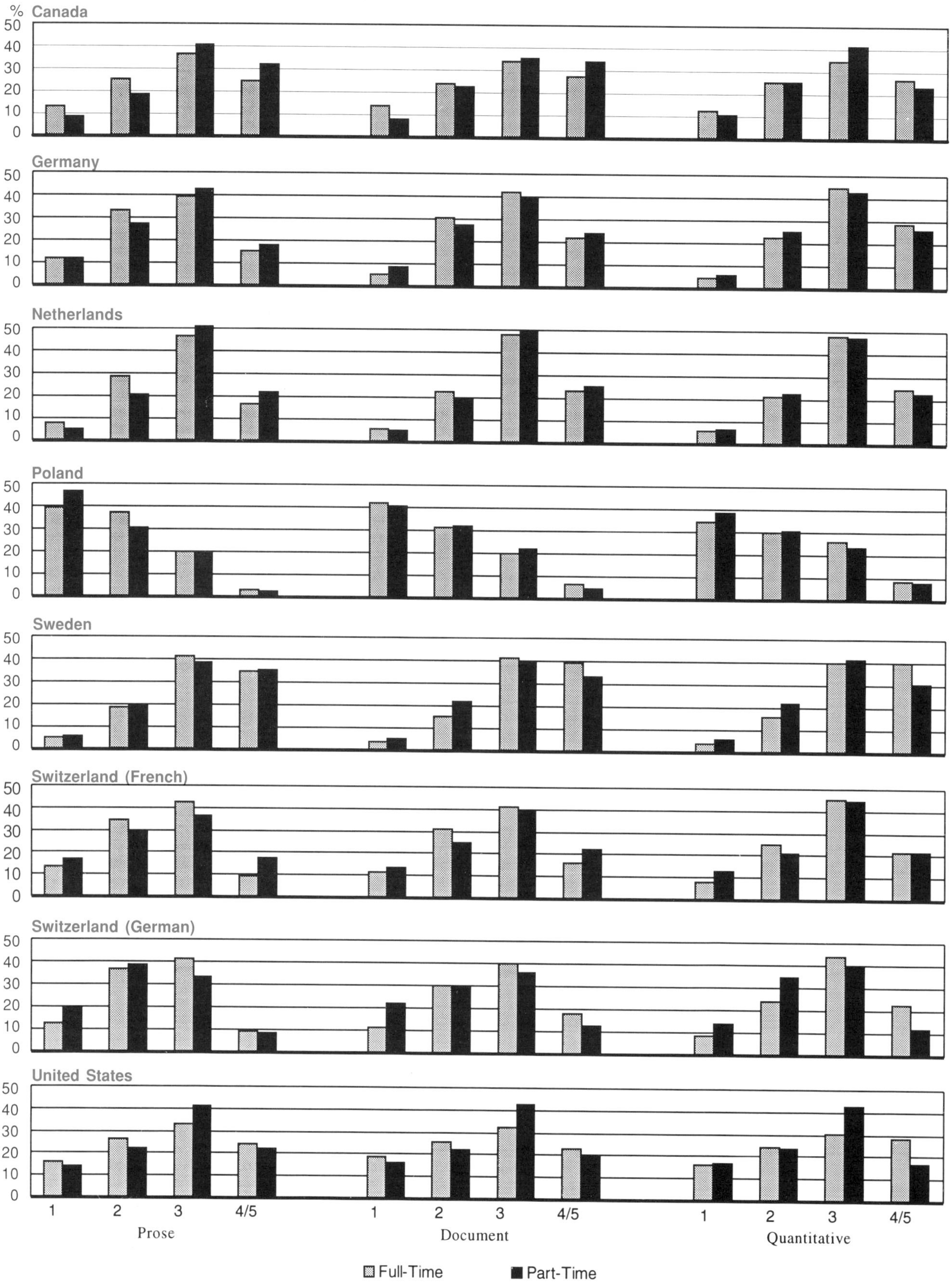

Full-Time   Part-Time

Studies on training show that...

Adult and continuing education

The increasing demand for highly skilled workers in the 1990s has been accompanied by a growing interest in training; specifically, the training employees receive to prepare them—and their employers—for changes in the work environment, processes and products. In this way the existing work force is yet another source of higher skilled workers when their skills are enhanced. This is particularly important as at least 80% of the post-2000 labour force is already at work.

A number of studies in OECD countries of adult education have shown that training tends to be concentrated on individuals with higher skill levels (Statistics Canada 1992; Australian Bureau of Statistics 1993). Yet, at the same time, employers worry that they will be unable to bring new technology to their workplace because some of their employees have such low literacy levels that the cost of training them would be prohibitive. But, one can also argue that continuing education allows individuals to broaden their skill. Much of the reading employees do each day is routine and there is some evidence that workers, particularly those with low literacy skills, develop reading skills that are narrowly specific to the regular reading they do. It is in training that new—and therefore challenging—reading activities occur, offering the opportunity to expand and deepen the literacy skills the individual ordinarily uses.

Table 3.6

Proportion of population at each literacy level who participated in adult education in the last year, document scale

	Level 1	Level 2	Level 3	Level 4/5
	Percentage			
Canada	19.3	35.3	44.6	65.1
Netherlands	19.8	30.2	44.8	57.2
Poland	8.7	15.6	23.2	34.2
Sweden	28.9	38.9	52.2	59.4
Switzerland (French)	20.9	27.6	41.8	47.7
Switzerland (German)	20.2	39.1	52.0	70.2
United States	21.4	36.0	53.1	62.8

In every country individuals with lower literacy skills were less likely to participate in adult education than those at higher levels.

...the more skilled a person is...

The IALS data point to considerable similarity between countries both in terms of the proportion of the work force that receives training (Figure 3.7) and in the way training is distributed by literacy skill (Table 3.6). Poland is a clear exception; here the proportion of the sample population reporting having received any training is notably small. Independent data are not available to confirm the IALS figures for Poland. However, it is likely that the IALS figures are appropriate and that because of Poland's transition to a market economy, employee training has yet to play an important role there.[10]

---

[10] Figures for Germany are not included in this discussion. The training data for the IALS sample were inconsistent with other data from Germany. When the wording of the relevant question used in the German questionnaire was reviewed, it was found that it would likely lead respondents to report only training that occurred in formal institutions; this undoubtedly led to under-reporting.

Figure 3.7
Literacy levels for those who received training, document scale

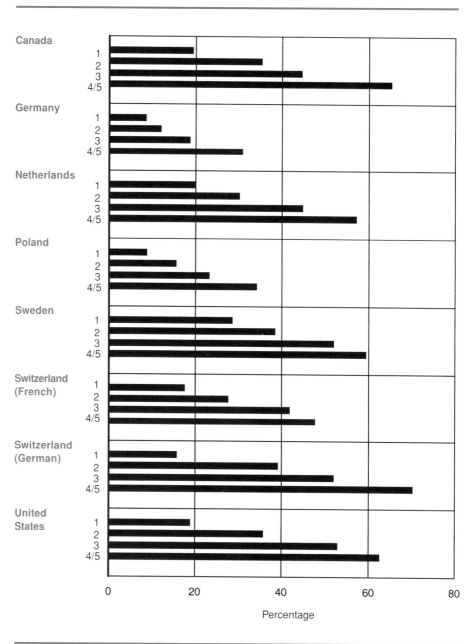

In short, for countries other than Poland, the more skilled a person is the more likely he or she has had some training or educational opportunity in the last year. Indeed, in all countries except Poland the majority of those at Level 4/5[11] had some training opportunity; only in Sweden did those at Level 1 have similar opportunities (25%). In all countries, the higher the literacy level—whatever the scale—the greater the likelihood that those studied received some training in the previous year. Consequently, this may be creating an increasing societal division based on skill. If training adds to skill, then clearly those who already have high-level skills will have these skills enhanced. At the other extreme, those with fewer skills have fewer opportunities to benefit from training; that is, to improve both their general literacy and specific, job-related skills. If their ordinary activities provide few opportunities for literate activities, or little variety in those that do occur, then their skills may even decline. The data explored in the next chapter strongly suggest that this is, indeed, the case.

Immigration

For many countries, immigration is a source of new workers. Some, such as Canada, have a significant proportion of immigrants in their 16- to 65-year-old population (approximately 20% in Canada), while others—Poland, the Netherlands and Germany in particular—have under 10%. While immigration often meets labour force demands, immigrants may be expected to have an impact on the distribution of literacy in at least three ways:

- they may have different educational experiences than the native-born population

- they may have learned an official language only as a second language

- they may be less familiar with the literate culture of the country.

Table 3.7 displays the distribution of literacy among immigrant and native-born populations.

Table 3.7

Proportion of population who are immigrants and who are native born at each literacy level, document scale

		Level 1	Level 2	Level 3	Level 4/5
		Percentage			
Canada	Born in Canada	14.8	25.6	35.4	24.2
	Immigrant	31.1	21.3	19.3	28.3
Germany	Born in Germany	7.8	32.1	40.7	19.4
	Immigrant	23.2	40.1	24.8	11.9
Netherlands	Born in the Netherlands	8.9	25.4	45.2	20.5
	Immigrant	27.4	30.8	30.0	11.8
Sweden	Born in Sweden	4.3	18.0	40.3	37.3
	Immigrant	24.7	27.3	30.8	17.2
Switzerland (French)	Born in Switzerland	10.2	29.3	42.6	18.0
	Immigrant	31.5	28.1	29.4	11.0
Switzerland (German)	Born in Switzerland	8.7	31.3	41.9	18.1
	Immigrant	56.6	20.7	14.5	8.2
United States	Born in the United States	17.5	27.4	34.0	21.2
	Immigrant	54.2	19.7	19.1	6.9

---

[11] The only exception is that just slightly less than half those at this level on the quantitative and document scales in French-speaking Switzerland received training.

...which is reflected in the literacy skill distribution of the population.

In all but one country, Canada, immigrants account for higher proportions at Level 1 and lower proportions at Level 4/5.[12] In Switzerland and the United States, immigrants are more likely to have lower educational attainment than those born in the country, but proportions with low education are similar between native- and foreign-born residents in Germany, the Netherlands and Sweden. At the same time, there is little difference in any of these countries between immigrants and native-born residents in the proportion with tertiary education. In these cases, other explanations, such as language or culture, are necessary.

Canada has relatively more immigrants at Level 4/5...

The exception to these observations is Canada. While there, too, the proportion of immigrants with low literacy skills is greater than the proportion of native-born residents, there are proportionately more immigrants at Level 4/5 than there are native born (26% compared with 22% on the prose scale, 28% compared with 24% on document, and 28% compared with 21% on quantitative). While the differences in proportions are not large, what is notable is that native born are not more prevalent than immigrants at Level 4/5 as they are in countries other than Canada. At the same time, a greater proportion of immigrants is at Level 1.

...which can be directly attributed to a policy that seeks high-level skills.

It appears that Canada, somewhat unlike the other IALS countries, has significant numbers of both low- and high-skilled immigrants. While it is difficult to directly compare immigration policies, it is important to note that Canada has long had a dual immigration policy; that is, one that actively seeks immigrants with high skills under one program, while accepting significant numbers of immigrants under other programs (refugee and family reunification). The IALS data reflect this dual policy. Because none of the other countries participating in the IALS actively recruit high-skilled immigrants, no others have large numbers of immigrants at Level 4/5.

If the IALS data are viewed in broad perspective, it can be concluded that the processes of literacy and employment work to increase the skill disparity in a society. Highly skilled people are more likely to find employment and are more likely to find it in positions that offer greater opportunity to use their skill. Therefore, opportunities to use literacy and opportunities to develop skill fall disproportionately to those with higher skill levels.

The highly skilled receive more training and this may increase worker skill disparity...

...a disparity that may limit economic growth.

If economies require increasing numbers of highly skilled workers to expand, then growth may well be limited by existing practices. Instead of enlarging the pool of highly skilled workers, the tendency is to increase the skills of the already skilled. The reserve employment pool, made up of the unemployed and those working in declining industrial sectors, is a low-skilled pool. Policies directed towards providing more educational opportunities and increasing skills in that pool must be a necessary part of any industrial growth strategy.

Background to literacy

Many factors influence the opportunity to access literacy enhancing activities...

Some of the factors included in the IALS study can be seen as more or less directly affecting the skill a particular individual possesses. These are not proposed as simple causes of literacy (or the lack thereof) but as factors that most directly influence an individual's opportunity to participate in literacy and literacy learning activities. Education is the most prominent of these, but others, such as age, knowledge of the official language (or languages) of the country, and familiarity with literacy practices also have an effect. It must be acknowledged that these factors are also important consequences of literacy; individuals with low skill are more likely to leave school early, for example. It is convenient, nonetheless, to start by thinking about these characteristics as a background to the distribution of literacy in a society.

---

[12]   Poland is excluded from this analysis because the proportion of the IALS population who reported being born outside Poland was less than 2%, making the distribution by level for this subgroup too unreliable.

Education

Although literacy is closely tied to education, it is not the same as education. Because the IALS countries have quite different patterns of educational attainment, it should be expected that these differences play some role in the differences in literacy. Table 3.8 presents, on the document scale, the proportion at each literacy level for specific levels of educational attainment[13] (tables for the other scales are in Appendix B). Figure 3.8 presents the same information.

Table 3.8

Proportion of population at each level of educational attainment who are at each literacy level, document scale

		Level 1	Level 2	Level 3	Level 4/5
Canada	Less than ISCED 02	73.6	15.4	9.7	1.3
	ISCED 02	23.2	40.2	26.3	10.3
	ISCED 03	10.5	28.4	36.9	24.1
	ISCED 05	4.2	17.6	39.1	39.1
	ISCED 06/07	3.3	10.1	38.5	48.1
Germany	Less than ISCED 02	55.5	30.2	14.3	0.0
	ISCED 02	10.5	38.3	39.2	12.0
	ISCED 03	4.7	26.7	43.5	25.1
	ISCED 05	4.7	20.2	48.3	26.8
	ISCED 06/07	1.1	17.9	34.8	46.2
Netherlands	Less than ISCED 02	36.0	38.7	19.2	6.2
	ISCED 02	11.2	36.9	43.1	8.8
	ISCED 03	2.9	18.2	52.4	26.5
	ISCED 05	N/A	N/A	N/A	N/A
	ISCED 06/07	1.3	13.8	50.0	34.9
Poland	Less than ISCED 02	74.6	18.8	5.2	1.4
	ISCED 02	46.9	33.9	15.2	4.0
	ISCED 03	27.8	38.3	27.2	6.8
	ISCED 05	16.4	35.5	36.1	12.1
	ISCED 06/07	15.6	29.6	32.8	22.0
Sweden	Less than ISCED 02	22.5	38.1	33.2	6.2
	ISCED 02	6.8	16.9	45.5	30.8
	ISCED 03	3.9	19.1	42.1	34.9
	ISCED 05	1.1	11.1	37.8	50.1
	ISCED 06/07	0.7	8.1	29.8	61.4
Switzerland (French)	Less than ISCED 02	41.9	39.7	16.4	2.0
	ISCED 02	31.1	46.9	19.9	2.1
	ISCED 03	9.0	31.1	45.1	14.8
	ISCED 05	2.0	19.5	47.9	30.6
	ISCED 06/07	4.9	7.1	47.9	40.1
Switzerland (German)	Less than ISCED 02	72.6	16.7	10.6	0.0
	ISCED 02	31.6	40.2	17.9	10.3
	ISCED 03	9.7	30.9	42.9	16.5
	ISCED 05	5.1	24.9	49.1	20.9
	ISCED 06/07	6.8	15.7	39.1	38.4
United States	Less than ISCED 02	74.0	18.8	6.3	1.0
	ISCED 02	45.2	27.9	21.1	5.9
	ISCED 03	21.2	33.7	32.5	12.6
	ISCED 05	11.7	25.0	39.4	24.0
	ISCED 06/07	6.7	13.3	38.9	41.1

---

[13] In order to compare educational attainment across countries, the IALS used the ISCED system. The full ISCED system distinguishes eight levels, but only five are used here. The numbers at each of the lowest levels (less than secondary) are quite small and do not support subgroup analysis singly; they are combined here. At the other end of the continuum, ISCED 07, education beyond the first university degree is also small and is combined with ISCED 06. The levels can roughly be interpreted as:

ISCED 10/00/01	Primary or less
ISCED 02	Some secondary education, but not completed
ISCED 03	Secondary education completed
ISCED 05	Tertiary, non-university education
ISCED 06/07	Tertiary, university education

It should be noted that the Netherlands does not use ISCED 05 in reports on its education system.

Figure 3.8

Distribution in each country of literacy level by educational attainment, document scale

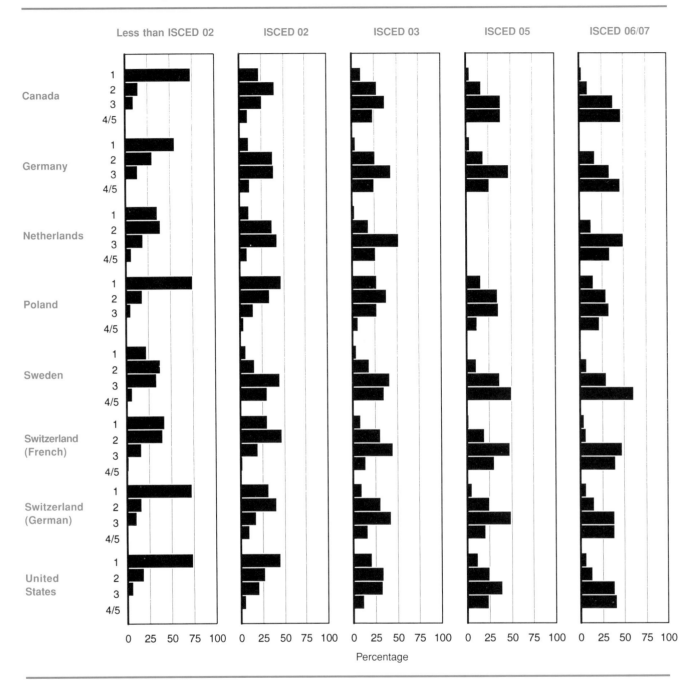

Table 3.9a

Comparison of the proportions in Canada and Germany at each level of educational attainment who are at each literacy level, prose scale

		Level 1	Level 2	Level 3	Level 4/5
		Percentage			
Canada	Less than ISCED 02	67.5	22.1	9.9	0.5
	ISCED 02	22.2	36.8	33.0	8.1
	ISCED 03	10.0	29.3	41.2	19.5
	ISCED 05	4.4	20.9	46.9	27.7
	ISCED 06/07	0.2	10.8	29.8	59.1
Germany	Less than ISCED 02	67.7	14.5	17.8	0.0
	ISCED 02	17.5	38.6	36.0	7.9
	ISCED 03	7.9	33.6	44.5	14.0
	ISCED 05	4.1	14.0	49.2	32.6
	ISCED 06/07	4.0	17.0	39.4	39.6

Table 3.9b

Comparison of the proportions in Canada and Germany at each level of educational attainment who are at each literacy level, document scale

		Level 1	Level 2	Level 3	Level 4/5
		Percentage			
Canada	Less than ISCED 02	73.6	15.4	9.7	1.3
	ISCED 02	23.2	40.2	26.3	10.3
	ISCED 03	10.5	28.4	36.9	24.1
	ISCED 05	4.2	17.6	39.1	39.1
	ISCED 06/07	3.3	10.1	38.5	48.1
Germany	Less than ISCED 02	55.5	30.2	14.3	0.0
	ISCED 02	10.5	38.3	39.2	12.0
	ISCED 03	4.7	26.7	43.5	25.1
	ISCED 05	4.7	20.2	48.3	26.8
	ISCED 06/07	1.1	17.9	34.8	46.2

Individuals in Germany with lower educational attainment are less likely to be at low literacy levels than are those in Canada. Conversely, individuals in Canada with postsecondary education (ISCED 05 and 06/07) are more likely to be at Level 4/5 than those with similar education in Germany.

Table 3.9c

Comparison of the proportions in Canada and Germany at each level of educational attainment who are at each literacy level, quantitative scale

		Level 1	Level 2	Level 3	Level 4/5
		Percentage			
Canada	Less than ISCED 02	69.4	18.5	11.3	0.8
	ISCED 02	23.1	41.5	27.6	7.8
	ISCED 03	8.8	31.7	42.8	16.6
	ISCED 05	4.2	20.7	48.6	26.4
	ISCED 06/07	2.2	4.4	29.4	64.0
Germany	Less than ISCED 02	42.5	20.8	29.2	7.5
	ISCED 02	7.6	31.0	44.1	17.2
	ISCED 03	4.1	21.0	49.3	25.7
	ISCED 05	2.7	11.1	59.4	26.9
	ISCED 06/07	2.0	13.2	28.6	56.2

It is no surprise that as the level of education increases, the proportion at Level 4/5 grows and the proportion at Level 1 decreases.

This connection offers some explanation for the differences between countries: their literacy levels differ because their educational attainment levels differ. For example, a much larger proportion of the Canadian (33%) than of the German population (14%) has completed some form of tertiary education. As this is the level of educational attainment with the largest proportion at literacy Level 4/5, it follows that Canada should have a larger proportion at literacy Level 4/5 (see Tables 3.9a to 3.9c which compare the two countries on all three scales). That is the case for the prose and document scales, but not for the quantitative scale.

...and large differences in literacy skills are to be expected.

At the same time, a larger proportion of the Canadian population falls at the lowest ISCED level, the group that has not attended secondary school (12% compared with 1% in Germany); this is the educational attainment level with the largest proportion at Level 1. In this case, there are larger proportions of Canadians at this level on the document and quantitative scales, as the difference in educational attainment would suggest, but the numbers are quite similar for the prose scale. Thus, there are grounds for proposing that while some of the differences between countries on the literacy measures are associated with differences between them on educational attainment, not all are. In this particular case, there seems to be a different connection between education and quantitative literacy and between education and prose literacy in Germany compared to Canada. One important conclusion from this is that the literacy measures produce a more richly textured picture of skill differences than simple educational attainment scales.

Figure 3.8 shows how the relation between literacy and education varies in the IALS countries. At the lowest education level (less than ISCED 02), the largest portion of the population is at Level 1 in all countries except Sweden and the Netherlands, where the largest portion is at Level 2. Level 2 (Level 3 in Sweden) is the predominant level for those at ISCED 02 (not completed secondary school) except in Poland and the United States where a larger number with this level of education are at Level 1.[14]

By the completion of secondary school, ISCED 03, Level 3 is dominant, except in Poland; only in the Netherlands and Sweden are the numbers in Level 3 strikingly larger than those in Level 2. It is in tertiary education levels (ISCED 05 and 06/07) that Level 3 is the largest group in all countries. In Canada, Sweden and the United States on all scales, and in Germany on the document and quantitative scales, 4/5 is the most common level for those with university education (ISCED 06/07).

Earlier it was noted that while Canada and Germany had similar mean scores on the prose scale, Germany had higher document and quantitative averages and that education was related to literacy in different ways in the two countries (Tables 3.9a to 3.9c provide some insight into this). On the quantitative scale in Germany, only ISCED 02 is required for Level 3 to be dominant (44%); only with tertiary education is this large a Level 3 proportion reached in Canada. A similar pattern, though with somewhat smaller proportions, occurs on the document scale; 39% of those at ISCED 02 in Germany are at Level 3, but it is only at ISCED 05 that there is this large a proportion in Canada. Explanations for these differences are not available in the IALS data. It makes sense to start by looking at differences in school curricula. A large body of material documents curriculum differences between Canada and Germany (and among other IALS countries); the conclusions of most of that literature are consistent with the findings of higher levels of literacy skill being attained at lower levels of education in Germany. (For comparisons of reading instruction, see Lundberg 1994.)

[14] This reflects, in some respects, inconsistencies in the way education is classified in the ISCED system.

Education is, by itself, not a satisfactory or simple proxy for literacy. Not only does every country have some proportion of its least educated population at Levels 3 and 4/5 on each literacy scale (and some proportion of its most educated at Level 1), but the relationship between education and literacy is not the same in every country and not the same from scale to scale. In the Netherlands and Sweden, and to some extent for the French-speaking population in Switzerland, the proportion of those with low education at Level 1 on the prose scale is small (less than 40% for the first two) compared with the other countries (all over 60%). As well, although Germany and Canada have the same proportions of those with low educational attainment at Level 1 on the prose scale (68% in both cases), Germany has a smaller proportion of this population at Level 1 on the document scale (Germany, 56%; Canada, 74%), with even larger differences on the quantitative scale (Germany, 43%; Canada, 69%). These both suggest that comparisons based solely on educational attainment may incorrectly estimate true skill differences.

Further, it should be noted that a direct test of literacy, such as the IALS, gives a different picture of the distribution of literacy than do classifications based on educational attainment (the UNESCO criteria, for example).[15] In the Netherlands some 324,000 adults who had never attended secondary school would be classified as having low literacy levels by UNESCO, even though they scored at Levels 3 and 4/5 on the IALS test. On the other hand, 474,000 adults who had at least started secondary school in the Netherlands would be classified as having high literacy skills although their scores on the IALS test put them at Level 1. In Canada, some 222,000 adults who scored at Levels 3 and 4/5 would be classified as low-skilled based on their educational attainment and 1.6 million of those at Level 1 would meet UNESCO's high literacy criteria because they had attended secondary school. In the Netherlands, approximately 7% of the population and, in Canada, 10%, would be misclassified using educational attainment alone.

Parents' education

It has long been recognized that an individual's educational attainment and literacy level are influenced by the parents' educational attainment. As Table 3.10 demonstrates, there is a relationship, but it is not the same in all cases.[16] For example, more Canadians than Germans whose parents have relatively low levels of education nonetheless attain Level 4/5. In general, one could argue, there is a closer relationship between parents' education and literacy in Germany than in Canada. This, in part, is likely a consequence of the considerable growth in tertiary education in Canada, which permits a significant number of Canadians to attain higher levels of education than their parents.

Although not directly a focus of the IALS, it is worth noting, once the connection between parents' education and literacy is established, that the IALS countries are remarkably varied in the parents' education. Over 30% of the respondents in the Netherlands reported that their parents had not attended secondary school, but only 2% of the German respondents reported their parents' education at the lowest levels.

---

[15] The UNESCO criteria classify individuals based on educational attainment:
    Less than Grade 4: basic illiterate
    Less than Grade 9, but more than Grade 4: functional literate
    Grade 9 and higher: fully literate.

[16] Table 3.10 is based on the education of the parent with the highest level of attainment.

Table 3.10

Proportion of population who are at each literacy level for each level of parents' educational attainment, document scale

		Level 1	Level 2	Level 3	Level 4/5
			Percentage		
Canada	Less than ISCED 02	28.3	30.1	29.6	12.0
	ISCED 02	8.9	23.8	29.5	37.8
	ISCED 03	8.6	15.1	46.2	30.1
	ISCED 05	9.9	16.7	29.4	44.0
	ISCED 06/07	8.4	19.3	31.2	41.0
Germany	Less than ISCED 02	37.5	35.6	23.6	3.2
	ISCED 02	9.6	34.7	37.8	17.8
	ISCED 03	4.3	27.4	47.2	21.2
	ISCED 05	1.8	21.9	56.2	20.1
	ISCED 06/07	1.9	18.7	40.8	38.6
Netherlands	Less than ISCED 02	18.4	33.9	36.7	11.0
	ISCED 02	5.3	25.9	46.4	22.4
	ISCED 03	2.0	21.0	51.9	25.2
	ISCED 05	N/A	N/A	N/A	N/A
	ISCED 06/07	3.1	10.4	48.7	37.8
Poland	Less than ISCED 02	54.1	29.8	12.9	3.3
	ISCED 02	37.4	35.4	22.0	5.3
	ISCED 03	22.2	31.6	34.8	11.4
	ISCED 05	25.7	28.6	33.2	12.5
	ISCED 06/07	16.7	27.3	30.4	25.6
Sweden	Less than ISCED 02	8.6	23.1	40.3	28.0
	ISCED 02	1.6	15.3	42.5	40.6
	ISCED 03	2.4	14.3	39.6	43.7
	ISCED 05	1.3	14.6	34.5	49.6
	ISCED 06/07	0.4	8.0	35.4	56.2
Switzerland (French)	Less than ISCED 02	24.5	36.3	29.1	10.1
	ISCED 02	14.8	34.9	40.0	10.3
	ISCED 03	8.4	26.2	47.4	18.0
	ISCED 05	10.1	19.5	46.4	24.1
	ISCED 06/07	5.6	19.1	40.8	34.5
Switzerland (German)	Less than ISCED 02	50.9	24.2	20.9	4.0
	ISCED 02	16.4	38.6	35.8	9.2
	ISCED 03	7.7	29.6	43.2	19.4
	ISCED 05	1.7	32.3	42.4	23.5
	ISCED 06/07	8.2	25.1	36.0	30.7
United States	Less than ISCED 02	33.6	30.6	26.5	9.3
	ISCED 02	22.7	30.8	36.5	9.9
	ISCED 03	14.0	25.8	35.1	25.1
	ISCED 05	9.0	16.5	32.3	42.3
	ISCED 06/07	8.4	18.6	41.5	31.5

Parents' education has some impact on literacy skill. However, individuals whose parents completed postsecondary education are not necessarily at high literacy levels.

Table 3.11

Proportion of population in each age group who are at each literacy level, document scale

		Level 1	Level 2	Level 3	Level 4/5
			Percentage		
Canada	16-25	10.4	22.3	36.4	31.0
	26-35	13.5	25.3	33.8	27.5
	36-45	13.8	22.0	36.8	27.4
	46-55	23.0	31.0	23.6	22.4
	56-65	43.8	23.7	23.8	8.7
Germany	16-25	5.2	29.0	43.0	22.8
	26-35	5.9	29.2	40.0	24.9
	36-45	9.5	30.6	38.5	21.4
	46-55	7.4	35.0	43.1	14.5
	56-65	17.7	40.9	32.6	8.8
Netherlands	16-25	6.1	16.8	51.1	26.0
	26-35	5.9	19.2	45.7	29.3
	36-45	9.2	24.2	49.5	17.1
	46-55	12.6	35.7	38.0	13.7
	56-65	22.6	40.5	30.1	6.8
Poland	16-25	32.2	33.1	26.2	8.5
	26-35	39.2	33.8	19.7	7.4
	36-45	42.6	33.6	18.1	5.7
	46-55	55.6	27.0	13.3	4.1
	56-65	70.1	20.9	7.6	1.4
Sweden	16-25	3.1	16.6	39.6	40.7
	26-35	3.9	10.4	38.1	47.6
	36-45	6.6	18.2	39.8	35.4
	46-55	6.8	19.7	43.1	30.3
	56-65	12.2	33.3	36.0	18.5
Switzerland (French)	16-25	8.7	24.9	40.4	26.0
	26-35	11.5	22.4	44.5	21.6
	36-45	19.2	32.9	34.2	13.7
	46-55	18.0	29.8	42.4	9.7
	56-65	27.5	38.1	29.8	4.6
Switzerland (German)	16-25	7.1	25.7	41.0	26.3
	26-35	17.4	20.7	38.8	23.1
	36-45	21.5	30.3	36.3	12.0
	46-55	21.0	33.8	35.0	10.2
	56-65	22.8	39.9	30.6	6.7
United States	16-25*	24.7	30.9	28.4	16.1
	26-35	21.6	22.9	34.5	21.0
	36-45	23.5	19.7	31.4	25.4
	46-55	21.4	28.2	33.2	17.3
	56-65	29.3	32.9	26.0	11.7

In most countries, the number at Level 1 increases with increasing age. It is not always the case, however, that the proportion at Level 4/5 decreases. Instead it appears that some experience is required to reach this level.

* The proficiency of United States' postsecondary students has been underestimated due to a sampling anomaly. This note also pertains to Figures 3.2c and 3.9.

Age

Educational attainment is not only distributed differently between the countries, but it is also distributed differently by age within each country. For example, only 49% of the Canadian population aged 55 to 64 has completed secondary education, while 81% of those aged 25 to 34 have that level of education. In comparison, in Germany 69% of those aged 55 to 64 have attained this level and 89% of those aged 25 to 34 (OECD 1995). Literacy is related to age independently of education as well. Recent Canadian data (Statistics Canada 1992) showed that groups of individuals with similar educational attainment, but of different ages, did not have the same literacy distribution, while older Canadians have lower skills than younger Canadians with the same education. There are no marked disparities among the countries with respect to the age makeup of the study population, so this by itself would not account for the differences, yet the relationship between age and literacy is itself an important question.[17] Table 3.11 and Figure 3.9 present the basic age data for each country on the document scale.

Table 3.12

Proportion of population in two age groups whose highest level of education is secondary graduation who are at each literacy level

		Level 1	Level 2	Level 3	Level 4/5
			Percentage		
Switzerland (French)					
Prose	18-24	7.8	19.1	60.6	12.6
	25-30	18.0	34.9	44.8	1.5
Document	18-24	2.9	25.9	55.5	15.7
	25-30	17.8	27.4	46.4	8.3
Quantitative	18-24	7.8	11.6	65.0	15.7
	25-30	3.5	44.8	43.4	8.3
Germany					
Prose	18-24	8.0	29.3	54.8	8.0
	25-30	8.3	29.6	36.1	25.9
Document	18-24	5.8	16.4	52.0	25.8
	25-30	3.0	20.4	40.6	35.9
Quantitative	18-24	5.8	20.3	56.3	17.6
	25-30	3.0	11.7	48.4	36.9
United States					
Prose	18-24	11.3	59.2	23.4	6.1
	25-30	21.2	28.4	34.1	16.2
Document	18-24	18.2	42.2	37.2	2.4
	25-30	27.9	20.3	36.9	14.9
Quantitative	18-24	13.7	46.7	33.1	6.4
	25-30	21.2	18.8	34.5	25.5

---

[17] Because there is an age effect on education, a breakdown of literacy scores by age and education together would be interesting, but sample sizes in most countries are too small to support three-way (age by education by literacy) analyses.

Figure 3.9
Literacy by age, document scale

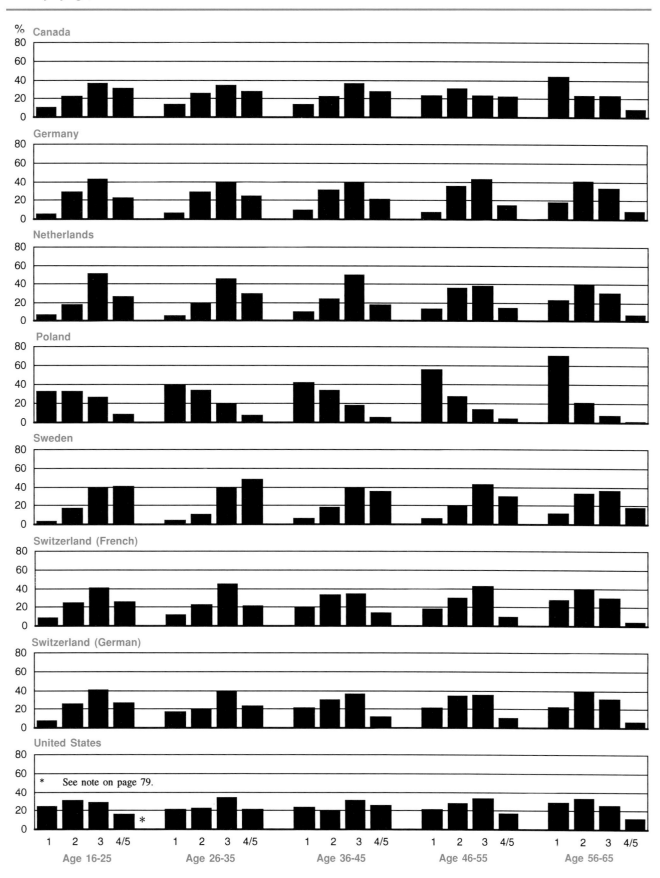

...because countries differ greatly in how much education each age group received...

...and even young people are not always at the highest skill levels.

The data also provide evidence of skill acquisition and...

The relationship between age and literacy is slightly more complex than that between education and literacy. In all countries, at older ages, the proportion at Level 1 is larger on all three scales,[18, 19] though there is not always a regular decrease; for example, the proportion at level one does not increase between the ages of 36 to 45 and 46 to 55 in either Swiss language group and there is no significant change at this level between the ages of 26 to 35 and 46 to 55 in the United States.[20] It is generally the case, though, that fewer—in many cases significantly fewer— young adults are at the lowest level on any scale. The exception to this is the United States, where the youngest age group has a slightly larger proportion than other age groups at Level 1 on all scales.[21]

This does not mean, however, that proportionally more young adults are at Level 4/5. Indeed, the relation between the proportion of 16- to 25-year-olds at Level 4/5 and the proportion of 25- to 36-year-olds at that level is quite mixed. Seldom does one age group have a substantially higher proportion than the other. In assessing this information, it must be noted that many of those aged 16 to 25 are still in school and that the 26-to-35 age group in many countries naturally includes more individuals with tertiary education; in some countries over 40% of the youngest age group have not yet completed secondary education. One interpretation of the data is that increases in educational attainment, and perhaps even in educational effectiveness, at the primary and secondary levels (the levels most likely attained by the youngest age group) are successful at raising skills to Levels 2 and 3, but that further education or life experience is necessary for Level 4/5. This interpretation is consistent with the findings discussed above under education, where it was seen that tertiary education is most commonly associated with the highest literacy level.

Even when those who have only completed secondary school are considered (Table 3.12) the picture is not consistent across countries. In Switzerland, among the French-speaking population, the 25-to-30 age group typically has larger numbers at the lower levels than the 18-to-24 age group and smaller numbers at Level 4/5. One interpretation of this pattern is that literacy skills decline after individuals leave school.

In contrast, the 25- to 30-year-old group in Germany consistently has larger numbers at literacy Level 4/5. A sensible interpretation of this pattern is that post-school experience raises literacy skills in Germany. It is particularly noteworthy that the proportions at Levels 1 and 2 are the same for the two age groups, further suggesting that the increase in Level 4/5 comes from increasing the skills of those at Level 3 after they have left secondary school even when there is no further formal education.

---

[18] The sole exception is the United States where the proportions at Level 1 are similar for all age groups. A greater proportion of the United States 16-to-25 sample are still in secondary school than in any other country, perhaps providing some explanation for that age group. This, however, does not explain why the proportion is the same for other age groups when this is not the case in the other countries.

[19] A traditional explanation for the lower scores in older age groups might invoke a notion of intellectual decline with age. Recent research suggests that this is unlikely to be a major factor.

[20] The 1992 National Adult Literacy Study in the United States found this same pattern for these three age groups (26 to 35, 36 to 45, 46 to 55).

[21] At least some of the explanation for the United States results here may lie in an under-coverage of university students. In this country more of respondents who reported being in school were in secondary school than in tertiary education; in the other countries students were more likely to be in a postsecondary program.

...surprisingly, considerable skill loss...

...suggesting complex interactions with work and society.

Unlike the pattern for school tests...

...women in the IALS do not consistently outperform men.

While the German pattern shows a consistent gain in skill and the Switzerland (French) pattern a regular decrease, the United States shows both an increase and a decrease. In the United States there are larger numbers at Levels 3 and 4/5, and at Level 1 for the 25- to 30-year-old group. This suggests that some Level 2 secondary school graduates are able to increase their skill to Level 3 (and some at Level 3 may improve to Level 4/5), while others see a decline in skill to Level 1. If this is the appropriate analysis for the United States, it adds to our understanding of why the United States is characterized by large numbers at both extreme literacy levels and small numbers at the middle levels.

The mixed results one sees in Table 3.12 demonstrate that adult literacy is a result not just of school experience, but also of life experience. In turn, this implies that the IALS results are not an appropriate measure of school effectiveness, but rather a measure of the culture of literacy in a particular society.

It is safe to say that in all cases the proportion of young adults, those just entering the work force (aged 16 to 25) or at the beginning of their careers (aged 26 to 35), have notably higher skills than older workers, who will be retiring from the work force.

Gender

Studies of school reading, such as the IEA Reading Literacy Study (Elley 1994), routinely find a gender effect, with girls typically scoring somewhat higher than boys, although in some studies boys have scored higher on reading tasks that are more practically oriented. As Tables 3.13a to 3.13c show, there is also a gender effect, small in some countries, large in others, but that effect is not the same on all the scales or for all countries on a scale.

- On the prose scale (Table 3.13a) women slightly outscore men in some countries (most notably in Canada and the United States), but the advantage is not large in any of them. In other countries the scores are so similar that no real difference can be claimed; in some cases the mean scores are a couple of points higher for women, in others, for men.

- On the document scale (Table 3.13b), in some countries men score higher than women, but there are still a number where there is no difference, though this group includes those for which there was a female advantage on the prose scale.

- On the quantitative scale (Table 3.13c), men outscore women in every country, though the difference in Canada is too small to be significant. In some cases, however, the differences are relatively large; in Sweden, there is a 16-point difference.

In general then, as one moves across prose to document to quantitative scales, men's scores increase relative to women's. In some countries, women's scores decrease through this progression of scales, but even when they do increase they do so more slowly than those of men. The predominant explanation for the difference between sexes points to different patterns of course enrolments in school. However, the IALS did not collect data on this young population. Men, particularly older men, tend to have more education than women, but this would only serve as an explanation if men outscored women on all scales. One might try to argue that the quantitative scale is more sensitive to education than is the prose scale (that is, an increase in education leads to a relatively greater improvement on quantitative), but the data do not strongly support this. It may also be that differences in employment, particularly in type of occupation, may play a role. Occupations that were historically filled more by women than by men, such as clerks, are characterized by greater frequencies of reading and writing (prose and document) than of numeracy (quantitative), while those more often filled by men, technicians and skilled craft workers, for example, are associated with more frequent numeracy tasks.

Table 3.13a

Proportion of each sex who are at each level of literacy, prose scale

		Level 1	Level 2	Level 3	Level 4/5
			Percentage		
Canada	Male	19.0	26.6	37.0	17.4
	Female	14.3	24.7	33.2	27.8
Germany	Male	15.4	31.8	37.9	15.4
	Female	13.3	36.7	38.0	12.0
Netherlands	Male	10.5	31.3	43.6	14.6
	Female	10.5	28.8	44.6	16.0
Poland	Male	43.3	35.4	18.7	2.6
	Female	42.0	33.7	20.8	3.5
Sweden	Male	7.9	20.9	39.9	31.3
	Female	7.1	19.8	39.5	33.6
Switzerland (French)	Male	17.1	31.2	40.9	10.8
	Female	18.2	36.2	36.4	9.2
Switzerland (German)	Male	17.9	32.9	40.0	9.2
	Female	20.7	38.4	32.1	8.7
United States	Male	22.2	28.0	29.8	20.0
	Female	19.3	23.9	34.7	22.1

Table 3.13b

Proportion of each sex who are at each level of literacy, document scale

		Level 1	Level 2	Level 3	Level 4/5
			Percentage		
Canada	Male	17.0	25.7	31.8	25.0
	Female	19.3	23.8	32.3	24.7
Germany	Male	7.8	31.0	38.7	22.4
	Female	10.1	34.4	40.2	15.3
Netherlands	Male	8.5	23.9	45.0	22.7
	Female	11.9	27.7	43.3	17.1
Poland	Male	43.7	31.1	18.7	6.4
	Female	47.0	30.4	17.4	5.2
Sweden	Male	5.0	16.8	39.6	38.6
	Female	7.3	21.0	39.3	32.4
Switzerland (French)	Male	14.0	27.0	40.3	18.7
	Female	18.5	30.6	37.5	13.4
Switzerland (German)	Male	15.2	26.7	39.7	18.4
	Female	21.1	31.4	33.6	13.9
United States	Male	25.2	24.9	30.4	19.5
	Female	22.4	26.7	32.3	18.5

Table 3.13c

Proportion of each sex who are at each level of literacy, quantitative scale

		Level 1	Level 2	Level 3	Level 4/5
			Percentage		
Canada	Male	17.2	24.9	33.8	24.1
	Female	16.6	27.2	35.9	20.2
Germany	Male	5.7	22.7	42.9	28.7
	Female	7.6	30.5	43.5	18.4
Netherlands	Male	8.2	20.8	46.4	24.6
	Female	12.4	30.4	42.1	15.1
Poland	Male	36.2	29.7	26.1	8.0
	Female	42.0	30.6	21.7	5.7
Sweden	Male	5.2	15.3	37.6	41.9
	Female	8.0	21.8	40.4	29.8
Switzerland (French)	Male	11.0	19.8	43.8	25.4
	Female	14.8	29.1	40.7	15.5
Switzerland (German)	Male	12.2	22.2	41.9	23.7
	Female	16.1	30.2	39.6	14.2
United States	Male	20.9	22.2	29.9	27.1
	Female	21.0	28.1	32.5	18.4

Summary

This chapter has laid out some of the factors that relate to literacy, but are not in and of themselves literacy activities. The most notable points are that there are differences among the countries, not simply on average scores, but on how literacy is distributed within the society. It also seems clear that policy decisions do have effects. Canada's policy of actively recruiting highly skilled immigrants gives it a quite different pattern of immigrant literacy. There also appear to be differences resulting from education policy; that is, individuals with similar levels of education have different patterns of literacy across the three scales when countries are compared.

Further, it has been shown that differences in literacy have consequences. Low-skill adults are more likely to be unemployed, or if employed, to be employed in industries that are declining. High-skill adults are likely to have higher incomes.

What has not been examined in this chapter are the actual literacy practices with which individuals are engaged. That is the topic we turn to in the next chapter.

References

Australian Bureau of Statistics. *Training and Education Experience*. Canberra, 1993.

Elley, Warwick B., ed., *The International Association for the Evaluation of Educational Achievement (IEA) Study of Reading Literacy: Achievement and Instruction in Thirty-two School Systems*. Oxford: Pergamon Press, 1994.

Lundberg, Ingvar. "The teaching of reading." In *The International Association for the Evaluation of Educational Achievement (IEA) Study of Reading Literacy: Achievement and Instruction in Thirty-two School Systems*. Edited by Warwick B. Elley. Oxford: Pergamon Press, 1994.

Organisation for Economic Co-operation and Development. *Education at a Glance: OECD Indicators*, 1995 Edition. Paris, 1995.

Statistics Canada. Adult Education and Training Survey. Ottawa, 1992.

Chapter 4

The practice(s) of literacy

Stan Jones, Centre for the Study of Adult Literacy, Carleton University, Ottawa, Canada

This chapter looks at the practices of literacy, within and between countries, and its impact on literacy skills...

...both inside and outside work.

The International Adult Literacy Survey (IALS) collected a broad range of information about the literacy practices and other daily activities of the respondents. This information is, in and of itself, of considerable comparative interest. The IALS also provides new insights into the differences in the distribution of literacy within and between countries.

This chapter discusses literacy practices at work and in the community:

- Literacy practices at work

  Most adults must face some literacy tasks at work, though these differ from job to job and individuals may differ in how successful they think they are in dealing with them. IALS respondents were asked a series of questions about their literacy practices at work and how they felt about their ability to carry them out successfully.

- Literacy practices in the community

  Everyone, whether employed or not, can engage in literacy activities as part of their daily life outside the workplace. Here, too, IALS respondents were asked to report on their everyday reading and writing tasks and to judge how well their abilities served them.

A key question is how literacy skill and literacy activity reinforce each other.

In each case both the range of practices and the relation of the practice to literacy were examined. A key question is: How do literacy skill and literacy activities interact? It seems likely that individuals who demonstrate higher literacy skills are more likely to be assigned and more willing to undertake more complex literacy activities. These activities in turn, by providing opportunities to practise and perhaps expand literacy skills, allow these individuals to maintain, and often to improve, their skills. If literacy is a fragile skill, one that requires continued use, the practices considered in this chapter constitute that continued use.

Literacy at work

Literacy practices

There are some connections between literacy skill and the frequency of performing certain tasks...

The IALS participants were asked a series of questions about the frequency with which they engaged in a variety of reading, writing and numeracy tasks. These tasks are conveniently grouped into three categories.

...such as reading journals...

1. Reading. Respondents were asked how frequently they read or used information from six types of texts as part of their job:

   a. Letters or memos

   b. Reports, articles, magazines or journals

   c. Manuals or reference books, including catalogues

d.   Diagrams or schematics

e.   Bills, invoices, spreadsheets or budget tables

f.   Directions or instructions for medicines, recipes or other products

2.   Writing. Respondents were asked how often they wrote or filled out four types of text as part of their job:

a.   Letters or memos

b.   Forms or things such as bills, invoices or budgets

c.   Reports or articles

d.   Estimates or technical specifications

3.   Numeracy. They were asked about two kinds of arithmetic:

a.   Measuring or estimating the size or weight of objects

b.   Calculating prices, costs or budgets

The relation between skill and frequency is unlikely to be a strong one, particularly in Levels 2, 3 and 4/5,[1] because frequency by itself does not equate to difficulty. As the test items themselves show, some tasks using a text can be relatively easy, while others are more difficult. For example, consider written directions, one of the literacy tasks surveyed. Directions can be simple (connecting two pieces of equipment, for example) or they can be difficult (such as instructions on installing a new furnace). Still, as in other studies of the relationship of frequency to skill, the IALS data show some connections.

---

[1] Because the proportion at Level 5 is under 5% in most countries, Levels 4 and 5 have been combined in the analyses presented in this chapter and in Chapter 3. For many of the analyses, then, a reliable estimate could not be made for the subgroup proportions at this level. Rather than simply leave blank cells in tables, Level 5 was combined with Level 4. As well, there seems to be no compelling policy interest in the relative proportions at Levels 4 and 5. As the data presented here show, even the difference between Level 3 and Level 4/5 is of minor interest. Given the large numbers at Levels 1 and 2 for which lack of literacy skill has a large impact, the pressing policy concern is how to increase Level 3 relative to Levels 1 and 2.

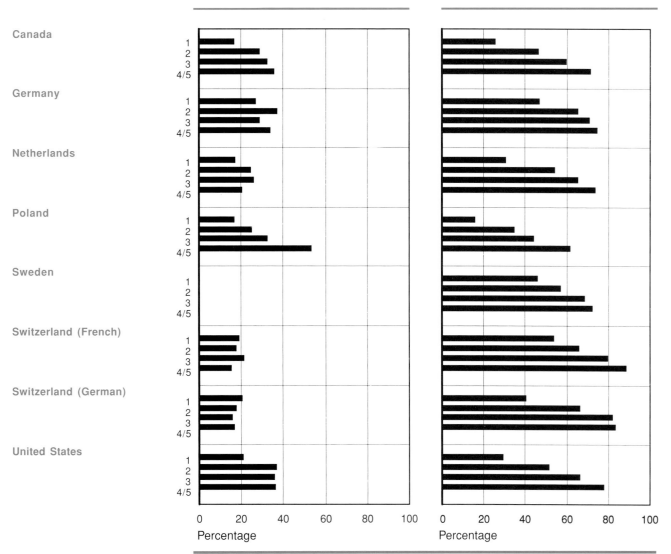

Figure 4.1a

Read directions or instructions for products as part of job at least once a week, prose scale

Figure 4.1b

Read reports, articles, magazines, journals as part of job at least once a week, prose scale

Table 4.1

Proportion of population in each country who reported engaging in each of several workplace reading tasks at least once a week

	Directions or instructions for medicines, recipes or other products	Bills, invoices, spreadsheets or budget tables	Diagrams or schematics	Manuals or reference books, including catalogues	Reports, articles, magazines or journals	Letters or memos
	Percentage					
Canada	30.4	48.0	32.5	49.2	55.4	70.2
Germany	31.9	62.0	51.4	60.8	66.9	80.4
Netherlands	23.8	43.2	39.9	52.1	61.5	66.7
Poland	24.1	28.2	21.0	27.0	29.9	33.6
Sweden	N/A	57.6	63.2	71.9	66.6	78.5
Switzerland (French)	19.1	56.8	38.2	50.3	72.3	72.9
Switzerland (German)	17.0	61.2	31.8	56.1	70.4	81.0
United States	33.8	47.6	37.6	61.6	59.8	71.6

...and reading directions and manuals.

These connections are strongest between tasks and the pertinent literacy domain...

...and for tasks with a narrow range of difficulty.

Since the job you do influences your practices, it also determines how your skills develop...

Figures 4.1a and 4.1b and 4.2a to 4.2d portray the relation between literacy ability and the frequency of various reading tasks at work. Table 4.1 reports the overall frequencies of the tasks for each country. There is a general tendency, across countries, scales and tasks, for individuals at higher literacy skill levels to report that they carry out a practice more frequently. For example, in Poland only 18% of those at Level 1 on the document scale reported reading directions as frequently as at least once a week, but 46% of those at Level 4/5 reported doing so. The differences are even larger for tasks that are likely to involve more complex texts, such as manuals and reference books; 17% of the Polish respondents at Level 1 (prose scale) said they did this at least once a week in contrast to 50% of those at Level 4/5. Similar differences are found for the reading of reports: Of those at Level 1 on the prose scale, 16% said they read reports at least once a week; of those at Level 4/5 on the prose scale, 62% did so.

Whether there are different frequencies reported at different levels on a particular scale may be related to the connection between the task and the scale. In Germany, respondents at Levels 2, 3 and 4/5 on the prose scale reported about the same frequency for reading diagrams and schematics. This type of task, however, is more typically a document task and, on this scale, there are some differences in reported frequency across these three levels, though not large ones. Similarly, in all countries there is no consistent relationship between level (except at Level 1) and frequency of use of bills, invoices and spreadsheets on the prose and document scales, but those at higher levels on the quantitative scale consistently report more frequent use of these texts.

It might also be expected that those tasks that might occur regularly at varying levels of difficulty are less likely to show a strong relationship than those that likely have narrower ranges of difficulty. Thus reading directions and instructions, which can show a wide range of complexity, is inconsistently related to level (in some countries, on some scales, Level 2 respondents may report more frequent use than Level 4/5 respondents). On the other hand, a task such as reading a manual or a reference book—which usually has a higher level of complexity—shows a consistent relationship between skill and frequency (in all countries, on all scales, Level 3 respondents reported performing this task more often than those at Level 2 and less often than those at Level 4/5).

The frequency of reading tasks varies by occupation, as should be expected (see Table 4.2). In French-speaking Switzerland, for example, 83% of the clerks reported reading memos and letters at least once a week, but only 54% of the skilled craft workers said they read them this frequently. Also in Switzerland, 68% of clerks reported working with bills or invoices weekly, while 55% of the technicians said that they did; in contrast, 42% of the technicians, compared with 23% of the clerks, used diagrams and schematics this often. Thus literacy practices are a key element in the connection between literacy skill and occupation, as demonstrated in the previous chapter. If literacy practices do maintain and enhance skill, then work organization itself can contribute to literacy skill. Common sense would suggest that if a job is organized to place few demands on worker's skills, then that worker's skills are likely to decline. Conversely, when a job allows regular exercise of literacy skill, incumbents can expect to maintain and increase that skill.

Table 4.2

Proportion of workers in each occupational group who reported engaging in each of several workplace reading tasks at least once a week

		Letters or memos	Reports, articles, magazines or journals	Manuals or reference books, including catalogues	Diagrams or schematics	Bills invoices, spreadsheets or budget tables	Directions or instructions for medicines, recipes or other products
					Percentage		
Canada	Professionals/Managers	93.4	84.0	81.6	51.5	65.2	45.0
	Technicians	77.2	69.9	48.3	28.5	45.3	28.2
	Clerks	84.1	52.9	45.9	14.7	52.2	17.2
	Service workers	58.4	41.4	32.3	15.0	43.8	34.9
	Skilled crafts workers	42.5	29.9	36.7	48.2	32.8	22.6
	Machinery operators	56.5	40.9	31.8	32.6	33.5	21.3
	Agriculture	42.0	31.7	29.7	23.1	38.4	25.3
Germany	Professionals/Managers	91.5	85.9	67.8	61.8	57.9	25.6
	Technicians	93.2	89.1	66.6	53.7	69.3	38.9
	Clerks	95.6	78.9	63.5	39.0	76.5	26.1
	Service workers	74.5	63.4	59.3	32.8	64.4	38.3
	Skilled crafts workers	68.6	42.8	59.4	73.1	54.4	31.5
	Machinery operators	68.3	44.4	50.9	49.9	50.8	39.6
	Agriculture	44.8	31.1	35.4	22.2	40.2	29.6
Netherlands	Professionals/Managers	86.6	86.9	70.8	55.0	59.7	25.8
	Technicians	81.8	74.2	62.2	43.5	50.7	34.1
	Clerks	79.9	58.9	50.8	37.3	49.6	17.5
	Service workers	44.5	43.0	32.4	18.8	37.0	28.7
	Skilled crafts workers	38.2	37.0	50.7	39.9	23.1	16.3
	Machinery operators	54.5	42.6	34.6	38.5	18.3	15.7
	Agriculture	27.0	27.3	14.6	18.5	17.1	10.7
Poland	Professionals/Managers	72.4	78.6	70.7	42.5	48.1	50.6
	Technicians	65.1	61.0	51.6	34.5	41.5	38.7
	Clerks	61.0	43.6	34.9	12.7	64.0	27.5
	Service workers	27.9	20.1	24.0	3.5	52.8	32.4
	Skilled crafts workers	16.6	10.7	13.3	28.6	8.0	15.2
	Machinery operators	23.9	11.8	10.1	19.9	23.2	11.5
	Agriculture	8.5	10.9	7.6	3.8	9.0	9.5
Sweden	Professionals/Managers	91.5	91.8	81.9	76.9	62.1	N/A
	Technicians	87.9	89.0	76.8	70.2	63.5	N/A
	Clerks	90.0	84.1	79.2	53.3	66.5	N/A
	Service workers	74.6	77.0	69.2	53.7	63.6	N/A
	Skilled crafts workers	57.0	61.5	62.4	50.4	41.9	N/A
	Machinery operators	55.2	57.1	44.7	47.2	42.7	N/A
	Agriculture	49.5	53.3	46.8	38.0	38.7	N/A
Switzerland (French)	Professionals/Managers	86.1	88.4	54.9	49.7	78.2	13.6
	Technicians	79.8	77.5	54.7	42.2	54.9	28.7
	Clerks	83.2	74.7	39.1	22.5	68.2	8.8
	Service workers	56.8	51.9	42.1	19.8	46.5	22.1
	Skilled crafts workers	54.3	61.7	55.1	56.2	47.0	20.6
	Machinery operators	62.5	57.9	38.3	30.8	34.7	17.6
	Agriculture	64.2	63.9	52.1	25.1	45.1	24.6
Switzerland (German)	Professionals/Managers	94.9	89.8	66.4	47.3	69.6	17.7
	Technicians	94.3	82.3	65.2	40.8	62.1	28.3
	Clerks	91.1	74.5	57.0	25.4	72.6	7.9
	Service workers	68.7	58.6	41.4	18.1	62.4	15.9
	Skilled crafts workers	69.4	55.5	62.8	31.8	54.9	15.3
	Machinery operators	54.3	39.2	27.2	12.3	46.8	16.6
	Agriculture	56.4	49.4	36.1	14.9	41.9	6.8
United States	Professionals/Managers	92.0	85.0	82.9	51.7	62.9	41.9
	Technicians	83.1	75.3	80.6	64.5	33.3	48.4
	Clerks	87.7	67.5	60.4	25.1	58.7	27.5
	Service workers	56.2	44.4	48.0	21.7	41.4	35.4
	Skilled crafts workers	53.0	39.1	53.4	57.5	34.6	26.4
	Machinery operators	43.5	29.2	42.3	28.3	21.3	20.7
	Agriculture	26.4	34.7	13.1	8.8	25.2	20.4

Figure 4.2a

Read bills, invoices, spreadsheets as part of job at least once a week, quantitative scale

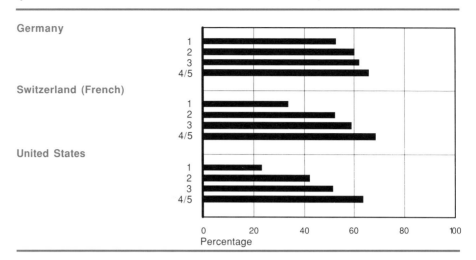

Figure 4.2b

Read diagrams or schematics as part of job, at least once a week, document scale

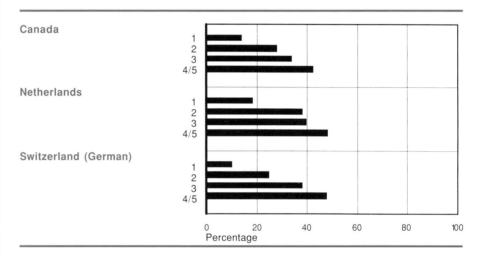

Figure 4.2c

Read manuals and reference books as part of job at least once a week, prose scale

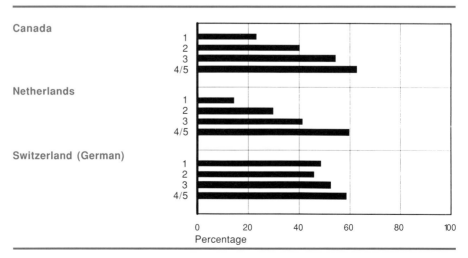

Figure 4.2d
Read letters or memos as part of job at least once a week, prose scale

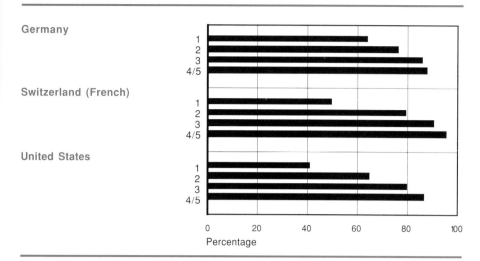

...with different occupations practising different tasks.

Overall, the occupational category with the highest reported frequencies across tasks is the professional/manager group. Clerks and technicians report the second most frequent use for many tasks, but for tasks closely associated with an occupation, these two groups differ. Thus, clerks read diagrams less frequently than technicians who, in turn, are less likely to read bills or invoices than clerks. Service workers, skilled craft workers and machine operators typically report reading less frequently than clerks, technicians and professionals/managers, but even in these occupations certain tasks occur with greater frequency. Skilled craft workers and machine operators read diagrams and schematics more frequently than clerks and service workers, and they must deal with bills and invoices relatively often. These are logical differences. Agricultural and other primary workers, for every task, reported the least frequent use of work-related reading materials.

With writing too, skill level and frequency of practice vary according to task...

As with reading, the relation between frequency of writing activities and skill varies from task to task (see Figures 4.3a, 4.3b, 4.4a and 4.4b). Overall frequencies in each country are presented in Table 4.3. In some countries, there is little difference among those at Levels 2, 3 and 4/5 on writing estimates (even Level 1 respondents report comparatively high weekly frequencies on this task) and on using bills and invoices (Level 1 is somewhat lower here). In contrast, in all countries respondents at Level 4/5 are considerably more likely than those at Level 2 to write letters and memos; they are also somewhat more likely to write reports and articles. For both types of writing, Level 3 frequencies are somewhere between those for Levels 2 and 4/5, and Level 1 frequencies are lower than Level 2. Again, as the task becomes more complex—writing letters and reports is usually more complicated than filling in forms—there is a stronger relationship between frequency and level of skill.

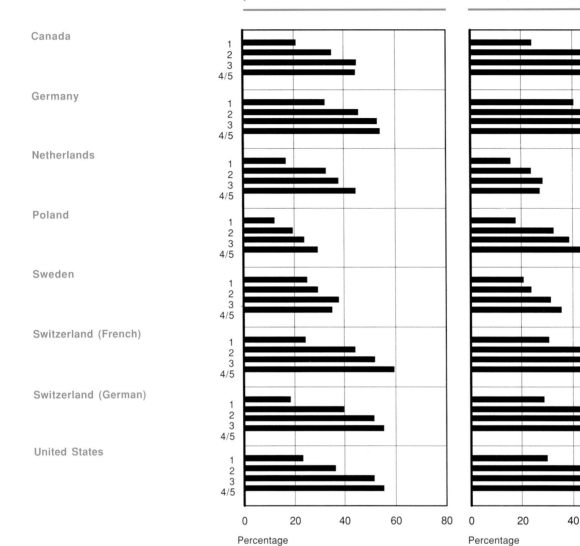

Figure 4.3a
Write reports or articles as part of job at least once a week, prose scale

Figure 4.3b
Write or fill in forms, bills or invoices as part of job at least once a week, document scale

Table 4.3

Proportion of population in each country who reported engaging in each of several workplace writing tasks at least once a week

	Letters or memos	Forms or things such as bills, invoices or budgets	Reports or articles	Estimates or technical specifications
		Percentage		
Canada	53.8	47.2	39.4	26.6
Germany	72.4	57.8	48.3	27.0
Netherlands	53.4	26.4	36.1	30.8
Poland	29.6	28.8	17.7	8.3
Sweden	74.0	47.8	54.6	30.2
Switzerland (French)	60.8	47.0	46.1	24.4
Switzerland (German)	79.0	57.3	42.8	25.3
United States	58.7	51.8	44.2	29.2

Figure 4.4a

Write estimates or technical specifications as part of job at least once a week, document scale

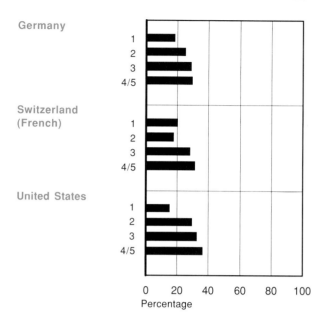

Figure 4.4b

Write letters or memos as part of job at least once a week, prose scale

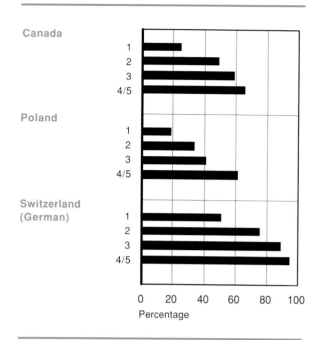

...with predictable occupational differences.

Different kinds of mathematics skills are also used in various occupations...

Here too there are natural differences among occupations (Table 4.4). Professionals/managers, technicians, and clerks reported the most frequent use of a variety of tasks. Notably, clerks are more likely than any of the other occupations to process bills and invoices; service workers reported as much use of these kinds of tasks as professionals/managers and technicians.

IALS respondents were asked to report on how often they used two different sets of mathematics skills in their job. One set comprised those required to deal with money (budget math) and the second those necessary to carry out measurements. There are some interesting correlational differences between these two activities (see Figures 4.5a and 4.5b and Table 4.5). Level 1 respondents reported using measurement math more often than budget math, though the overall frequencies of the two types are similar in all countries (except Germany, which reported more frequent budget math and Poland with more frequent measurement math). Correspondingly, those at Level 4/5 reported more budget than measurement math. The proportions for the two sets of math tasks are almost identical in both Levels 2 and 3, although higher frequencies were uniformly reported for Level 3, compared with Level 2.

Table 4.4

Proportion of workers in each occupational group who reported engaging in each of several workplace writing tasks at least once a week

		Letters or memos	Forms or things such as bills, invoices or budgets	Reports or articles	Estimates or technical specifications
		Percentage			
Canada	Professionals/Managers	83.6	58.0	65.4	42.8
	Technicians	49.1	37.2	37.0	24.1
	Clerks	64.2	62.5	33.9	13.7
	Service workers	41.0	46.1	26.9	15.1
	Skilled crafts workers	32.6	29.0	27.7	35.8
	Machinery operators	36.2	41.3	37.3	27.9
	Agriculture	28.4	34.3	15.0	12.2
Germany	Professionals/Managers	90.7	60.2	64.2	27.3
	Technicians	87.2	70.5	69.8	33.6
	Clerks	84.4	73.4	59.5	33.6
	Service workers	68.3	59.6	36.1	14.5
	Skilled crafts workers	58.0	43.1	34.2	35.3
	Machinery operators	58.1	55.8	26.6	17.2
	Agriculture	29.3	23.6	10.2	8.2
Netherlands	Professionals/Managers	69.6	32.4	52.3	43.9
	Technicians	72.1	32.1	47.5	29.5
	Clerks	64.9	30.5	28.0	22.2
	Service workers	35.4	29.9	25.0	18.3
	Skilled crafts workers	26.6	16.1	24.3	39.7
	Machinery operators	29.5	11.0	18.8	32.1
	Agriculture	19.6	8.9	10.7	12.5
Poland	Professionals/Managers	66.4	48.6	33.2	20.1
	Technicians	59.1	47.8	33.0	15.2
	Clerks	51.3	68.6	36.0	11.3
	Service workers	21.3	47.1	21.2	7.7
	Skilled crafts workers	15.4	10.0	8.0	5.6
	Machinery operators	20.9	23.6	14.3	4.2
	Agriculture	6.7	7.1	3.9	1.6
Sweden	Professionals/Managers	87.8	53.1	65.0	39.0
	Technicians	86.1	49.0	59.0	22.8
	Clerks	83.2	61.1	55.6	23.2
	Service workers	66.5	51.5	50.3	20.7
	Skilled crafts workers	48.0	37.1	43.1	43.2
	Machinery operators	48.9	32.1	35.0	21.6
	Agriculture	48.5	31.0	32.3	18.5
Switzerland (French)	Professionals/Managers	78.8	77.7	60.4	31.2
	Technicians	64.6	45.5	52.3	28.8
	Clerks	79.5	65.2	41.1	18.2
	Service workers	43.1	34.8	28.4	10.5
	Skilled crafts workers	42.3	36.7	45.9	43.1
	Machinery operators	48.3	47.9	42.1	8.3
	Agriculture	37.7	30.2	36.1	11.5
Switzerland (German)	Professionals/Managers	91.8	66.6	64.8	38.3
	Technicians	90.5	64.7	52.6	29.4
	Clerks	90.6	64.0	43.5	21.4
	Service workers	68.1	62.2	27.4	18.6
	Skilled crafts workers	70.0	38.5	26.6	28.2
	Machinery operators	50.3	49.1	22.1	1.0
	Agriculture	55.1	36.8	26.6	11.7
United States	Professionals/Managers	83.1	64.4	65.1	38.7
	Technicians	74.0	44.3	48.7	47.2
	Clerks	72.6	57.8	49.2	19.4
	Service workers	43.9	43.9	29.0	20.4
	Skilled crafts workers	40.6	48.1	35.3	46.0
	Machinery operators	21.3	33.8	23.0	18.4
	Agriculture	19.7	24.0	6.0	9.0

Literacy, Economy and Society

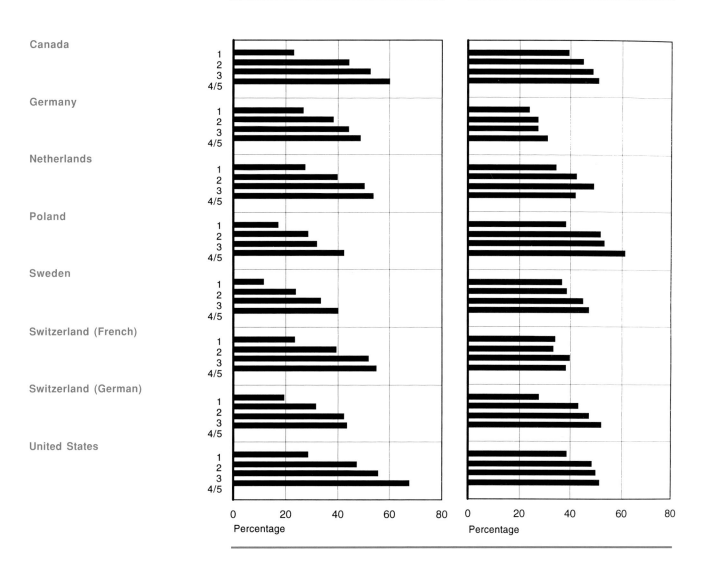

Figure 4.5a

Use mathematics to calculate costs, prices or budgets as part of job at least once a week, quantitative scale

Figure 4.5b

Use mathematics to measure things as part of job at least once a week, quantitative scale

Table 4.5

Proportion of population in each country who reported engaging in each of two workplace numeracy tasks at least once a week

	Measure or estimate the size or weight of objects	Calculate prices, costs or budgets
	Percentage	
Canada	47.2	48.9
Germany	28.3	43.3
Netherlands	44.9	47.2
Poland	48.1	26.8
Sweden	53.2	48.8
Switzerland (French)	37.2	46.7
Switzerland (German)	45.3	37.4
United States	47.9	52.3

97

Table 4.6

Proportion of workers in each occupational group who reported engaging in each of two workplace numeracy tasks at least once a week

		Measure or estimate the size or weight of objects	Calculate prices, costs or budgets
		Percentage	
Canada	Professionals/Managers	48.2	30.5
	Technicians	30.8	40.0
	Clerks	40.7	51.5
	Service workers	41.5	56.5
	Skilled crafts workers	65.9	40.6
	Machinery operators	55.2	29.7
	Agriculture	48.5	37.9
Germany	Professionals/Managers	33.5	48.0
	Technicians	29.2	49.3
	Clerks	18.3	63.0
	Service workers	11.4	48.7
	Skilled crafts workers	48.6	30.5
	Machinery operators	21.4	14.0
	Agriculture	15.3	21.9
Netherlands	Professionals/Managers	49.9	58.5
	Technicians	41.2	50.0
	Clerks	35.4	49.3
	Service workers	39.3	52.3
	Skilled crafts workers	61.2	41.4
	Machinery operators	52.5	31.0
	Agriculture	33.0	18.2
Poland	Professionals/Managers	51.1	42.9
	Technicians	50.9	35.0
	Clerks	40.9	45.9
	Service workers	65.7	52.9
	Skilled crafts workers	58.5	9.8
	Machinery operators	42.1	15.9
	Agriculture	31.2	16.4
Sweden	Professionals/Managers	57.0	51.7
	Technicians	35.5	52.6
	Clerks	30.5	46.7
	Service workers	53.6	66.5
	Skilled crafts workers	78.2	31.3
	Machinery operators	56.6	33.5
	Agriculture	48.4	29.7
Switzerland (French)	Professionals/Managers	32.6	56.5
	Technicians	40.0	49.2
	Clerks	20.3	44.7
	Service workers	25.3	47.3
	Skilled crafts workers	69.5	37.1
	Machinery operators	43.7	33.4
	Agriculture	34.4	40.1
Switzerland (German)	Professionals/Managers	43.7	52.9
	Technicians	53.1	41.3
	Clerks	24.3	34.3
	Service workers	24.9	33.1
	Skilled crafts workers	75.2	29.2
	Machinery operators	56.3	16.0
	Agriculture	35.3	23.6
United States	Professionals/Managers	45.4	64.2
	Technicians	60.7	34.8
	Clerks	32.8	54.0
	Service workers	41.5	54.5
	Skilled crafts workers	74.3	50.2
	Machinery operators	57.7	23.0
	Agriculture	50.2	31.9

...with more "budgeting" in some, and more "measuring" in others.

The pattern for countries in the practice of literacy is similar for different tasks...

Table 4.6 presents data on the frequency of these mathematical tasks for different occupations. Clerks and service workers, as might be expected, reported using budget math more frequently. On the other hand, skilled craft workers, machine operators, and agricultural workers used measurement math more frequently. Technicians and professionals/managers reported similar frequencies for the two maths.

There are differences between the countries in the frequencies reported for the different literacy tasks, but these differences are mostly consistent from task to task. Swedish respondents almost always reported the most frequent use of literacy tasks at work and Polish respondents the least frequent. Except for the quantitative tasks, Polish respondents report the second least frequent use of each task.

Figure 4.6a
Employment growth and literacy patterns, Germany

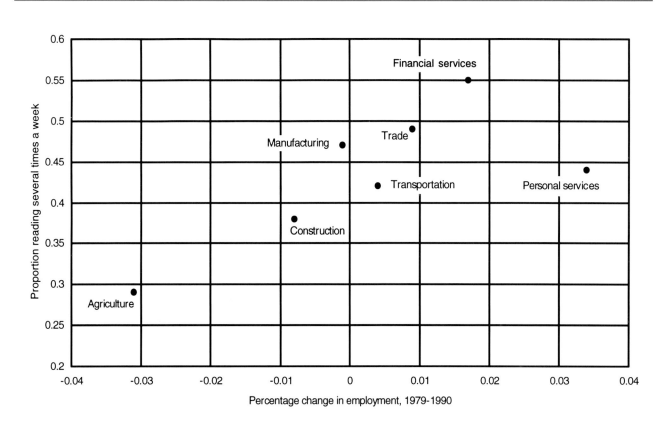

...reflecting variations in how many workers belong to occupations that make more or less use of literacy.

The differences reflect the countries' different occupational distributions. In general, respondents in Poland used all the literacy skills the least, and this country—at least among the survey countries—has the largest proportion of workers in the occupations requiring the fewest literacy skills: agriculture and other primary occupations. At the same time, Poland recorded the smallest proportions in the occupations requiring the most frequent use of literacy: managers, technicians, and clerks.[2]

Figure 4.6b

Employment growth and literacy patterns, Canada

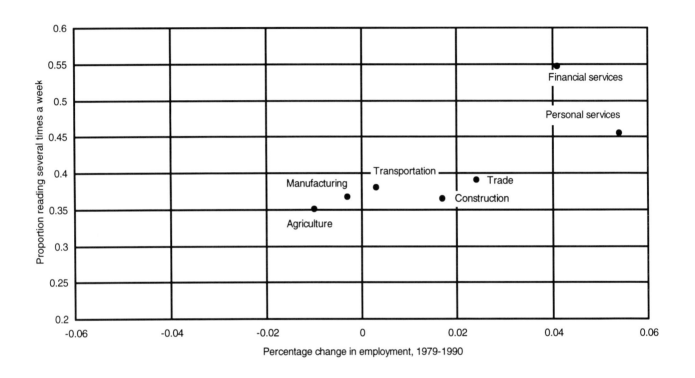

---

2   Sweden also has a small proportion of clerks, but this is offset by a very large number of managers.

Also, workers in growth sectors tend to use literacy more than those in declining ones.

Most people do not recognize that they have a literacy problem...

There is not only a connection between literacy level and the ongoing changes in employment patterns, but there is also a connection between the frequency with which job incumbents deal with literacy tasks and those changes. Figures 4.6a and 4.6b show, using Canada and Germany as examples, the relationship between changes in employment patterns and the average proportion across all tasks who reported engaging in that task several times a week. The proportions of workers in those industries that recorded growth between 1979 and 1990 and reported performing certain work-related literacy tasks several times a week are larger than those in the industries that recorded no or declining growth.

Self-assessment of skills at work

Respondents were also asked to judge how well their literacy skills served them in the workplace, particularly in relation to their current job and their ability to improve their job (see Figures 4.7a - 4.7c). It should be no surprise that few people rated their literacy skills for their current work as poor or even moderate. The largest proportion doing so are in the Netherlands (20%). It must be noted that here and in Poland, there is a general tendency for lower ratings than in the other countries.[3]

Figure 4.7a
Self-rating of reading skills for main job, document scale

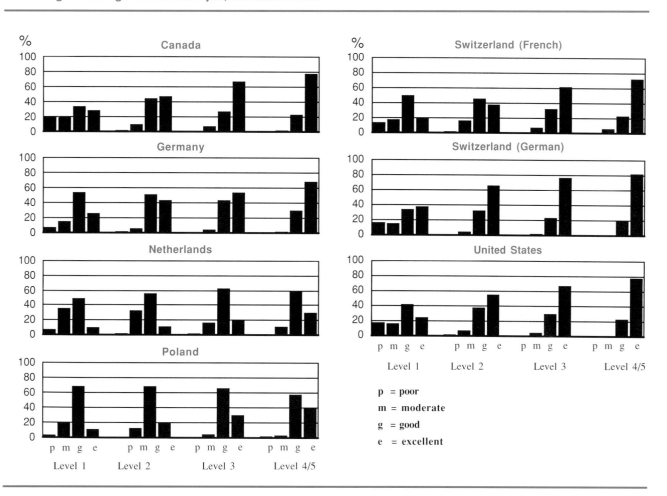

---

[3]   Sweden did not collect self assessments of skill.

Literacy, Economy and Society

Figure 4.7b
Self-rating of writing skills for main job, prose scale

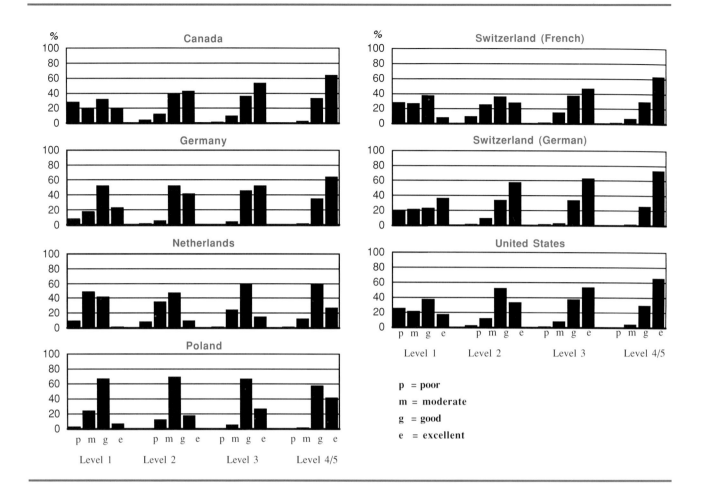

Figure 4.7c

Self-rating of mathematical skills for main job, quantitative scale

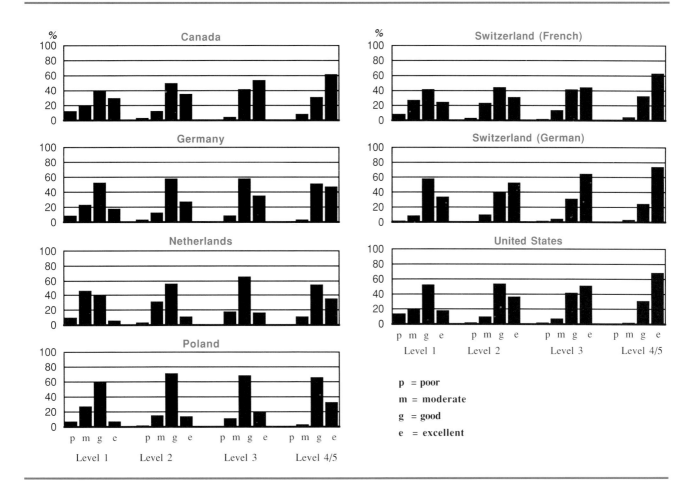

...and those with higher skills are particularly impressed with their skills...

...although this self-confidence is higher in reading than in writing or numeracy...

...but few people feel that low skills limit their prospects...

In general, fewer than two-thirds of the respondents felt their literacy skills at work were excellent, though there was a tendency for those at higher skill levels to rate their own skills as excellent. This effect is found for all three skills—reading, writing and numeracy—on all three scales.

In all countries more people rated their reading ability higher than their writing and numeracy abilities. The latter two were either similarly rated, or numeracy received slightly lower ratings. In North America, most programs that provide workplace-relevant literacy training focus on reading. The IALS data suggest that more adults have, or regard themselves as having, lower writing and numeracy skills. Therefore, examining how well such programs meet the perceived needs of potential participants would be valuable.

Relatively few people (fewer than 20% in most countries; Germany and Switzerland had poor response to this question) felt their skills limited their opportunities, although in many countries those at Level 1 were much more likely to indicate some problems (Poland and the Netherlands are the exceptions). Figures 4.8a to 4.8c show the patterns of responses.

Figure 4.8a
Reading skills limiting job opportunities, document scale

Figure 4.8b
Writing skills limiting job opportunities, prose scale

Figure 4.8c
Mathematical skills limiting job opportunities, quantitative scale

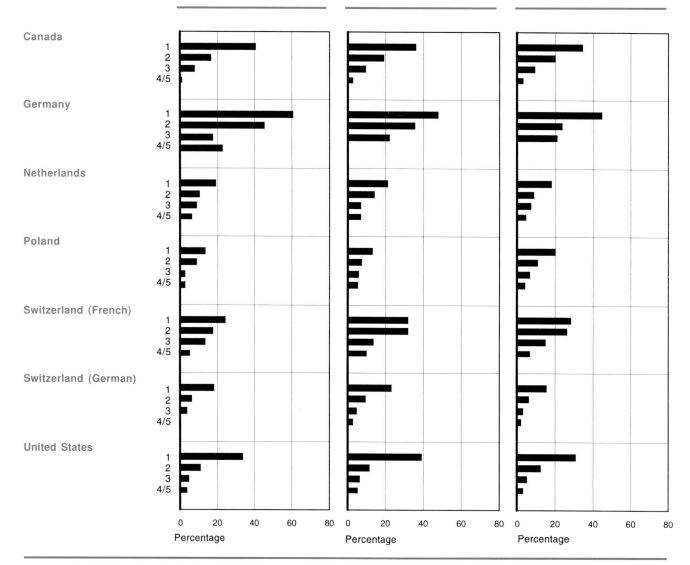

...which might help explain low scores in Poland, where development of literacy skills may suffer through lack of demand...

...especially among small-scale farmers.

Workplace literacy trends are mirrored outside work and...

...whether you read a daily newspaper is more likely to depend on your nationality than on your literacy level...

...with book reading far behind...

If these perceptions are accurate, they may provide some additional evidence for the low scores in Poland. In this country, respondents reported the least frequent engagement in literacy tasks at work compared with respondents in other countries. Researchers who have explored literacy in other industrialized jurisdictions with low literacy levels have argued that literacy skill is demand driven. That is, if the need for literacy is low, then there is little motive to improve literacy skill. Further, pursuing higher education, which delays entering the work force, is not an economically wise decision: there is no payoff. And investing time and money in additional training does not necessarily lead to a better job or greater productivity. The evidence from Poland may indicate that in this country the demand for literacy is lower, relative to other countries, because low-skill individuals report fewer perceived limitations based on their own literacy skill. Hence, if literacy is demand driven, it is not surprising that lower skill averages are found in Poland. It will be important to see whether, as the market economy develops more fully in Poland, there is an increase in demand and in skill.

Why the demand might be lower is, of course, an interesting question. Undoubtedly the changing economic base in Poland plays a large role. There is a relatively large agricultural population in Poland. And the data from the occupational analysis suggest that agricultural occupations are associated with lower literacy skills. In addition, to the extent that agriculture is often a small enterprise, it is unlikely that Polish farmers will need to access information from complex texts.

Literacy in the community

Literacy, of course, is not only interesting because of its role in work—it is essential to full civic participation. Much literacy activity takes place outside the workplace. The IALS asked respondents a variety of questions about their everyday literacy practices and their participation in other social and community activities. They were also asked to evaluate their own literacy skill outside work. The results from this battery of questions mirror those from the workplace literacy questions.

Literacy practices

The survey asked about four specific home and community literacy activities: newspaper reading, book and magazine reading, library use, and letter writing. The patterns of everyday literacy practices are shown in Figures 4.9a to 4.9d. Almost everyone reads a newspaper at least once a week (over 80% of respondents in every country reported doing so; over 90% in some countries), but daily readership varies from country to country from lows of 60% in Poland and 62% in the United States to a high of 90% in Sweden. Literacy level has only a small effect on newspaper reading, probably because this task covers a broad range of skills. The National Adult Literacy Survey in the United States (Kirsch et al. 1993), for example, found great level-to-level variation in the newspaper sections that were read regularly. Nonetheless, those at Level 1 are less likely to read newspapers, particularly on a daily basis. In those countries with large numbers of second-language speakers in Level 1 (Canada, the United States and Switzerland) the proportion of Level 1 newspaper readers is smaller, most likely a consequence of the scarcity of daily papers in the languages these individuals speak most fluently. Reading newspapers is the most common literacy activity; no other task attracted such frequent readers.

Much less common are literacy activities that might be thought of as less functional, more "literate," than reading newspapers. Fewer than 40% of respondents in any country reported reading books daily; about 66% at least once a month. Reading books has a strong effect on the level of literacy. Uniformly, more of those at Level 4/5 reported reading books every day, with smaller numbers at each lower level. In Germany more than 50% of those at Level 1 said they read books monthly.

There are small differences in letter writing from country to country. About half of respondents reported writing letters at least once a month. There are significant differences across literacy level for all frequencies of letter writing.

Many libraries have programs designed to help adults at low literacy levels improve their skill. The IALS data suggest that most such programs likely serve the already highly skilled. In all countries individuals at Level 4/5 are most likely to report frequent library visits, though in the Netherlands those at Level 3 have almost the same frequency. Fewer than one-fifth of Level 1 adults said they visit a library even once a month. There are large country-to-country variations in the use of libraries. Swedish and Dutch residents are the most frequent users of libraries; Swiss residents reported the least use.

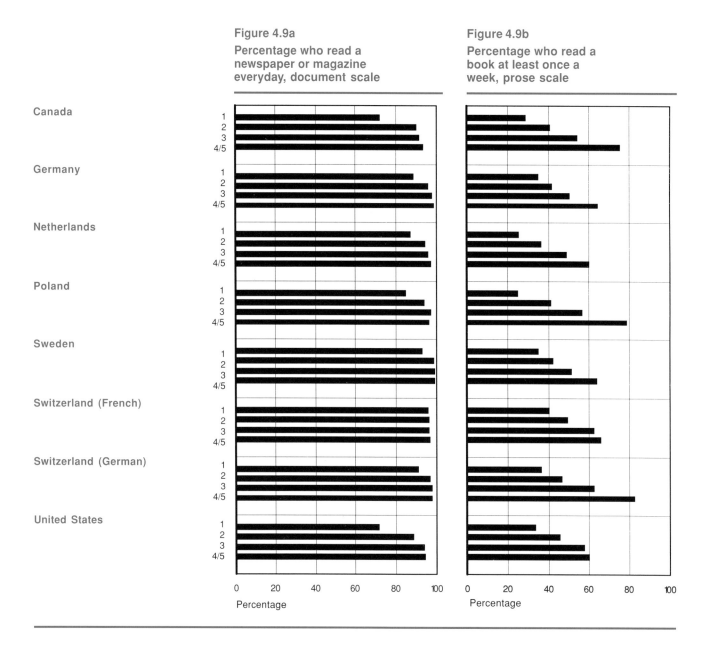

Figure 4.9a

Percentage who read a newspaper or magazine everyday, document scale

Figure 4.9b

Percentage who read a book at least once a week, prose scale

Figure 4.9c

Percentage who write a letter
at least once a week, prose scale

Figure 4.9d

Percentage who use a public library
at least once a month, prose scale

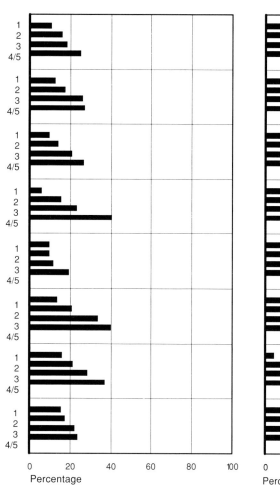

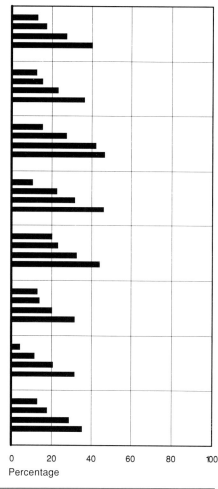

Remarkably consistent links exist between practice and skill.

Overall, adults in those countries where the average scores are highest (notably Sweden and the Netherlands) also report the greatest daily use of literacy-related tasks and those in countries with the lowest scores the least use. It is important, nonetheless, to note that the Polish are closer to the middle in library visits. Still, one is impressed by the overall consistency, in everyday and workplace contexts, in the connections between practice and skill, both on an individual and a population level. Such consistency should not be unexpected, of course, and that it is so strongly reflected in the IALS data is further evidence of the quality of that data.

Activities related to literacy

Lower literacy groups watch television more...

The IALS examined a number of practices that, while not direct evidence of literacy, are widely thought to be associated with it, or with its absence. For example, it is a widespread public belief that television watching and literacy are somehow incompatible. The IALS data demonstrates a noticeable—and negative—link between the two (see Figure 4.10). Those most likely to watch television for significant periods of time are usually at lower literacy levels. Over 10% of those in Level 1 reported watching more than five hours of television each day, except in Poland and Switzerland where television viewing is generally low, in part because television ownership is low. Over 20% of those at Level 4/5 watched television less than one hour a day.

...perhaps because it pre-empts reading time and reduces reading demands.

Higher level literates participate more in community activities...

...and for all these activities, the clearest differences are between Level 1 and the rest.

The frequency of television viewing varies by country. About 10% of all respondents in Germany and the United States reported watching over five hours a day, but only 5% in the Netherlands and Poland watch this much television daily.[4] Television may interfere with literacy in two ways: the time it occupies might have been spent reading; and it provides easy access to everyday information, reducing the need to read.

There is some country-to-country difference in how literacy relates to community participation (see Figure 4.11). In Canada and the United States such participation is higher among respondents at Levels 3 and 4/5 than for Levels 1 and 2. Among the German-speaking population in Switzerland, those at Level 4/5 reported more regular community participation than those at Level 3. In other countries, however, there is no difference across the highest three levels. In all cases, a small number at Level 1 reported frequent participation in their communities.

Throughout these participation questions, however, the clearest difference is between Level 1 and the others. Sometimes Level 2 differs from 3 and sometimes Level 3 differs from 4/5, but there are also instances where the differences between these three levels are relatively small. In all, however, Level 1 is distinct with respect to community participation. This further suggests that a single approach to studying literacy is unwarranted; the effects are different at different levels. However, there are effects at all levels.

Figure 4.10

Percentage watching two hours of television per day, prose scale

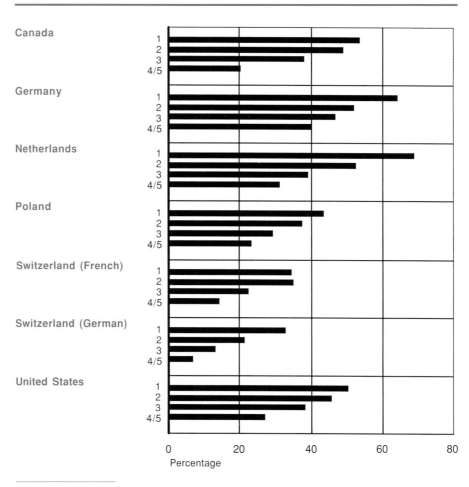

4 A large number of Swiss respondents did not answer this question.

108

Figure 4.11

Percentage participating in community organizations at least once a month by literacy level, document scale

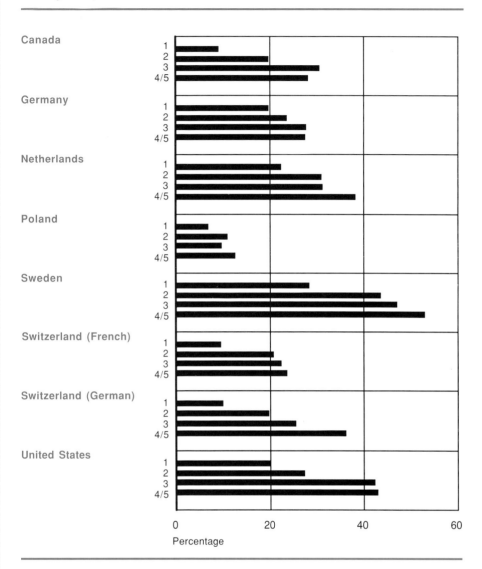

Self-assessment

In addition to evaluating their workplace literacy skills, IALS respondents were asked to evaluate how well their literacy skills served them in daily life. And just as in the workplace, most think their skills are satisfactory (Figures 4.12a to 4.12c). Over 80% of the respondents in every country rated their reading in daily life as good or excellent. Although there is a clear relationship between level and self-rating, many of those at Level 1 rated their skill as excellent. Only a handful of Level 3 or Level 4/5 respondents—often only one person—in any country rated their skills as poor.

Although not specifically asked to judge the adequacy of their literacy skill in daily life, this may well have been the criteria that many respondents used. Numerous studies have shown how adults with low literacy skills are able to construct their daily lives so that literacy is not a part of it and therefore, they can legitimately claim that their skills serve them well . These coping mechanisms often lead to individuals being dependent on others to meet their literacy needs.

As for work, people were more confident in their reading skills than in writing or mathematics.

In most countries, more individuals were willing to rate their reading skills as excellent, but they did not give the same rating to their writing skills. There were fewer people who rated their mathematics skills higher than their reading skills, but the assessments for writing and mathematics were similar in all countries.

Figure 4.12a
Self-rating of reading skills for daily life, document scale

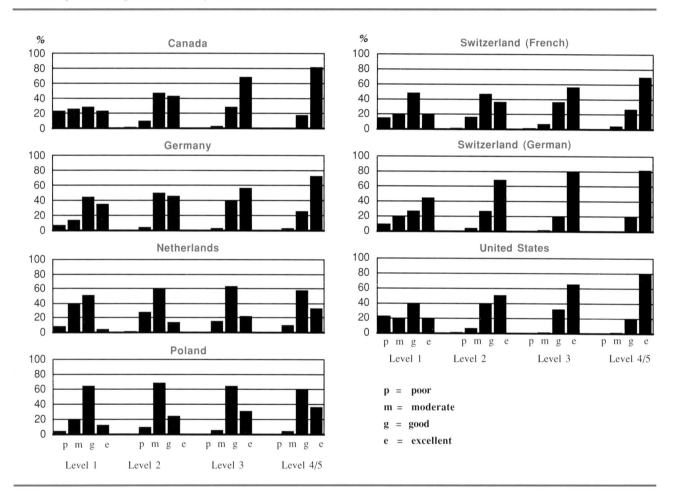

p = poor
m = moderate
g = good
e = excellent

Figure 4.12b
Self-rating of writing skills for daily life, prose scale

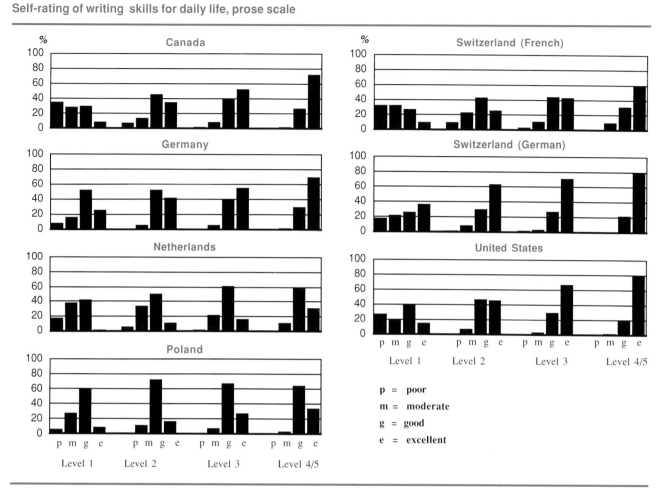

p = poor
m = moderate
g = good
e = excellent

Figure 4.12c

Self-rating of mathematical skills for daily life, quantitative scale

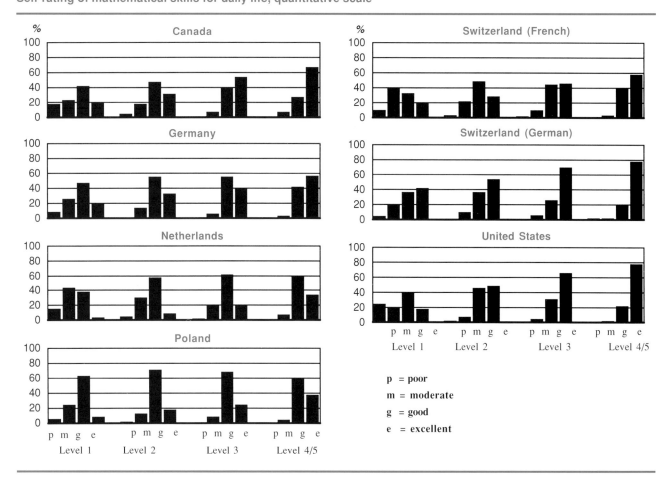

p = poor
m = moderate
g = good
e = excellent

So practices and skills are mutually reinforcing...

...and the importance of practice makes it possible for adults to build their skills.

Summary

Literacy practices are intimately related to literacy skill: each reinforces the other. In some ways, jobs can be designed to fit the literacy skills of the people available to fill them, but clearly, employees with low levels of literacy skills are less able to adapt to changes efficiently through the use of printed text either for self-study or for more formal instruction. Significant numbers of Level 1 respondents in all countries said that their literacy skills made it difficult for them to advance or change their jobs.

If the formal education system provides the raw material from which adult literacy is created, the practices explored in this chapter are at the centre of that creation. It is possible to imagine that those individuals with lower educational attainment but high literacy skill are those who found—or had thrust on them—ways to practise literacy, and to sustain and develop it. At the same time, those with higher educational attainment and lower skills may well be those who could not find opportunities, or did not act on opportunities, or who found themselves in situations where opportunities were not available; therefore, they were not actively engaged in literacy activities. With this view, the judgement on the education system is not whether it produces literate adults, but whether it yields graduates who can sustain and augment their literacy levels. The judgement on a society is whether it offers opportunities for, or whether it values, high literacy levels for all. Widespread high levels of adult literacy are the result of what adults do, not necessarily what students do.

References

Kirsch, Irwin S., et al. *Adult Literacy in America: A First Look at the Results of the National Adult Literacy Survey.* Washington, D.C.: National Center for Education Statistics, U.S. Department of Education, 1993.

Chapter 5

International Adult Literacy Survey: insights and prospects

T. Scott Murray, Statistics Canada, Ottawa, Canada

This survey has broken new ground...

The International Adult Literacy Survey (IALS) has broken new ground in the understanding of literacy, its distribution and its implications. When the project was conceived in 1991, there were reservations about the potential for comparing literacy proficiency across languages and cultures. In practice, the richness and validity of the data obtained exceeded even the expectations of the project's most enthusiastic supporters.

...by demonstrating that literacy can be compared internationally.

The IALS demonstrated that modern measurement technology is capable of making valid estimates of adults' abilities across countries. Both the theories of literacy and the measurement scales that have been devised in national contexts have proven to be robust when adapted to accommodate multiple languages and cultures. Such a breakthrough will have implications beyond the measurement of literacy. It is the first time that a reliable means has been found for comparing the competences of different countries' adult populations. In a world in which the abilities of the work force are thought to be crucial in determining well-being and economic performance, the demand for such knowledge is immense.

The findings

This publication identifies a first set of conclusions:

This report has made only a start in interpreting the IALS data. The main work of interpretation and application will need to be carried out within each of the participating countries. But already, there are some strong conclusions. The most important findings are that:

National averages differ, but distribution is important.

- *Important differences in literacy skills do exist across and within nations.* These differences are large enough to matter both socially and economically. They concern not only the overall levels of literacy skill in particular countries, but also the distribution of those levels. In some countries, most of the population clusters into a relatively narrow band of proficiency; in others, there is a wide range of difference between adults with low and high levels of literacy.

Literacy is a problem for many;

- *Literacy skill deficits are found not just among marginalized groups, but affect large proportions of the entire adult population.* Over half of adults in some countries fail to move beyond the two basic levels (Levels 1 and 2) of literacy. There is a need to consider methods for improving the skills of entire populations as well as seeking remedial measures for selected groups.

Literacy helps you prosper;

Education is not everything;

Literacy takes practice.

Low-level literates may deny their problem.

Cross-national differences must be understood in context...

- *Literacy is strongly correlated with life chances and use of opportunities.* While the processes that lead to this result are certainly complex, there can be no doubt about its importance to employment stability, the incidence of unemployment, and income. Moreover, in most countries the structural adjustment that is reducing the economic prospects of adults with low literacy levels is far from complete. Therefore, those with low literacy levels will have even fewer opportunities in the future.

- *Literacy is not synonymous with educational attainment.* Not surprisingly, people with more education tend, on average, to have higher literacy levels. But the length of initial schooling and further education is shown to be only one factor contributing to literacy in adulthood—in two ways. First, in every country there are many cases of poorly educated people who perform well, and a smaller but still significant number of highly educated people who perform poorly on the literacy scales. The implication is that although formal education yields an immense advantage, there is also scope for individuals to improve their literacy through their own efforts and behaviour. Second, there are considerable differences between countries in terms of the likelihood that someone with a particular quantity of education will perform at a particular level. The implication is that schooling provides no more than a "start in life" when it comes to acquiring literacy skills, and it appears to provide a more effective start in some countries than in others.

- *Literacy skills, like muscles, are maintained and strengthened through regular use.* Formal education systems provide only the raw material for adult literacy. The evidence shows that the lack of application of literacy in daily activities is associated with lower levels of performance. Some supportive contexts at home and at work seem to reinforce literacy practices and applications better than others. One reason for optimism is that some areas of high employment growth in OECD countries, such as financial and other service sectors, tend to create environments that reinforce literacy. Others, such as manufacturing, may become better at doing so through restructuring. But the transition to information-based economies is not a smooth one, and a strong effort will be needed to ensure that literacy practices are improved within organizations of all kinds. The creation of environments that favour lifelong learning will require strong commitment from individuals, employers and governments.

- *Adults with low literacy levels do not usually acknowledge or recognize they have a problem.* Survey participants at all literacy levels, when asked whether their reading skills were sufficient to meet their everyday needs, replied overwhelmingly that they were. For those designing programs to reduce the dependence of low-level literates on others, this denial has important implications.

International differences

In supporting these conclusions, the IALS offers a unique set of cross-national data. It is important, however, to ensure that any direct comparisons across countries incorporate an understanding of international differences. This contextual understanding has two dimensions. On the one hand, it is necessary to appreciate the cultural and societal norms that make each country specific. On the other hand, it is important to account for different structural characteristics of societies including, in particular, the demographic composition, the make-up of their industrial base and the degree of urban-rural disparities. For example, a country's immigration pattern may influence its distribution of literacy proficiency.

...but may potentially be remedied through policy action...

...provided that there is wide collaboration to do so.

The IALS is a useful model to develop in the future...

...by surveying more industrialized countries...

The relative importance of text-based information and the traditional use of written materials in homes and workplaces will have important effects on each country's results.

But at the same time, national differences in literacy patterns cannot simply be dismissed as cultural phenomena beyond control. It is essential to recognize that government policies can have important long-term effects on literacy levels. In most European countries, it is striking to note the increase in literacy levels among succeeding generations, as shown by the much higher performance of 16- to 24-year-olds compared with their elders. A straightforward explanation of this would be the expansion and improvement of upper-secondary and tertiary education in these countries during recent years. It is also striking to note that in Germany, one of the few European countries that has traditionally stressed the development of literacy skills even for those secondary education students destined for technical jobs, relatively few adults of any age have low literacy scores. A striking contrast between North America and Europe, which may be related to their education systems, is that North Americans score higher in prose than in document literacy; in Europe, the reverse is true. A plausible explanation for this could be found in the domination of narrative textbooks in North America, and the greater exposure of students in many European countries to written materials that impart information.

What is evident, however, is that the interactions between national policies and the shapes of national performance profiles are in many cases complex, and policies do not always fall into a single area of responsibility. To address literacy-related problems therefore requires broad co-ordination between several bodies, to devise strategies for long-term cumulative impact. In Canada, an inter-ministerial effort, co-ordinated by the National Literacy Secretariat (National Literacy Secretariat 1990), followed the country's first national study of adult literacy (Montigny et al. 1991). Any strategy for addressing a nation's literacy problems, moreover, needs to find an appropriate combination of actions—involving all interested parties—that address literacy locally, followed by larger policies, including any necessary changes to the education system.

The next steps

This first International Adult Literacy Survey has established an interesting model under which collaboration between governments and researchers can produce, in a period of three years, a rich and complex source of cross-national data providing a solid information base for policy decisions. A general renewed interest by governments in human capital indicators is associated with the need to demonstrate that investment in human resource development can pay off. Having created a robust methodology, the IALS therefore offers a useful instrument for governments wanting to make similar comparisons in the future.

While the present report was going to press, plans were already under way to conduct parallel studies in a number of countries, including Australia, New Zealand and the United Kingdom. One reason for encouraging the participation of other OECD member countries in such surveys in the coming months and years is that they will provide a cumulative set of comparisons. The average skill levels of adults can be expected to change very slowly compared with those of school-age populations, who are more immediately affected by a cycle of educational reform. So it will be reasonable to compare the data from the seven countries who participated in the 1994 IALS with that of other countries undertaking a similar survey, say, two years later.

Furthermore, there is a need to build links with other agencies to explore the viability of applying aspects of the IALS methodology in less developed countries. Current methods of measuring literacy in such countries might be refined using the insights gained from this survey. The accelerating pace of development in some regions demands a gradual shift in concern from policies for fighting illiteracy to those addressing problems of low literacy.

...and extending the depth and scope of similar surveys in the future.

Finally, there is ample room for improving the quality and scope of this kind of survey in the future. Governments need to work with researchers to build the next generation of assessments. To achieve a richer understanding of the factors associated with literacy, three improvements could be made. First, the inclusion of more domains of literacy skill would allow a better understanding of the relationships between various skills. Second, larger population samples would allow more information on detailed statistically valid breakdowns of results. Finally, if assessments could be administered to samples of workers within individual firms, and those workers and firms were followed over time, a detailed understanding of the links between workers' skills, job success and company performance might be obtained. The reward would be a micro-level understanding of the contribution made by adult literacy to macro-economic performance.

References

Montigny, Gilles, Karen Kelly and Stan Jones. *Adult Literacy in Canada: Results of a National Study.* Ottawa: Minister of Industry, Science and Technology (Statistics Canada, Catalogue no. 89-525E), 1991.

National Literacy Secretariat. *Partners in Literacy, National Literacy Program: An Overview of Projects.* Multiculturalism and Citizenship Canada (Catalogue no. ci96-52/1990).

Appendix A

Participants in the International Adult Literacy Survey project

As mentioned in the Introduction, many people have contributed to this study. This appendix lists the names of the country representatives, policy makers, researchers and experts in literacy assessment and scaling who have actively taken part in the preparatory work leading to the publication of the study.

International management and co-ordination

Mr. T. Scott Murray, International Study Director, Statistics Canada, Ottawa

Prime technical contractors

Mr. Donald Hirsch, Consultant, London

Mr. Stan Jones, Carleton University, Ottawa

Mr. Irwin Kirsch, ETS, Princeton

Mr. Archie Lapointe, ETS, Princeton

Mr. Andy Latham, ETS, Princeton

Mr. Georges Lemaître, OECD, Paris

Ms. Nancy Mead, ETS, Princeton

Ms. Mary Michaels, ETS, Princeton

Mr. Kentaro Yamamoto, ETS, Princeton

Representatives of national and support agencies

Canada	Mr. Jim Page, National Literacy Secretariat, Ottawa
	Mr. Doug Giddings, Human Resources Development Canada, Ottawa
	Ms. Cathy Chapman, Human Resources Development Canada, Ottawa
Germany	Mr. Michael Hirsch, Federal Ministry of Education, Science, Research and Technology, Bonn
Ireland	Mr. Padraig Bennis, Ministry of Education, Dublin
Netherlands	Mr. Peter van den Dool, Ministry of Education, Culture and Science, Amsterdam
Poland	Mr. Jerzy Wisniewski, Ministry of National Education, Warsaw
Sweden	Mr. Ulf Lundgen, National Agency for Education, Stockholm
Switzerland	Mr. Uri Peter Trier, Swiss National Science Foundation, National Research Programme 33, Bern
United States	Mr. Eugene Owen, National Center for Education Statistics, Washington, D.C.

National study teams

Canada
Mr. Jean Pignal, National Study Director, Statistics Canada, Ottawa
Mr. Richard Porzuczek
Mr. Paul Labelle
Ms. Debbie Calcutt
Ms. Huguette Demers
Ms. Anna Maneiro
Ms. Lia Gendron
Ms. Claire Bradshaw
Ms. Linda Bélanger

Germany
Mr. Rainer Lehmann, National Study Director, Humboldt University, Berlin
Mr. Rainer Peek
Ms. Barbara L. von Harder

Ireland
Mr. Brendan L. Hickey (deceased), National Study Director, St. Patrick's College, Dublin
Mr. Mark Morgan, National Study Director, St. Patrick's College, Dublin
Ms. Anne Cronin
Mr. David Millar
Mr. Ronan Reilly
Ms. Anna Gacquin
Ms. Clare Fitzpatrick

Netherlands
Mr. Willem Houtkoop, National Study Director, Max Goote Expert Center for Vocational and Continuing Education and Training, Amsterdam
Mr. Max van der Kamp
Ms. Ellen Couvret
Mr. Jan Bouts
Mr. van Assema

Poland
Mr. Ireneusz Bialecki, National Study Director, Warsaw University, Warsaw
Ms. Hanna Gulczynska, Deputy National Study Director, Warsaw University
Ms. Ewa Swierzbowska-Kowalik
Mr. Zbigniew Sawinski

Sweden	Mr. Mats Myrberg, National Study Director, National Agency for Education, Stockholm
	Ms. Eva Josefsson
	Ms. Birgitta Järpsten
	Ms. Ann-Charlotte Ocka
	Mr. Stefan Persson
	Ms. Helena Sjösvärd
	Ms. Harriet Stenvall
	Ms. Sonja Tiderman
	Ms. Monica Åtting

Switzerland	Mr. François Stoll, National Study Director, University of Zurich, Zurich
	Mr. Philipp Notter, National Study Director, University of Zurich, Zurich
	Mr. Denis Ribeaud
	Mr. Claude Fischli

United States	Ms. Marilyn Binkley, National Study Director, National Center for Education Statistics, Washington, D.C.
	Ms. Gail Hoff
	Ms. Karen Monroe
	Ms. Marilyn Monahan

Key supporters

Mr. Paul Bélanger, UNESCO Institute for Education, Hamburg

Mr. Michail Skaliotis, EUROSTAT, Luxembourg

Ms. Bettina Knauth, EUROSTAT, Luxembourg

Mr. Norman Davis, Consultant, European Union Task Force on Human Resources, Education, Training and Youth, Brussels

Mr. Albert Tuijnman, OECD, Paris

Ms. Jeanne Griffith, National Center for Education Statistics, Washington, D.C.

Independent quality review team

Mr. Graham Kalton, WESTAT, Rockville

Mr. Lars Lyberg, Statistics Sweden, Stockholm

Mr. Jean Michel Rempp, INSEE, Paris

Appendix B

Tables: distribution of literacy

Table B-1a

Proportion of each labour force category at each literacy level, prose scale

		Level 1	Level 2	Level 3	Level 4/5
			Percentage		
Canada	Employed	11.5	24.7	37.5	26.4
	Unemployed	24.7	36.9	20.9	14.2
	Student	37.5	20.9	39.7	26.1
	Other out of labour force	26.4	14.2	26.1	12.8
Germany	Employed	0.7	33.3	40.5	15.4
	Unemployed	9.3	40.5	25.4	4.5
	Student	1.2	15.4	4.5	28.6
	Other out of labour force	15.4	4.5	28.6	8.9
Netherlands	Employed	6.9	26.5	48.6	18.0
	Unemployed	22.7	46.2	28.6	2.5
	Student	6.8	19.0	50.4	23.9
	Other out of labour force	18.1	39.0	34.4	8.5
Poland	Employed	39.4	36.4	20.7	3.5
	Unemployed	65.0	26.4	8.4	0.2
	Student	16.5	37.3	38.0	8.2
	Other out of labour force	46.5	35.4	16.8	1.4
Sweden	Employed	5.5	19.5	41.0	33.9
	Unemployed	25.6	37.1	28.7	8.6
	Student	3.5	15.1	39.7	41.7
	Other out of labour force	13.6	21.5	38.2	26.7
Switzerland (French)	Employed	13.9	33.6	41.9	10.6
	Unemployed	36.3	37.6	23.4	2.7
	Student	5.5	30.4	43.7	20.4
	Other out of labour force	21.3	41.0	32.2	5.5
Switzerland (German)	Employed	15.0	37.8	38.4	8.8
	Unemployed	36.5	43.5	18.5	1.4
	Student	3.3	16.8	51.6	28.2
	Other out of labour force	22.2	41.5	30.8	5.5
United States	Employed	15.0	26.2	34.1	24.8
	Unemployed	23.1	36.4	27.6	12.9
	Student	26.9	25.0	34.5	13.5
	Other out of labour force	34.8	22.8	29.6	12.7

For example, 40.5% of the employed in Germany are at Level 3 on this scale.

Table B-1b

Proportion of each labour force category at each literacy level, document scale

		Level 1	Level 2	Level 3	Level 4/5
			Percentage		
Canada	Employed	11.9	24.0	34.5	29.6
	Unemployed	38.9	23.1	23.3	14.7
	Student	8.1	26.0	31.9	33.9
	Other out of labour force	35.3	26.6	26.8	11.3
Germany	Employed	5.3	30.7	41.6	22.4
	Unemployed	19.0	38.2	37.9	5.0
	Student	5.5	17.9	37.4	39.3
	Other out of labour force	14.0	38.8	35.9	11.3
Netherlands	Employed	5.7	21.7	48.5	24.0
	Unemployed	18.8	47.3	29.5	4.4
	Student	4.7	14.4	47.1	33.8
	Other out of labour force	20.5	35.0	35.5	9.0
Poland	Employed	41.3	31.0	20.6	7.1
	Unemployed	67.4	24.5	6.7	1.3
	Student	22.7	34.7	31.5	11.1
	Other out of labour force	50.1	33.5	13.0	3.4
Sweden	Employed	4.8	16.7	40.6	37.9
	Unemployed	17.7	37.9	33.3	11.1
	Student	2.6	16.4	39.8	41.2
	Other out of labour force	12.2	23.6	34.3	29.8
Switzerland (French)	Employed	12.0	30.3	41.1	16.6
	Unemployed	27.5	30.7	35.7	6.1
	Student	2.0	19.7	49.7	28.5
	Other out of labour force	24.6	31.8	30.8	12.8
Switzerland (German)	Employed	14.1	30.6	38.4	16.9
	Unemployed	18.9	34.2	42.1	4.7
	Student	1.9	16.4	41.9	39.8
	Other out of labour force	22.6	33.6	34.1	9.6
United States	Employed	17.8	25.5	33.9	22.7
	Unemployed	26.8	43.2	24.7	5.3
	Student	23.6	25.8	33.8	16.9
	Other out of labour force	40.3	24.8	25.3	9.6

For example, 47.3% of the unemployed in the Netherlands are at Level 2 on this scale.

Table B-1c

Proportion of each labour force category at each literacy level, quantitative scale

		Level 1	Level 2	Level 3	Level 4/5
			Percentage		
Canada	Employed	11.4	25.0	36.0	27.6
	Unemployed	29.3	32.9	25.5	12.4
	Student	7.5	26.6	45.3	20.6
	Other out of labour force	33.2	27.4	29.5	9.9
Germany	Employed	4.3	22.9	45.2	27.6
	Unemployed	12.1	37.2	40.7	10.0
	Student	3.9	20.4	37.8	37.9
	Other out of labour force	10.3	32.4	41.2	16.2
Netherlands	Employed	6.0	21.2	48.0	24.8
	Unemployed	13.2	36.1	43.0	7.8
	Student	6.1	19.3	49.7	24.9
	Other out of labour force	20.8	35.7	34.4	9.1
Poland	Employed	34.5	30.5	25.6	9.3
	Unemployed	57.7	24.0	16.4	1.8
	Student	19.1	36.6	36.4	7.9
	Other out of labour force	47.1	31.1	18.2	3.6
Sweden	Employed	4.7	17.4	39.8	38.1
	Unemployed	19.9	31.0	35.4	13.6
	Student	5.0	17.6	38.1	39.2
	Other out of labour force	12.3	19.0	36.1	32.7
Switzerland (French)	Employed	8.7	24.7	45.6	20.9
	Unemployed	20.9	33.2	35.3	10.5
	Student	3.3	13.8	46.4	36.5
	Other out of labour force	18.9	30.5	33.8	16.9
Switzerland (German)	Employed	10.4	26.3	42.3	21.0
	Unemployed	21.5	24.1	41.0	13.5
	Student	1.9	19.9	42.4	35.8
	Other out of labour force	13.6	35.3	41.6	9.5
United States	Employed	15.9	24.4	32.5	27.1
	Unemployed	15.0	31.6	39.4	13.9
	Student	25.2	27.4	36.7	10.7
	Other out of labour force	36.9	26.7	25.1	11.3

For example, 7.9% of the students in Poland are at Level 4/5 on this scale.

Table B-2a

Proportion of those working full time and those working part time at each literacy level, prose scale

		Level 1	Level 2	Level 3	Level 4/5
			Percentage		
Canada	Full time	13.5	25.3	36.7	24.6
	Part time	8.9	18.4	40.6	32.1
Germany	Full time	11.8	33.6	39.1	15.5
	Part time	11.8	27.6	42.9	17.7
Netherlands	Full time	7.8	28.6	47.0	16.6
	Part time	5.6	20.5	51.8	22.0
Poland	Full time	39.3	37.2	20.1	3.3
	Part time	46.4	30.5	20.3	2.9
Sweden	Full time	5.1	18.9	41.2	34.8
	Part time	5.8	19.7	38.9	35.6
Switzerland (French)	Full time	13.7	34.7	42.4	9.2
	Part time	17.0	29.1	36.3	17.6
Switzerland (German)	Full time	12.5	37.0	41.1	9.4
	Part time	19.5	38.4	33.6	8.5
United States	Full time	15.9	26.5	33.0	24.6
	Part time	14.0	22.3	41.1	22.6

For example, 20.3% of those working part time in Poland are at Level 3 on this scale.

Table B-2b

Proportion of those working full time and those working part time at each literacy level, document scale

		Level 1	Level 2	Level 3	Level 4/5
			Percentage		
Canada	Full time	14.0	24.3	34.2	27.5
	Part time	7.8	23.0	35.1	34.1
Germany	Full time	5.6	30.6	41.7	22.1
	Part time	8.5	27.3	39.9	24.3
Netherlands	Full time	6.3	22.5	47.7	23.5
	Part time	5.5	19.5	49.9	25.1
Poland	Full time	42.1	31.2	19.9	6.8
	Part time	41.0	31.9	22.3	4.7
Sweden	Full time	4.3	15.5	41.1	39.1
	Part time	5.4	22.1	39.4	33.1
Switzerland (French)	Full time	11.4	31.3	41.1	16.2
	Part time	13.2	25.1	39.5	22.1
Switzerland (German)	Full time	11.4	30.2	40.2	18.1
	Part time	22.1	29.3	36.1	12.4
United States	Full time	18.7	25.9	32.2	23.2
	Part time	16.3	22.1	42.3	19.4

For example, 24.3% of those working full time in Canada are at Level 2 on this scale.

Table B-2c

Proportion of those working full time and those working part time at each literacy level, quantitative scale

		Level 1	Level 2	Level 3	Level 4/5
			Percentage		
Canada	Full time	12.7	25.5	34.9	26.9
	Part time	10.5	25.1	41.3	23.1
Germany	Full time	4.5	22.5	44.6	28.4
	Part time	6.2	25.1	43.0	25.7
Netherlands	Full time	6.3	21.1	48.1	24.6
	Part time	6.6	23.0	47.6	22.8
Poland	Full time	35.0	30.3	25.8	8.9
	Part time	38.4	30.8	23.1	7.7
Sweden	Full time	4.1	16.3	39.8	39.8
	Part time	6.1	22.0	41.5	30.4
Switzerland (French)	Full time	7.9	25.3	45.2	21.5
	Part time	12.8	20.8	44.6	21.7
Switzerland (German)	Full time	8.8	24.3	44.1	22.8
	Part time	14.3	34.7	39.1	11.9
United States	Full time	16.3	24.4	30.6	28.7
	Part time	16.9	23.6	42.5	17.0

For example, 44.6% of those working part time in Switzerland (French) are at Level 3 on this scale.

Table B-3a

Proportion of each income group at each literacy level, prose scale

		Level 1	Level 2	Level 3	Level 4/5
			Percentage		
Canada	No income	29.9	29.7	29.0	11.4
	Quintile 1	14.3	25.7	38.0	22.0
	Quintile 2	20.6	24.4	34.2	20.8
	Quintile 3	13.7	22.1	37.3	26.9
	Quintile 4	7.9	29.2	34.9	27.9
	Quintile 5	4.4	18.5	37.7	39.4
Germany	No income	14.2	35.4	37.9	12.6
	Quintile 1	14.2	32.0	39.5	14.3
	Quintile 2	21.5	36.3	34.2	8.0
	Quintile 3	14.6	37.4	35.3	12.8
	Quintile 4	10.0	38.0	40.4	11.6
	Quintile 5	7.8	25.2	43.6	23.4
Netherlands	No income	17.0	37.0	35.5	10.5
	Quintile 1	7.6	24.2	49.1	19.1
	Quintile 2	9.5	22.9	51.7	15.8
	Quintile 3	9.9	28.2	44.6	17.2
	Quintile 4	7.2	34.6	42.3	15.9
	Quintile 5	2.1	20.4	55.5	22.0
Poland	No income	0.0	0.0	0.0	0.0
	Quintile 1	44.2	37.7	16.0	2.1
	Quintile 2	45.0	34.4	18.7	2.0
	Quintile 3	36.2	39.3	21.2	3.3
	Quintile 4	28.9	40.8	25.3	5.0
	Quintile 5	36.5	30.9	26.7	5.8
Sweden	No income	29.6	31.1	27.3	12.0
	Quintile 1	3.1	11.5	38.7	46.7
	Quintile 2	10.2	22.8	39.8	27.2
	Quintile 3	9.0	23.1	36.8	31.1
	Quintile 4	5.7	24.0	43.2	27.1
	Quintile 5	3.7	14.5	40.6	41.2
Switzerland (French)	No income	N/A	N/A	N/A	N/A
	Quintile 1	15.6	39.4	34.4	10.6
	Quintile 2	18.3	36.9	31.5	13.3
	Quintile 3	15.3	32.6	41.9	10.1
	Quintile 4	12.0	32.8	46.5	8.7
	Quintile 5	4.7	28.8	49.4	17.1
Switzerland (German)	No income	N/A	N/A	N/A	N/A
	Quintile 1	18.7	34.9	33.9	12.5
	Quintile 2	21.0	40.8	31.3	6.9
	Quintile 3	13.5	44.1	32.7	9.8
	Quintile 4	15.3	33.2	46.0	5.5
	Quintile 5	3.4	31.0	47.5	18.1
United States	No income	32.4	29.9	27.3	10.4
	Quintile 1	23.4	26.3	32.4	17.9
	Quintile 2	17.8	26.9	35.3	20.0
	Quintile 3	8.4	21.9	41.6	28.0
	Quintile 4	3.8	15.8	41.0	39.4
	Quintile 5	1.2	14.9	28.4	55.5

For example, 10.2% of those at Quintile 2 in Sweden are at Level 1 on this scale.

Table B-3b

Proportion of each income group at each literacy level, document scale

		Level 1	Level 2	Level 3	Level 4/5
			Percentage		
Canada	No income	36.8	26.4	25.1	11.7
	Quintile 1	13.8	26.7	32.6	26.9
	Quintile 2	23.5	22.7	30.4	23.4
	Quintile 3	9.9	26.9	41.3	21.9
	Quintile 4	6.1	21.5	40.3	32.1
	Quintile 5	6.2	21.2	27.3	45.3
Germany	No income	10.8	33.4	39.8	15.9
	Quintile 1	5.6	37.6	37.6	19.1
	Quintile 2	14.0	35.6	34.1	16.2
	Quintile 3	7.0	39.2	36.3	17.5
	Quintile 4	6.4	27.4	46.2	20.0
	Quintile 5	2.6	19.9	45.0	32.5
Netherlands	No income	18.3	32.7	35.2	13.8
	Quintile 1	7.8	20.3	51.0	20.8
	Quintile 2	5.9	21.6	53.7	18.8
	Quintile 3	9.9	25.1	43.7	21.4
	Quintile 4	5.0	25.4	46.6	22.9
	Quintile 5	1.0	16.4	50.6	32.0
Poland	No income	0.0	0.0	0.0	0.0
	Quintile 1	50.4	25.5	20.0	4.1
	Quintile 2	43.8	33.2	17.8	5.2
	Quintile 3	36.5	33.4	22.5	7.7
	Quintile 4	35.8	36.7	18.8	8.7
	Quintile 5	38.6	25.3	25.5	10.7
Sweden	No income	46.0	0.0	31.1	22.9
	Quintile 1	1.7	16.0	36.9	45.4
	Quintile 2	9.7	25.4	37.8	27.1
	Quintile 3	6.9	19.3	43.5	30.3
	Quintile 4	5.1	20.9	42.9	31.1
	Quintile 5	1.9	10.9	40.3	46.9
Switzerland (French)	No income	N/A	N/A	N/A	N/A
	Quintile 1	17.9	28.2	35.4	18.5
	Quintile 2	17.9	30.6	39.0	12.6
	Quintile 3	11.7	32.2	38.3	17.8
	Quintile 4	8.1	29.8	42.7	19.4
	Quintile 5	3.9	22.9	50.2	23.0
Switzerland (German)	No income	N/A	N/A	N/A	N/A
	Quintile 1	17.0	30.2	33.6	19.1
	Quintile 2	23.5	34.7	28.2	13.7
	Quintile 3	13.7	28.7	38.2	19.4
	Quintile 4	13.1	28.0	42.4	16.5
	Quintile 5	2.8	30.3	42.8	24.0
United States	No income	35.7	31.2	24.2	8.9
	Quintile 1	26.1	25.8	33.9	14.2
	Quintile 2	17.9	31.1	31.8	19.2
	Quintile 3	12.4	24.7	36.5	26.4
	Quintile 4	4.8	19.0	41.3	34.9
	Quintile 5	3.1	11.0	37.9	48.0

For example, 27.4% of those at Quintile 4 in Germany are at Level 2 on this scale.

Table B-3c

Proportion of each income group at each literacy level, quantitative scale

		Level 1	Level 2	Level 3	Level 4/5
			Percentage		
Canada	No income	33.2	27.9	29.6	9.3
	Quintile 1	14.1	26.9	43.1	15.8
	Quintile 2	17.1	31.0	35.0	17.0
	Quintile 3	13.8	28.8	27.1	30.3
	Quintile 4	5.0	16.7	49.2	29.1
	Quintile 5	3.6	21.8	32.0	42.6
Germany	No income	7.8	29.5	42.7	19.9
	Quintile 1	6.2	32.5	42.7	18.6
	Quintile 2	8.9	30.0	41.4	19.7
	Quintile 3	6.4	28.3	44.4	21.0
	Quintile 4	5.0	19.5	47.9	27.7
	Quintile 5	3.2	16.3	43.8	36.7
Netherlands	No income	17.8	31.5	38.1	12.6
	Quintile 1	10.7	21.6	47.9	19.8
	Quintile 2	6.2	25.5	53.1	15.2
	Quintile 3	8.6	24.7	45.9	20.8
	Quintile 4	5.2	25.0	46.2	23.6
	Quintile 5	1.0	13.4	46.1	39.5
Poland	No income	0.0	0.0	0.0	0.0
	Quintile 1	45.5	27.4	22.5	4.6
	Quintile 2	37.2	32.3	25.7	4.8
	Quintile 3	31.6	30.8	27.5	10.0
	Quintile 4	25.4	35.6	26.8	12.1
	Quintile 5	30.8	24.7	28.8	15.8
Sweden	No income	46.0	0.0	43.1	10.9
	Quintile 1	3.5	14.4	38.0	44.2
	Quintile 2	10.1	23.3	40.1	26.4
	Quintile 3	6.6	23.7	42.0	27.7
	Quintile 4	6.0	18.9	43.9	31.3
	Quintile 5	1.3	11.0	37.5	50.2
Switzerland (French)	No income	N/A	N/A	N/A	N/A
	Quintile 1	13.5	25.5	38.9	22.1
	Quintile 2	11.5	26.5	44.3	17.8
	Quintile 3	11.7	29.4	46.0	12.8
	Quintile 4	3.8	21.1	52.7	22.4
	Quintile 5	3.2	15.8	38.8	42.2
Switzerland (German)	No income	N/A	N/A	N/A	N/A
	Quintile 1	12.4	28.7	40.7	18.2
	Quintile 2	15.3	41.6	28.8	14.2
	Quintile 3	11.7	26.1	42.8	19.4
	Quintile 4	8.6	21.3	51.0	19.1
	Quintile 5	0.9	19.3	44.3	35.6
United States	No income	32.9	28.0	28.0	11.1
	Quintile 1	25.6	26.8	33.4	14.2
	Quintile 2	18.9	30.2	30.8	20.0
	Quintile 3	9.3	22.9	37.2	30.7
	Quintile 4	1.8	13.6	36.7	48.0
	Quintile 5	1.2	8.4	33.3	57.1

For example, 46% of those with no income in Sweden are at Level 1 on this scale.

Table B-4a

Proportion of each literacy level in each income quintile, prose scale

		Level 1	Level 2	Level 3	Level 4/5
			Percentage		
Canada	No income	46.0	30.0	21.6	12.6
	Quintile 1	13.8	16.3	17.8	15.3
	Quintile 2	18.0	14.0	14.5	13.2
	Quintile 3	11.2	11.9	14.9	15.9
	Quintile 4	7.1	17.1	15.1	17.9
	Quintile 5	3.9	10.7	16.2	25.1
Germany	No income	34.0	34.3	33.2	31.5
	Quintile 1	8.6	7.9	8.8	9.1
	Quintile 2	24.3	16.7	14.2	9.5
	Quintile 3	15.2	15.7	13.4	13.9
	Quintile 4	10.2	15.6	15.0	12.3
	Quintile 5	7.6	9.8	15.4	23.6
Netherlands	No income	52.0	39.9	25.9	21.6
	Quintile 1	7.6	8.6	11.8	13.0
	Quintile 2	9.5	8.0	12.2	10.6
	Quintile 3	19.5	19.5	20.9	22.8
	Quintile 4	8.7	14.6	12.1	12.8
	Quintile 5	2.7	9.3	17.1	19.3
Poland	No income	0.2	0.0	0.0	0.0
	Quintile 1	22.9	20.3	14.7	11.5
	Quintile 2	22.0	17.5	16.2	10.1
	Quintile 3	21.3	24.1	22.1	20.2
	Quintile 4	14.4	21.2	22.3	26.3
	Quintile 5	19.1	16.9	24.8	32.0
Sweden	No income	1.8	0.6	0.2	0.1
	Quintile 1	7.4	8.6	13.7	18.9
	Quintile 2	21.8	15.3	12.6	9.9
	Quintile 3	28.2	22.8	17.2	16.6
	Quintile 4	21.4	28.5	24.2	17.4
	Quintile 5	19.5	24.2	32.0	37.1
Switzerland (French)	No income	N/A	N/A	N/A	N/A
	Quintile 1	26.3	26.3	19.7	20.9
	Quintile 2	26.8	21.4	15.6	22.7
	Quintile 3	23.0	19.3	21.2	17.7
	Quintile 4	18.3	19.7	24.0	15.4
	Quintile 5	5.5	13.3	19.5	23.3
Switzerland (German)	No income	N/A	N/A	N/A	N/A
	Quintile 1	34.9	25.2	23.4	30.2
	Quintile 2	19.1	14.4	10.5	8.1
	Quintile 3	20.7	26.3	18.6	19.5
	Quintile 4	20.5	17.3	22.8	9.5
	Quintile 5	4.8	16.8	24.6	32.7
United States	No income	45.2	31.3	20.6	11.9
	Quintile 1	26.1	22.0	19.7	16.3
	Quintile 2	17.9	20.2	19.2	16.3
	Quintile 3	8.0	15.5	21.3	21.6
	Quintile 4	2.6	8.0	15.1	21.8
	Quintile 5	0.3	3.0	4.1	12.1

For example, 14.2% of those at Level 3 on this scale in Germany are in Quintile 2.

Table B-4b

Proportion of each literacy level in each income quintile, document scale

		Level 1	Level 2	Level 3	Level 4/5
			Percentage		
Canada	No income	51.7	27.7	20.3	11.9
	Quintile 1	12.1	17.6	16.5	17.2
	Quintile 2	18.8	13.6	13.9	13.6
	Quintile 3	7.4	15.1	17.8	11.9
	Quintile 4	5.0	13.1	18.8	18.9
	Quintile 5	5.0	12.8	12.7	26.5
Germany	No income	42.2	34.6	33.5	27.7
	Quintile 1	5.6	9.9	8.0	8.4
	Quintile 2	25.8	17.5	13.6	13.3
	Quintile 3	11.8	17.7	13.2	13.2
	Quintile 4	10.6	12.0	16.4	14.7
	Quintile 5	4.1	8.3	15.2	22.7
Netherlands	No income	58.0	41.2	25.7	22.0
	Quintile 1	8.2	8.4	12.2	10.9
	Quintile 2	6.1	8.8	12.7	9.7
	Quintile 3	20.1	20.2	20.5	21.8
	Quintile 4	6.2	12.5	13.3	14.2
	Quintile 5	1.4	8.8	15.6	21.5
Poland	No income	0.0	0.0	0.0	1.0
	Quintile 1	24.4	16.4	18.8	11.1
	Quintile 2	20.0	20.1	15.8	13.1
	Quintile 3	20.1	24.4	24.0	23.4
	Quintile 4	16.7	22.7	17.1	22.4
	Quintile 5	18.9	16.4	24.2	29.0
Sweden	No income	3.5	0.0	0.3	0.2
	Quintile 1	5.0	13.2	12.9	17.2
	Quintile 2	26.3	18.7	11.8	9.2
	Quintile 3	27.7	21.0	20.1	15.1
	Quintile 4	24.4	27.2	23.7	18.7
	Quintile 5	13.0	20.0	31.3	39.6
Switzerland (French)	No income	N/A	N/A	N/A	N/A
	Quintile 1	33.4	22.4	20.1	23.5
	Quintile 2	28.8	21.1	19.2	13.9
	Quintile 3	19.3	22.6	19.2	20.0
	Quintile 4	13.5	21.3	21.8	22.2
	Quintile 5	5.0	12.6	19.7	20.3
Switzerland (German)	No income	N/A	N/A	N/A	N/A
	Quintile 1	33.2	26.6	23.8	26.7
	Quintile 2	22.3	14.9	9.7	9.3
	Quintile 3	22.0	20.9	22.3	22.4
	Quintile 4	18.3	17.7	21.5	16.5
	Quintile 5	4.1	20.0	22.7	25.1
United States	No income	44.2	30.5	19.2	11.4
	Quintile 1	25.9	20.2	21.5	14.6
	Quintile 2	15.9	21.8	18.1	17.7
	Quintile 3	10.4	16.3	19.6	22.9
	Quintile 4	2.9	9.0	15.9	21.7
	Quintile 5	0.7	2.0	5.7	11.8

For example, 24.4% of those at Level 2 on this scale in Poland are in Quintile 3.

Table B-4c

Proportion of each literacy level in each income quintile, quantitative scale

		Level 1	Level 2	Level 3	Level 4/5
		Percentage			
Canada	No income	51.8	27.9	21.4	10.7
	Quintile 1	13.8	16.9	19.6	11.5
	Quintile 2	15.2	17.6	14.4	11.2
	Quintile 3	11.5	15.4	10.5	18.7
	Quintile 4	4.5	9.7	20.6	19.5
	Quintile 5	3.2	12.5	13.4	28.3
Germany	No income	39.6	37.4	32.8	28.6
	Quintile 1	8.0	10.4	8.3	6.8
	Quintile 2	21.3	17.9	15.0	13.4
	Quintile 3	14.0	15.5	14.8	13.1
	Quintile 4	10.7	10.4	15.6	16.8
	Quintile 5	6.5	8.3	13.5	21.3
Netherlands	No income	56.8	40.3	27.6	19.9
	Quintile 1	11.3	9.1	11.4	10.3
	Quintile 2	6.4	10.6	12.5	7.8
	Quintile 3	17.6	20.3	21.3	21.1
	Quintile 4	6.5	12.5	13.1	14.6
	Quintile 5	1.4	7.3	14.1	26.4
Poland	No income	0.0	0.0	0.0	0.8
	Quintile 1	26.4	18.0	16.9	9.5
	Quintile 2	20.4	20.0	18.2	9.3
	Quintile 3	20.9	23.0	23.5	23.5
	Quintile 4	14.2	22.5	19.4	24.1
	Quintile 5	18.1	16.4	21.9	32.8
Sweden	No income	3.3	0.0	0.4	0.1
	Quintile 1	10.0	11.9	13.4	16.6
	Quintile 2	26.1	17.3	12.7	8.9
	Quintile 3	25.1	25.9	19.6	13.7
	Quintile 4	27.3	24.7	24.5	18.6
	Quintile 5	8.3	20.3	29.4	42.1
Switzerland (French)	No income	N/A	N/A	N/A	N/A
	Quintile 1	34.2	24.5	20.2	22.5
	Quintile 2	25.2	22.0	20.0	15.7
	Quintile 3	26.4	24.9	21.2	11.6
	Quintile 4	8.7	18.2	24.7	20.5
	Quintile 5	5.5	10.5	14.0	29.7
Switzerland (German)	No income	N/A	N/A	N/A	N/A
	Quintile 1	34.1	28.6	25.4	22.4
	Quintile 2	20.5	20.2	8.8	8.5
	Quintile 3	26.5	21.5	22.1	19.6
	Quintile 4	17.0	15.2	22.9	16.8
	Quintile 5	1.8	14.4	20.7	32.7
United States	No income	44.2	29.6	22.2	12.1
	Quintile 1	27.6	22.6	21.2	12.4
	Quintile 2	18.3	22.9	17.6	15.7
	Quintile 3	8.5	16.3	19.9	22.6
	Quintile 4	1.2	6.9	14.1	25.4
	Quintile 5	0.3	1.7	5.0	11.9

For example, 14.1% of those at Level 3 on this scale in the United States are in Quintile 4.

Table B-5a

Proportion of each occupational group at each literacy level, prose scale

		Level 1	Level 2	Level 3	Level 4/5
			Percentage		
Canada	Manager/Professional	3.2	17.4	36.5	42.9
	Technician	4.3	26.4	26.3	43.0
	Clerk	6.0	27.8	51.2	15.1
	Sales/Service	10.9	29.2	34.5	25.4
	Skilled crafts workers	29.7	23.1	33.4	13.8
	Machine operator/Assembler	29.1	19.6	39.9	11.4
	Agriculture/Primary	18.6	27.9	39.6	13.8
Germany	Manager/Professional	4.5	19.1	44.4	32.0
	Technician	3.9	22.9	49.0	24.2
	Clerk	9.6	39.0	38.9	12.5
	Sales/Service	10.4	36.9	36.3	16.5
	Skilled crafts workers	14.4	35.6	42.9	7.1
	Machine operator/Assembler	21.6	52.8	20.0	5.7
	Agriculture/Primary	36.8	31.3	28.0	3.9
Netherlands	Manager/Professional	3.2	20.0	52.1	24.7
	Technician	2.7	19.6	54.4	23.3
	Clerk	6.0	24.2	53.2	16.5
	Sales/Service	8.5	29.5	44.2	17.8
	Skilled crafts workers	10.4	44.6	37.8	7.1
	Machine operator/Assembler	19.1	36.5	36.8	7.6
	Agriculture/Primary	16.9	31.6	43.1	8.4
Poland	Manager/Professional	13.1	31.2	40.9	14.8
	Technician	23.4	45.1	28.0	3.6
	Clerk	25.1	43.3	28.5	3.1
	Sales/Service	30.5	43.4	22.0	4.2
	Skilled crafts workers	47.2	38.6	14.0	0.3
	Machine operator/Assembler	48.7	35.0	15.7	0.5
	Agriculture/Primary	62.9	27.8	8.5	0.7
Sweden	Manager/Professional	2.4	12.1	38.4	47.0
	Technician	3.3	16.5	43.1	37.1
	Clerk	3.4	18.5	43.2	35.0
	Sales/Service	6.6	22.4	38.8	32.1
	Skilled crafts workers	10.0	26.4	42.5	21.1
	Machine operator/Assembler	7.7	27.5	41.4	23.4
	Agriculture/Primary	11.6	30.0	39.4	19.0
Switzerland (French)	Manager/Professional	7.0	17.3	53.3	22.4
	Technician	8.4	29.5	48.5	13.5
	Clerk	3.5	39.1	45.7	11.6
	Sales/Service	27.0	45.7	24.6	2.6
	Skilled crafts workers	25.2	35.7	37.7	1.4
	Machine operator/Assembler	28.0	30.4	31.9	9.7
	Agriculture/Primary	24.8	48.2	24.2	2.8
Switzerland (German)	Manager/Professional	5.1	31.4	50.4	13.0
	Technician	3.5	29.9	52.6	14.0
	Clerk	6.3	38.0	40.4	15.3
	Sales/Service	15.9	44.3	34.7	5.0
	Skilled crafts workers	24.8	46.5	26.2	2.4
	Machine operator/Assembler	40.1	35.9	24.0	0.0
	Agriculture/Primary	33.3	43.9	20.5	2.3
United States	Manager/Professional	3.9	15.6	37.0	43.4
	Technician	2.4	16.3	47.3	34.0
	Clerk	7.3	29.8	41.7	21.2
	Sales/Service	24.2	26.1	32.3	17.4
	Skilled crafts workers	29.4	38.0	25.5	7.1
	Machine operator/Assembler	28.9	36.9	27.8	6.3
	Agriculture/Primary	31.7	21.2	24.5	22.7

For example, 27.8% of the clerks in Canada are at Level 2 on this scale.

Table B-5b

Proportion of each occupational group at each literacy level, document scale

		Level 1	Level 2	Level 3	Level 4/5
			Percentage		
Canada	Manager/Professional	2.6	14.9	32.4	50.1
	Technician	3.5	12.1	58.6	25.9
	Clerk	8.2	26.8	36.7	28.3
	Sales/Service	16.4	29.7	29.0	24.8
	Skilled crafts workers	24.7	30.5	28.8	16.1
	Machine operator/Assembler	27.7	31.3	26.4	14.6
	Agriculture/Primary	17.5	31.4	32.7	18.4
Germany	Manager/Professional	1.5	20.0	36.4	42.1
	Technician	2.3	14.0	54.2	29.6
	Clerk	5.4	31.1	44.2	19.3
	Sales/Service	5.5	37.3	39.3	17.9
	Skilled crafts workers	6.7	33.0	46.5	13.7
	Machine operator/Assembler	11.7	48.3	32.1	7.8
	Agriculture/Primary	19.0	39.1	28.7	13.2
Netherlands	Manager/Professional	2.3	17.1	52.5	28.0
	Technician	2.6	15.1	49.6	32.7
	Clerk	5.0	20.3	55.1	19.5
	Sales/Service	7.1	24.1	49.0	19.8
	Skilled crafts workers	9.1	36.2	39.1	15.6
	Machine operator/Assembler	12.8	33.4	36.2	17.5
	Agriculture/Primary	16.4	24.2	43.7	15.7
Poland	Manager/Professional	19.2	28.4	33.9	18.4
	Technician	22.2	39.2	29.8	8.8
	Clerk	33.1	31.7	28.1	7.1
	Sales/Service	34.3	32.9	25.8	6.9
	Skilled crafts workers	47.1	30.4	16.6	5.9
	Machine operator/Assembler	57.7	27.3	12.7	2.3
	Agriculture/Primary	60.5	29.3	8.9	1.3
Sweden	Manager/Professional	1.6	13.7	38.2	46.4
	Technician	2.8	14.8	41.7	40.8
	Clerk	2.2	15.8	41.1	40.9
	Sales/Service	5.9	21.5	41.3	31.3
	Skilled crafts workers	8.4	17.3	44.5	29.8
	Machine operator/Assembler	7.3	19.3	45.3	28.1
	Agriculture/Primary	11.0	25.5	37.8	25.8
Switzerland (French)	Manager/Professional	5.4	15.9	49.0	29.7
	Technician	6.9	30.4	47.9	14.8
	Clerk	6.3	31.2	46.1	16.4
	Sales/Service	16.7	39.5	34.9	8.9
	Skilled crafts workers	21.8	28.8	32.0	17.3
	Machine operator/Assembler	27.9	34.7	23.3	14.1
	Agriculture/Primary	19.6	45.1	28.5	6.7
Switzerland (German)	Manager/Professional	5.0	28.6	44.0	22.4
	Technician	4.4	22.4	47.7	25.4
	Clerk	7.1	32.0	42.4	18.5
	Sales/Service	20.1	38.1	36.0	5.8
	Skilled crafts workers	22.0	36.8	32.7	8.5
	Machine operator/Assembler	30.6	27.3	31.0	11.1
	Agriculture/Primary	31.3	31.9	24.6	12.2
United States	Manager/Professional	5.1	14.9	41.0	39.1
	Technician	4.2	17.0	48.7	30.1
	Clerk	11.1	34.0	33.1	21.8
	Sales/Service	26.6	25.4	32.8	15.2
	Skilled crafts workers	29.9	37.6	25.0	7.4
	Machine operator/Assembler	35.4	32.2	25.8	6.6
	Agriculture/Primary	36.4	12.2	27.3	24.1

For example, 40.8% of the technicians in Sweden are at Level 4/5 on this scale.

Table B-5c

Proportion of each occupational group at each literacy level, quantitative scale

		Level 1	Level 2	Level 3	Level 4/5
			Percentage		
Canada	Manager/Professional	2.2	15.0	36.4	46.4
	Technician	3.9	17.7	33.4	45.0
	Clerk	4.9	34.6	40.7	19.7
	Sales/Service	15.2	30.7	40.8	13.4
	Skilled crafts workers	22.2	34.5	29.3	13.9
	Machine operator/Assembler	29.0	28.6	33.7	8.8
	Agriculture/Primary	21.2	25.0	36.1	17.7
Germany	Manager/Professional	1.9	14.1	37.3	46.7
	Technician	1.7	15.4	51.6	31.3
	Clerk	5.2	26.1	45.6	23.1
	Sales/Service	5.0	25.2	44.5	25.3
	Skilled crafts workers	3.2	23.8	48.2	24.8
	Machine operator/Assembler	11.2	40.6	36.0	12.3
	Agriculture/Primary	17.6	27.2	38.5	16.7
Netherlands	Manager/Professional	1.9	15.1	48.9	34.2
	Technician	2.9	17.4	50.7	29.0
	Clerk	4.5	26.7	51.9	16.8
	Sales/Service	7.8	24.1	47.1	21.0
	Skilled crafts workers	10.1	31.9	44.4	13.6
	Machine operator/Assembler	13.4	24.8	41.5	20.3
	Agriculture/Primary	18.3	27.2	44.0	10.4
Poland	Manager/Professional	11.5	26.3	37.5	24.7
	Technician	18.5	32.7	36.1	12.7
	Clerk	27.5	31.7	29.5	11.3
	Sales/Service	28.2	36.8	28.1	6.8
	Skilled crafts workers	41.8	29.3	24.2	4.6
	Machine operator/Assembler	42.7	31.0	19.8	6.5
	Agriculture/Primary	54.3	28.5	15.2	2.0
Sweden	Manager/Professional	1.5	15.4	37.0	46.1
	Technician	3.5	15.0	41.5	40.0
	Clerk	3.9	14.7	42.1	39.4
	Sales/Service	7.3	21.4	39.8	31.5
	Skilled crafts workers	6.4	19.5	44.0	30.0
	Machine operator/Assembler	7.9	16.1	42.0	34.0
	Agriculture/Primary	8.0	26.5	39.1	26.4
Switzerland (French)	Manager/Professional	4.0	10.8	44.8	40.5
	Technician	3.7	18.7	57.6	20.0
	Clerk	3.2	25.1	52.0	19.6
	Sales/Service	19.7	36.3	34.4	9.6
	Skilled crafts workers	12.2	28.4	40.3	19.0
	Machine operator/Assembler	27.4	31.5	33.0	8.2
	Agriculture/Primary	18.6	39.0	36.7	5.7
Switzerland (German)	Manager/Professional	3.6	16.5	49.8	30.1
	Technician	2.6	20.5	49.4	27.5
	Clerk	8.5	26.4	45.4	19.7
	Sales/Service	12.1	38.8	38.2	10.9
	Skilled crafts workers	11.5	36.5	39.5	12.5
	Machine operator/Assembler	27.9	24.5	39.6	8.1
	Agriculture/Primary	26.2	32.7	27.0	14.0
United States	Manager/Professional	3.7	14.1	36.6	45.6
	Technician	2.3	10.8	44.4	42.5
	Clerk	10.6	31.7	35.5	22.1
	Sales/Service	25.1	28.5	29.3	17.2
	Skilled crafts workers	28.7	31.5	28.9	10.9
	Machine operator/Assembler	30.4	30.9	27.5	11.2
	Agriculture/Primary	33.6	9.5	42.5	14.4

For example, 24.8% of the machine operators in the Netherlands are at Level 2 on this scale.

Table B-6a

Proportion of workers in each industrial group at each literacy level, prose scale

		Level 1	Level 2	Level 3	Level 4/5
			Percentage		
Canada	Agriculture/Mining	16.1	24.7	44.0	15.2
	Manufacturing	25.1	17.3	42.9	14.7
	Construction/Transport	21.7	24.3	33.4	20.5
	Trade/Hospitality	12.3	30.5	37.1	20.1
	Financial services	2.0	26.1	46.7	25.2
	Personal services	6.9	21.0	33.1	39.0
Germany	Agriculture/Mining	30.6	38.4	14.7	16.3
	Manufacturing	11.9	37.7	36.4	14.0
	Construction/Transport	17.6	37.3	33.6	11.4
	Trade/Hospitality	13.7	36.1	37.5	12.6
	Financial services	6.4	26.8	54.0	12.7
	Personal services	6.8	26.0	44.5	22.8
Netherlands	Agriculture/Mining	14.0	33.3	43.3	9.4
	Manufacturing	10.1	32.5	45.1	12.2
	Construction/Transport	10.9	35.4	44.1	9.6
	Trade/Hospitality	7.9	33.8	45.5	12.7
	Financial services	4.4	20.4	49.8	25.3
	Personal services	4.4	17.6	53.1	24.8
Poland	Agriculture/Mining	61.1	30.3	8.0	0.7
	Manufacturing	41.0	35.1	21.1	2.8
	Construction/Transport	41.2	38.2	19.2	1.3
	Trade/Hospitality	30.9	46.5	19.9	2.8
	Financial services	22.2	33.9	29.9	13.9
	Personal services	31.0	37.5	26.1	5.4
Sweden	Agriculture/Mining	3.3	31.7	47.8	17.3
	Manufacturing	6.2	21.9	40.6	31.3
	Construction/Transport	7.5	19.6	44.1	28.9
	Trade/Hospitality	7.2	22.3	39.8	30.7
	Financial services	2.5	15.0	34.0	48.4
	Personal services	4.5	17.1	41.1	37.3
Switzerland (French)	Agriculture/Mining	13.2	54.6	29.5	2.6
	Manufacturing	20.9	35.3	39.2	4.5
	Construction/Transport	24.4	26.8	45.1	3.7
	Trade/Hospitality	16.1	42.8	36.5	4.6
	Financial services	5.3	26.2	54.6	13.9
	Personal services	10.4	29.8	43.0	16.7
Switzerland (German)	Agriculture/Mining	25.7	50.6	17.7	6.0
	Manufacturing	12.5	42.6	37.8	7.1
	Construction/Transport	14.8	43.4	36.6	5.1
	Trade/Hospitality	17.0	44.3	33.7	4.9
	Financial services	0.9	29.9	52.8	16.5
	Personal services	13.5	30.4	43.6	12.5
United States	Agriculture/Mining	21.1	20.9	27.0	30.9
	Manufacturing	21.6	32.2	29.8	16.4
	Construction/Transport	17.7	27.4	37.8	17.1
	Trade/Hospitality	18.5	31.6	33.7	16.2
	Financial services	10.6	26.3	34.8	28.2
	Personal services	12.2	18.7	36.3	32.7

For example, 34.8% of those working in financial services in the United States are at Level 3 on this scale.

Table B-6b

Proportion of workers in each industrial group at each literacy level, document scale

		Level 1	Level 2	Level 3	Level 4/5
			Percentage		
Canada	Agriculture/Mining	16.9	27.6	32.8	22.7
	Manufacturing	21.6	24.0	31.3	23.2
	Construction/Transport	19.6	32.4	26.7	21.3
	Trade/Hospitality	13.9	29.0	32.4	24.7
	Financial services	3.3	15.7	33.7	47.4
	Personal services	7.9	19.7	40.4	32.0
Germany	Agriculture/Mining	8.5	49.1	18.8	23.5
	Manufacturing	5.6	29.3	43.5	21.5
	Construction/Transport	7.7	40.5	33.1	18.7
	Trade/Hospitality	6.7	33.2	39.2	21.0
	Financial services	5.6	19.7	52.7	21.9
	Personal services	5.1	23.5	44.5	27.0
Netherlands	Agriculture/Mining	9.8	19.8	48.3	22.1
	Manufacturing	6.5	28.3	43.7	21.5
	Construction/Transport	10.5	28.5	42.6	18.4
	Trade/Hospitality	5.7	24.5	52.3	17.5
	Financial services	4.7	13.5	50.7	31.1
	Personal services	4.6	18.4	49.3	27.7
Poland	Agriculture/Mining	60.5	26.4	10.8	2.3
	Manufacturing	49.8	28.6	15.0	6.7
	Construction/Transport	38.8	38.1	18.2	4.9
	Trade/Hospitality	30.3	38.4	24.7	6.7
	Financial services	27.3	25.5	29.4	17.9
	Personal services	33.1	30.9	26.9	9.1
Sweden	Agriculture/Mining	6.9	21.0	44.3	27.8
	Manufacturing	5.6	16.1	39.7	38.6
	Construction/Transport	4.0	14.4	42.4	39.1
	Trade/Hospitality	5.8	18.9	44.3	31.0
	Financial services	2.3	11.0	34.4	52.3
	Personal services	4.2	18.4	41.4	36.1
Switzerland (French)	Agriculture/Mining	5.2	58.0	26.1	10.7
	Manufacturing	16.3	34.1	38.6	11.0
	Construction/Transport	22.3	22.7	37.3	17.8
	Trade/Hospitality	11.8	39.2	39.2	9.8
	Financial services	2.9	22.0	52.6	22.4
	Personal services	8.9	25.6	43.6	22.0
Switzerland (German)	Agriculture/Mining	17.2	43.4	31.5	7.9
	Manufacturing	13.3	35.0	32.3	19.3
	Construction/Transport	17.5	26.6	42.2	13.7
	Trade/Hospitality	16.4	33.8	37.5	12.3
	Financial services	5.3	21.6	50.9	22.2
	Personal services	10.6	28.3	40.7	20.4
United States	Agriculture/Mining	22.1	19.9	26.1	32.0
	Manufacturing	25.0	28.3	30.6	16.2
	Construction/Transport	19.8	30.3	30.9	19.0
	Trade/Hospitality	22.5	28.0	32.0	17.5
	Financial services	12.4	24.7	35.5	27.4
	Personal services	14.2	20.8	38.2	26.8

For example, 27.0% of those working in personal services in Germany are at Level 4/5 on this scale.

Table B-6c

Proportion of workers in each industrial group at each literacy level, quantitative scale

		Level 1	Level 2	Level 3	Level 4/5
			Perc	entage	
Canada	Agriculture/Mining	17.2	28.2	37.8	16.8
	Manufacturing	20.4	27.9	30.3	21.4
	Construction/Transport	21.6	27.0	32.0	19.4
	Trade/Hospitality	12.8	33.9	37.7	15.5
	Financial services	1.5	19.9	35.6	43.0
	Personal services	7.5	19.6	39.6	33.3
Germany	Agriculture/Mining	3.8	22.0	44.9	29.3
	Manufacturing	3.5	28.2	44.7	23.6
	Construction/Transport	7.1	27.5	36.0	29.4
	Trade/Hospitality	6.8	24.6	42.7	25.9
	Financial services	2.9	12.2	57.4	27.4
	Personal services	4.4	18.6	44.9	32.1
Netherlands	Agriculture/Mining	8.6	17.7	56.5	17.2
	Manufacturing	6.9	24.0	49.2	19.9
	Construction/Transport	10.5	26.2	47.0	16.3
	Trade/Hospitality	6.5	26.0	49.8	17.7
	Financial services	4.8	15.6	44.7	34.9
	Personal services	5.1	19.6	47.1	28.2
Poland	Agriculture/Mining	53.2	26.3	18.3	2.2
	Manufacturing	39.1	30.9	21.5	8.5
	Construction/Transport	32.5	31.4	29.2	6.9
	Trade/Hospitality	25.2	35.3	29.7	9.8
	Financial services	20.0	22.8	35.1	22.2
	Personal services	27.9	31.1	28.8	12.2
Sweden	Agriculture/Mining	5.1	20.6	45.4	28.9
	Manufacturing	6.1	15.8	39.7	38.4
	Construction/Transport	2.9	15.0	40.3	41.8
	Trade/Hospitality	7.2	19.0	40.3	33.5
	Financial services	1.4	11.8	34.4	52.4
	Personal services	4.3	19.6	41.1	35.0
Switzerland (French)	Agriculture/Mining	8.8	32.2	50.1	9.0
	Manufacturing	9.6	36.5	38.4	15.5
	Construction/Transport	17.6	16.6	39.8	26.0
	Trade/Hospitality	7.8	33.3	41.1	17.8
	Financial services	2.1	19.0	53.6	25.3
	Personal services	7.2	20.3	47.4	25.1
Switzerland (German)	Agriculture/Mining	14.7	46.6	34.0	4.7
	Manufacturing	11.5	26.7	37.8	24.0
	Construction/Transport	9.4	30.8	43.8	16.0
	Trade/Hospitality	10.4	34.2	40.7	14.8
	Financial services	3.3	19.0	48.4	29.3
	Personal services	10.4	20.7	46.1	22.8
United States	Agriculture/Mining	20.4	6.4	42.4	30.8
	Manufacturing	20.1	26.5	30.6	22.8
	Construction/Transport	17.1	29.0	30.5	23.5
	Trade/Hospitality	20.6	30.0	30.5	18.8
	Financial services	13.0	21.8	37.2	27.9
	Personal services	13.5	20.7	34.3	31.6

For example, 40.3% of those working in the trade/hospitality sector in Sweden are at Level 3 on this scale.

Table B-7a

Proportion of those participating and not participating in adult education at each literacy level, prose scale

		Level 1	Level 2	Level 3	Level 4/5
			Percentage		
Canada	Participant	8.1	20.4	40.9	30.6
	Non-participant	23.0	29.5	30.7	16.7
Germany	Participant	6.3	28.7	39.4	25.7
	Non-participant	16.1	35.4	37.7	10.8
Netherlands	Participant	6.0	23.3	49.0	21.8
	Non-participant	13.7	34.8	40.7	10.8
Poland	Participant	24.5	36.0	31.0	8.5
	Non-participant	45.8	34.3	17.8	2.1
Sweden	Participant	4.3	16.4	40.9	38.4
	Non-participant	10.6	24.3	38.7	26.4
Switzerland (French)	Participant	8.5	27.7	47.5	16.3
	Non-participant	19.3	38.5	35.3	6.9
Switzerland (German)	Participant	8.0	31.4	46.2	14.4
	Non-participant	22.9	42.2	30.0	4.9
United States	Participant	7.9	20.5	38.9	32.7
	Non-participant	27.5	30.5	28.7	13.3

For example, 46.2% of those who participated in adult education in Switzerland (German) are at Level 3 on this scale.

Table B-7b

Proportion of those participating and not participating in adult education at each literacy level, document scale

		Level 1	Level 2	Level 3	Level 4/5
			Percentage		
Canada	Participant	8.2	20.4	33.4	38.1
	Non-participant	25.6	28.0	31.1	15.3
Germany	Participant	4.3	21.8	41.4	32.4
	Non-participant	10.0	35.1	39.0	15.9
Netherlands	Participant	4.9	19.0	48.3	27.8
	Non-participant	13.8	30.5	41.3	14.4
Poland	Participant	26.6	32.1	28.0	13.4
	Non-participant	48.7	30.5	16.3	4.5
Sweden	Participant	3.5	14.4	40.5	41.6
	Non-participant	8.9	23.3	38.4	29.4
Switzerland (French)	Participant	8.2	22.9	46.8	22.0
	Non-participant	17.2	33.3	36.1	13.4
Switzerland (German)	Participant	6.4	25.5	42.7	25.4
	Non-participant	22.0	34.5	34.2	9.3
United States	Participant	10.7	21.9	39.3	28.1
	Non-participant	30.3	30.1	26.8	12.9

For example, 25.6% of those who did not participate in adult education in Canada are at Level 1 on this scale.

Table B-7c

Proportion of those participating and not participating in adult education at each literacy level, quantitative scale

		Level 1	Level 2	Level 3	Level 4/5
			Percentage		
Canada	Participant	7.7	22.4	39.9	30.0
	Non-participant	23.8	28.9	31.0	16.3
Germany	Participant	2.6	22.9	41.1	33.4
	Non-participant	7.5	27.4	43.7	21.4
Netherlands	Participant	5.2	20.7	47.4	26.8
	Non-participant	13.8	28.9	42.2	15.1
Poland	Participant	23.9	26.7	35.8	13.7
	Non-participant	41.8	30.8	21.8	5.6
Sweden	Participant	3.8	15.6	39.8	40.7
	Non-participant	9.3	21.7	38.2	30.9
Switzerland (French)	Participant	5.3	19.1	47.8	27.8
	Non-participant	13.4	28.5	40.9	17.2
Switzerland (German)	Participant	5.1	21.0	44.9	29.0
	Non-participant	15.6	32.5	40.1	11.8
United States	Participant	10.1	20.5	37.6	31.8
	Non-participant	26.7	29.1	27.7	16.5

For example, 26.7% of those who participated in adult education in Poland are at Level 2 on this scale.

Table B-8a

Proportion of each literacy level who participated in adult education, prose scale

	Level 1	Level 2	Level 3	Level 4/5
		Percentage		
Canada	20.8	34.1	49.9	57.8
Germany	7.8	14.9	18.5	34.1
Netherlands	23.3	31.7	45.6	58.3
Poland	8.6	15.6	23.4	41.5
Sweden	29.4	41.1	52.2	60.1
Switzerland (French)	19.6	28.5	42.7	56.7
Switzerland (German)	23.2	39.3	57.2	71.9
United States	18.1	34.1	51.1	65.5

For example, of those who participated in adult education in Switzerland (French), 56.7% are at Level 4/5 on this scale.

Table B-8b

Proportion of each literacy level who participated in adult education, document scale

	Level 1	Level 2	Level 3	Level 4/5
		Percentage		
Canada	19.3	35.3	44.6	65.1
Germany	8.6	11.9	18.7	30.7
Netherlands	19.8	30.2	44.8	57.2
Poland	8.7	15.6	23.2	34.2
Sweden	28.9	38.9	52.2	59.4
Switzerland (French)	20.9	27.6	41.8	47.7
Switzerland (German)	20.2	39.1	52.0	70.2
United States	21.4	36.0	53.1	62.8

For example, of those who participated in adult education in the United States, 36% are at Level 2 on this scale.

Table B-8c

Proportion of each literacy level who participated in adult education, quantitative scale

	Level 1	Level 2	Level 3	Level 4/5
		Percentage		
Canada	19.6	36.7	49.1	58.0
Germany	7.1	15.3	17.0	25.3
Netherlands	20.8	33.2	43.8	55.2
Poland	9.1	13.2	22.4	29.9
Sweden	29.9	42.7	51.9	57.7
Switzerland (French)	18.0	27.1	39.3	47.2
Switzerland (German)	21.9	35.9	49.3	68.1
United States	22.6	35.2	51.1	59.9

For example, of those who participated in adult education in the Netherlands, 33.2% are at Level 2 on this scale.

Table B-9a

Proportion at each ISCED level for each literacy level, prose scale

		Level 1	Level 2	Level 3	Level 4/5
			Percentage		
Canada	Less than ISCED 02	67.5	22.1	9.9	0.5
	ISCED 02	22.2	36.8	33.0	8.1
	ISCED 03	10.0	29.3	41.2	19.5
	ISCED 05	4.4	20.9	46.9	27.7
	ISCED 06/07	0.2	10.8	29.8	59.1
Germany	Less than ISCED 02	67.7	14.5	17.8	0.0
	ISCED 02	17.5	38.6	36.0	7.9
	ISCED 03	7.9	33.6	44.5	14.0
	ISCED 05	4.1	14.0	49.2	32.6
	ISCED 06/07	4.0	17.0	39.4	39.6
Netherlands	Less than ISCED 02	37.8	42.1	17.2	3.0
	ISCED 02	11.9	44.8	38.3	4.9
	ISCED 03	2.7	23.3	55.2	18.8
	ISCED 05	N/A	N/A	N/A	N/A
	ISCED 06/07	1.3	11.9	52.3	34.5
Poland	Less than ISCED 02	75.2	19.0	5.7	0.2
	ISCED 02	42.5	39.7	15.9	1.8
	ISCED 03	24.9	44.4	28.5	2.3
	ISCED 05	11.8	38.8	40.7	8.6
	ISCED 06/07	11.2	30.4	42.0	16.4
Sweden	Less than ISCED 02	25.2	42.5	24.7	7.6
	ISCED 02	7.0	20.7	47.3	25.0
	ISCED 03	5.7	20.5	42.7	31.1
	ISCED 05	1.4	9.4	43.4	45.8
	ISCED 06/07	0.7	6.3	32.2	60.7
Switzerland (French)	Less than ISCED 02	48.8	34.7	14.9	1.6
	ISCED 02	28.9	51.5	19.6	0.0
	ISCED 03	11.1	36.4	43.5	9.1
	ISCED 05	7.0	25.6	56.8	10.7
	ISCED 06/07	4.8	13.4	49.4	32.4
Switzerland (German)	Less than ISCED 02	65.8	28.8	5.4	0.0
	ISCED 02	34.2	42.9	18.7	4.2
	ISCED 03	11.0	39.8	39.4	9.8
	ISCED 05	6.8	30.1	54.1	9.0
	ISCED 06/07	6.7	21.1	46.7	25.5
United States	Less than ISCED 02	69.3	19.9	8.9	1.8
	ISCED 02	44.7	30.1	22.3	2.8
	ISCED 03	16.9	33.7	35.4	13.9
	ISCED 05	9.5	24.8	39.9	25.8
	ISCED 06/07	4.9	11.9	35.7	47.5

For example, 39.6% of those at ISCED 06/07 in Germany are at Level 4/5 on this scale.

Table B-9b

Proportion at each ISCED level for each literacy level, document scale

		Level 1	Level 2	Level 3	Level 4/5
		Percentage			
Canada	Less than ISCED 02	73.6	15.4	9.7	1.3
	ISCED 02	23.2	40.2	26.3	10.3
	ISCED 03	10.5	28.4	36.9	24.1
	ISCED 05	4.2	17.6	39.1	39.1
	ISCED 06/07	3.3	10.1	38.5	48.1
Germany	Less than ISCED 02	55.5	30.2	14.3	0.0
	ISCED 02	10.5	38.3	39.2	12.0
	ISCED 03	4.7	26.7	43.5	25.1
	ISCED 05	4.7	20.2	48.3	26.8
	ISCED 06/07	1.1	17.9	34.8	46.2
Netherlands	Less than ISCED 02	36.0	38.7	19.2	6.2
	ISCED 02	11.2	36.9	43.1	8.8
	ISCED 03	2.9	18.2	52.4	26.5
	ISCED 05	N/A	N/A	N/A	N/A
	ISCED 06/07	1.3	13.8	50.0	34.9
Poland	Less than ISCED 02	74.6	18.8	5.2	1.4
	ISCED 02	46.9	33.9	15.2	4.0
	ISCED 03	27.8	38.3	27.2	6.8
	ISCED 05	16.4	35.5	36.1	12.1
	ISCED 06/07	15.6	29.6	32.8	22.0
Sweden	Less than ISCED 02	22.5	38.1	33.2	6.2
	ISCED 02	6.8	16.9	45.5	30.8
	ISCED 03	3.9	19.1	42.1	34.9
	ISCED 05	1.1	11.1	37.8	50.1
	ISCED 06/07	0.7	8.1	29.8	61.4
Switzerland (French)	Less than ISCED 02	41.9	39.7	16.4	2.0
	ISCED 02	31.1	46.9	19.9	2.1
	ISCED 03	9.0	31.1	45.1	14.8
	ISCED 05	2.0	19.5	47.9	30.6
	ISCED 06/07	4.9	7.1	47.9	40.1
Switzerland (German)	Less than ISCED 02	72.6	16.7	10.6	0.0
	ISCED 02	31.6	40.2	17.9	10.3
	ISCED 03	9.7	30.9	42.9	16.5
	ISCED 05	5.1	24.9	49.1	20.9
	ISCED 06/07	6.8	15.7	39.1	38.4
United States	Less than ISCED 02	74.0	18.8	6.3	1.0
	ISCED 02	45.2	27.9	21.1	5.9
	ISCED 03	21.2	33.7	32.5	12.6
	ISCED 05	11.7	25.0	39.4	24.0
	ISCED 06/07	6.7	13.3	38.9	41.1

For example, 33.9% of those at ISCED 02 in Poland are at Level 2 on this scale.

Table B-9c

Proportion at each ISCED level for each literacy level, quantitative scale

		Level 1	Level 2	Level 3	Level 4/5
		Percentage			
Canada	Less than ISCED 02	69.4	18.5	11.3	0.8
	ISCED 02	23.1	41.5	27.6	7.8
	ISCED 03	8.8	31.7	42.8	16.6
	ISCED 05	4.2	20.7	48.6	26.4
	ISCED 06/07	2.2	4.4	29.4	64.0
Germany	Less than ISCED 02	42.5	20.8	29.2	7.5
	ISCED 02	7.6	31.0	44.1	17.2
	ISCED 03	4.1	21.0	49.3	25.7
	ISCED 05	2.7	11.1	59.4	26.9
	ISCED 06/07	2.0	13.2	28.6	56.2
Netherlands	Less than ISCED 02	35.5	35.5	23.7	5.3
	ISCED 02	11.9	35.5	41.7	10.9
	ISCED 03	2.7	22.1	52.0	23.2
	ISCED 05	N/A	N/A	N/A	N/A
	ISCED 06/07	1.7	9.7	49.4	39.3
Poland	Less than ISCED 02	69.4	21.3	7.9	1.3
	ISCED 02	39.4	34.3	22.1	4.1
	ISCED 03	20.9	36.2	32.9	10.1
	ISCED 05	15.5	25.7	47.7	11.1
	ISCED 06/07	9.1	25.9	38.6	26.5
Sweden	Less than ISCED 02	21.7	32.0	35.3	11.1
	ISCED 02	7.1	21.0	40.8	31.1
	ISCED 03	4.8	18.5	41.9	34.8
	ISCED 05	0.6	14.6	38.5	46.3
	ISCED 06/07	1.0	5.9	29.3	63.7
Switzerland (French)	Less than ISCED 02	40.2	37.1	22.4	0.3
	ISCED 02	22.6	44.0	29.5	4.0
	ISCED 03	5.6	24.2	48.2	22.0
	ISCED 05	3.2	13.8	51.8	31.2
	ISCED 06/07	4.2	9.1	45.4	41.4
Switzerland (German)	Less than ISCED 02	51.0	26.3	19.7	3.0
	ISCED 02	22.0	44.0	21.3	12.7
	ISCED 03	6.9	27.2	46.7	19.2
	ISCED 05	3.7	14.3	54.2	27.9
	ISCED 06/07	6.8	18.3	36.0	38.9
United States	Less than ISCED 02	66.8	23.2	9.1	0.8
	ISCED 02	44.7	22.8	28.0	4.5
	ISCED 03	18.4	34.2	33.0	14.5
	ISCED 05	8.8	23.1	41.3	26.8
	ISCED 06/07	4.9	11.3	32.1	51.8

For example 11.3% of those at less than ISCED 02 in Canada are at Level 3 on this scale.

Table B-10a

Proportion by parents' education for each ISCED level at each literacy level, prose scale

		Level 1	Level 2	Level 3	Level 4/5
		Percentage			
Canada	Less than ISCED 02	26.0	25.9	34.8	13.3
	ISCED 02	7.9	25.0	43.3	23.9
	ISCED 03	10.8	23.0	33.6	32.5
	ISCED 05	3.9	20.2	38.6	37.3
	ISCED 06/07	7.2	20.8	33.1	38.9
Germany	Less than ISCED 02	53.6	34.1	9.6	2.6
	ISCED 02	15.2	36.2	36.0	12.6
	ISCED 03	8.5	32.8	45.5	13.2
	ISCED 05	2.5	21.4	55.6	20.4
	ISCED 06/07	5.4	19.0	45.3	30.2
Netherlands	Less than ISCED 02	17.8	41.0	34.1	7.1
	ISCED 02	7.1	26.7	48.1	18.1
	ISCED 03	3.5	20.8	54.8	21.0
	ISCED 05	N/A	N/A	N/A	N/A
	ISCED 06/07	2.6	16.5	53.3	27.5
Poland	Less than ISCED 02	52.5	33.1	13.0	1.4
	ISCED 02	33.0	39.5	25.4	2.1
	ISCED 03	17.8	38.5	36.6	7.2
	ISCED 05	31.0	21.7	40.8	6.4
	ISCED 06/07	12.6	30.1	38.9	18.4
Sweden	Less than ISCED 02	10.5	25.0	39.9	24.6
	ISCED 02	2.0	14.0	43.4	40.6
	ISCED 03	2.8	17.1	39.1	41.0
	ISCED 05	1.6	13.8	38.8	45.9
	ISCED 06/07	1.4	10.0	33.7	55.0
Switzerland (French)	Less than ISCED 02	26.3	39.4	31.5	2.8
	ISCED 02	17.7	37.3	37.6	7.4
	ISCED 03	10.2	33.3	44.7	11.9
	ISCED 05	9.3	22.5	52.8	15.4
	ISCED 06/07	5.8	18.9	50.0	25.3
Switzerland (German)	Less than ISCED 02	49.5	30.8	18.5	1.2
	ISCED 02	23.6	41.3	29.7	5.4
	ISCED 03	8.4	40.2	41.7	9.7
	ISCED 05	3.6	35.4	44.7	16.3
	ISCED 06/07	7.3	19.2	51.9	21.5
United States	Less than ISCED 02	32.2	28.9	28.0	10.9
	ISCED 02	18.5	26.9	39.1	15.6
	ISCED 03	10.6	24.3	38.0	27.1
	ISCED 05	6.3	29.2	33.6	31.0
	ISCED 06/07	7.7	16.0	37.9	38.4

For example, 39.4% of those whose parents' education is at less than ISCED 02 in Switzerland (French) are at Level 2 on this scale.

Table B-10b

Proportion by parents' education for each ISCED level at each literacy level, document scale

		Level 1	Level 2	Level 3	Level 4/5
			Percentage		
Canada	Less than ISCED 02	28.3	30.1	29.6	12.0
	ISCED 02	8.9	23.8	29.5	37.8
	ISCED 03	8.6	15.1	46.2	30.1
	ISCED 05	9.9	16.7	29.4	44.0
	ISCED 06/07	8.4	19.3	31.2	41.0
Germany	Less than ISCED 02	37.5	35.6	23.6	3.2
	ISCED 02	9.6	34.7	37.8	17.8
	ISCED 03	4.3	27.4	47.2	21.2
	ISCED 05	1.8	21.9	56.2	20.1
	ISCED 06/07	1.9	18.7	40.8	38.6
Netherlands	Less than ISCED 02	18.4	33.9	36.7	11.0
	ISCED 02	5.3	25.9	46.4	22.4
	ISCED 03	2.0	21.0	51.9	25.2
	ISCED 05	N/A	N/A	N/A	N/A
	ISCED 06/07	3.1	10.4	48.7	37.8
Poland	Less than ISCED 02	54.1	29.8	12.9	3.3
	ISCED 02	37.4	35.4	22.0	5.3
	ISCED 03	22.2	31.6	34.8	11.4
	ISCED 05	25.7	28.6	33.2	12.5
	ISCED 06/07	16.7	27.3	30.4	25.6
Sweden	Less than ISCED 02	8.6	23.1	40.3	28.0
	ISCED 02	1.6	15.3	42.5	40.6
	ISCED 03	2.4	14.3	39.6	43.7
	ISCED 05	1.3	14.6	34.5	49.6
	ISCED 06/07	0.4	8.0	35.4	56.2
Switzerland (French)	Less than ISCED 02	24.5	36.3	29.1	10.1
	ISCED 02	14.8	34.9	40.0	10.3
	ISCED 03	8.4	26.2	47.4	18.0
	ISCED 05	10.1	19.5	46.4	24.1
	ISCED 06/07	5.6	19.1	40.8	34.5
Switzerland (German)	Less than ISCED 02	50.9	24.2	20.9	4.0
	ISCED 02	16.4	38.6	35.8	9.2
	ISCED 03	7.7	29.6	43.2	19.4
	ISCED 05	1.7	32.3	42.4	23.5
	ISCED 06/07	8.2	25.1	36.0	30.7
United States	Less than ISCED 02	33.6	30.6	26.5	9.3
	ISCED 02	22.7	30.8	36.5	9.9
	ISCED 03	14.0	25.8	35.1	25.1
	ISCED 05	9.0	16.5	32.3	42.3
	ISCED 06/07	8.4	18.6	41.5	31.5

For example, 31.6% of those whose parents' education is at ISCED 03 in Poland are at Level 2 on this scale.

Table B-10c

Proportion by parents' education for each ISCED level at each literacy level, quantitative scale

		Level 1	Level 2	Level 3	Level 4/5
			Percentage		
Canada	Less than ISCED 02	23.9	33.3	32.3	10.5
	ISCED 02	7.5	24.4	41.3	26.8
	ISCED 03	10.3	18.9	40.4	30.4
	ISCED 05	6.1	21.2	39.9	32.8
	ISCED 06/07	8.2	16.4	33.7	41.7
Germany	Less than ISCED 02	37.5	35.4	26.5	0.5
	ISCED 02	7.0	28.2	42.6	22.2
	ISCED 03	4.3	22.0	50.0	23.6
	ISCED 05	0.7	8.2	51.9	39.2
	ISCED 06/07	2.4	16.2	44.1	37.3
Netherlands	Less than ISCED 02	17.6	32.7	37.3	12.3
	ISCED 02	6.3	24.5	46.9	22.4
	ISCED 03	3.4	21.5	52.3	22.7
	ISCED 05	N/A	N/A	N/A	N/A
	ISCED 06/07	2.6	12.4	51.8	33.2
Poland	Less than ISCED 02	46.6	30.1	18.9	4.5
	ISCED 02	32.0	33.5	26.5	8.0
	ISCED 03	18.2	28.5	43.1	10.2
	ISCED 05	22.9	28.0	36.7	12.5
	ISCED 06/07	14.7	23.3	40.5	21.5
Sweden	Less than ISCED 02	8.8	21.5	40.4	29.3
	ISCED 02	4.3	17.3	38.1	40.3
	ISCED 03	2.7	14.8	40.6	41.8
	ISCED 05	1.6	14.7	33.4	50.4
	ISCED 06/07	0.8	10.5	33.0	55.6
Switzerland (French)	Less than ISCED 02	17.8	31.7	39.7	10.8
	ISCED 02	10.7	27.5	40.2	21.6
	ISCED 03	6.5	20.9	47.5	25.2
	ISCED 05	7.3	19.5	50.0	23.3
	ISCED 06/07	6.6	11.8	45.2	36.3
Switzerland (German)	Less than ISCED 02	39.1	28.1	27.7	5.1
	ISCED 02	12.1	36.2	36.6	15.1
	ISCED 03	5.2	25.7	47.4	21.7
	ISCED 05	2.0	19.7	51.9	26.4
	ISCED 06/07	5.1	20.9	40.6	33.4
United States	Less than ISCED 02	31.3	25.7	29.3	13.7
	ISCED 02	19.9	33.2	36.8	10.2
	ISCED 03	11.9	24.0	34.5	29.6
	ISCED 05	9.1	23.2	39.9	27.7
	ISCED 06/07	7.7	15.0	36.0	41.3

For example, 15% of those whose parents' education is at ISCED 06/07 in the United States are at Level 2 on this scale.

Table B-11a

Proportion of those within each age group at each literacy level, prose scale

		Level 1	Level 2	Level 3	Level 4/5
			Percentage		
Canada	16-25	10.7	25.7	43.7	19.9
	26-35	12.3	28.5	33.1	26.1
	36-45	13.3	18.6	36.8	31.3
	46-55	20.6	30.2	30.9	18.4
	56-65	37.6	26.4	28.0	8.1
Germany	16-25	8.9	29.5	46.2	15.4
	26-35	12.4	30.6	37.3	19.7
	36-45	14.5	31.5	39.4	14.5
	46-55	14.2	37.4	37.5	10.9
	56-65	22.1	43.2	30.1	4.7
Netherlands	16-25	8.3	22.1	50.1	19.5
	26-35	6.4	20.5	50.6	22.5
	36-45	8.6	30.4	46.6	14.3
	46-55	13.9	38.8	37.5	9.8
	56-65	20.1	47.5	27.7	4.7
Poland	16-25	26.7	38.3	29.1	5.9
	26-35	35.0	39.0	22.2	3.7
	36-45	42.0	38.0	17.2	2.8
	46-55	53.5	29.6	16.0	1.0
	56-65	69.5	20.5	9.8	0.2
Sweden	16-25	3.8	16.7	39.8	39.7
	26-35	4.9	14.2	39.2	41.7
	36-45	7.1	19.7	41.5	31.7
	46-55	8.2	21.8	41.8	28.2
	56-65	15.9	32.7	35.3	16.2
Switzerland (French)	16-25	10.5	31.0	43.1	15.4
	26-35	11.1	29.4	46.5	13.0
	36-45	22.1	33.5	35.5	8.9
	46-55	20.9	35.1	36.1	7.9
	56-65	27.7	43.3	26.8	2.3
Switzerland (German)	16-25	7.3	35.5	43.4	13.8
	26-35	16.6	26.8	44.6	12.0
	36-45	24.2	34.3	32.4	9.1
	46-55	19.4	41.7	34.7	4.2
	56-65	30.4	46.0	19.5	4.1
United States	16-25	23.5	30.7	33.0	12.8
	26-35	19.6	23.2	35.7	21.6
	36-45	19.5	21.4	30.0	29.2
	46-55	18.3	25.7	32.2	23.8
	56-65	23.6	30.7	31.1	14.7

For example, 37.4% of those aged 46-55 in Germany are at Level 2 on this scale.

Table B-11b

Proportion of those within each age group at each literacy level, document scale

		Level 1	Level 2	Level 3	Level 4/5
				Percentage	
Canada	16-25	10.4	22.3	36.4	31.0
	26-35	13.5	25.3	33.8	27.5
	36-45	13.8	22.0	36.8	27.4
	46-55	23.0	31.0	23.6	22.4
	56-65	43.8	23.7	23.8	8.7
Germany	16-25	5.2	29.0	43.0	22.8
	26-35	5.9	29.2	40.0	24.9
	36-45	9.5	30.6	38.5	21.4
	46-55	7.4	35.0	43.1	14.5
	56-65	17.7	40.9	32.6	8.8
Netherlands	16-25	6.1	16.8	51.1	26.0
	26-35	5.9	19.2	45.7	29.3
	36-45	9.2	24.2	49.5	17.1
	46-55	12.6	35.7	38.0	13.7
	56-65	22.6	40.5	30.1	6.8
Poland	16-25	32.2	33.1	26.2	8.5
	26-35	39.2	33.8	19.7	7.4
	36-45	42.6	33.6	18.1	5.7
	46-55	55.6	27.0	13.3	4.1
	56-65	70.1	20.9	7.6	1.4
Sweden	16-25	3.1	16.6	39.6	40.7
	26-35	3.9	10.4	38.1	47.6
	36-45	6.6	18.2	39.8	35.4
	46-55	6.8	19.7	43.1	30.3
	56-65	12.2	33.3	36.0	18.5
Switzerland (French)	16-25	8.7	24.9	40.4	26.0
	26-35	11.5	22.4	44.5	21.6
	36-45	19.2	32.9	34.2	13.7
	46-55	18.0	29.8	42.4	9.7
	56-65	27.5	38.1	29.8	4.6
Switzerland (German)	16-25	7.1	25.7	41.0	26.3
	26-35	17.4	20.7	38.8	23.1
	36-45	21.5	30.3	36.3	12.0
	46-55	21.0	33.8	35.0	10.2
	56-65	22.8	39.9	30.6	6.7
United States	16-25	24.7	30.9	28.4	16.1
	26-35	21.6	22.9	34.5	21.0
	36-45	23.5	19.7	31.4	25.4
	46-55	21.4	28.2	33.2	17.3
	56-65	29.3	32.9	26.0	11.7

For example, 23.8% of those aged 56-65 in Canada are at Level 3 on this scale.

Table B-11c

Proportion of those within each age group at each literacy level, quantitative scale

		Level 1	Level 2	Level 3	Level 4/5
		Percentage			
Canada	16-25	10.1	28.6	44.6	16.7
	26-35	12.0	25.5	35.1	27.5
	36-45	11.9	22.4	35.6	30.1
	46-55	23.9	32.2	24.8	19.0
	56-65	39.7	21.5	31.4	7.4
Germany	16-25	4.4	26.4	47.1	22.0
	26-35	4.9	23.3	42.9	28.9
	36-45	6.5	22.9	44.3	26.3
	46-55	7.0	27.1	41.2	24.7
	56-65	10.8	34.9	40.8	13.5
Netherlands	16-25	7.7	21.0	50.1	21.1
	26-35	6.7	19.9	45.3	28.2
	36-45	10.1	25.0	46.0	18.9
	46-55	12.8	31.0	39.8	16.4
	56-65	17.6	36.2	36.9	9.3
Poland	16-25	29.6	32.6	31.0	6.7
	26-35	32.7	33.0	25.6	8.7
	36-45	36.1	32.1	23.4	8.4
	46-55	47.7	26.9	19.5	5.9
	56-65	60.8	21.4	15.6	2.2
Sweden	16-25	4.9	17.6	39.0	38.4
	26-35	4.0	14.3	36.3	45.4
	36-45	7.0	16.5	41.2	35.2
	46-55	5.8	19.7	40.5	34.0
	56-65	12.9	27.0	37.5	22.6
Switzerland (French)	16-25	6.2	21.4	47.0	25.4
	26-35	8.8	20.6	47.8	22.9
	36-45	16.6	25.2	36.4	21.8
	46-55	16.1	22.7	43.2	18.0
	56-65	19.2	36.0	33.8	11.0
Switzerland (German)	16-25	6.9	21.9	48.2	22.9
	26-35	13.1	20.7	40.8	25.4
	36-45	19.0	26.3	37.9	16.9
	46-55	14.8	28.5	41.2	15.5
	56-65	15.8	37.6	35.7	10.8
United States	16-25	26.5	30.8	29.2	13.5
	26-35	20.1	20.9	35.6	23.5
	36-45	18.2	23.2	26.9	31.6
	46-55	19.0	25.2	32.3	23.6
	56-65	22.4	29.6	32.0	16.0

For example, 7.7% of those aged 16-25 in the Netherlands are at Level 1 on this scale.

Table B-12a

Proportion of those who are immigrants and of those who are native born at each literacy level, prose scale

		Level 1	Level 2	Level 3	Level 4/5
			Percentage		
Canada	Born in Canada	12.9	26.4	38.9	21.8
	Immigrated to Canada	31.0	22.6	20.5	26.0
Germany	Born in Germany	12.3	34.3	39.1	14.2
	Immigrated to Germany	38.5	32.8	24.2	4.5
Netherlands	Born in the Netherlands	9.1	29.9	45.0	16.0
	Immigrated to the Netherlands	30.6	32.9	30.9	5.6
Sweden	Born in Sweden	5.1	20.1	40.4	34.3
	Immigrated to Sweden	30.9	22.2	32.5	14.4
Switzerland (French)	Born in Switzerland	11.3	34.0	43.4	11.3
	Immigrated to Switzerland	33.6	33.4	26.2	6.7
Switzerland (German)	Born in Switzerland	9.8	39.7	40.7	9.8
	Immigrated to Switzerland	58.1	19.7	16.7	5.5
United States	Born in the United States	14.0	27.3	35.0	23.7
	Immigrated to the United States	55.5	17.8	19.6	7.1

For example, 55.5% of those in the United States who are immigrants are at Level 1 on this scale.

Table B-12b

Proportion of those who are immigrants and of those who are native born at each literacy level, document scale

		Level 1	Level 2	Level 3	Level 4/5
			Percentage		
Canada	Born in Canada	14.8	25.6	35.4	24.2
	Immigrated to Canada	31.1	21.3	19.3	28.3
Germany	Born in Germany	7.8	32.1	40.7	19.4
	Immigrated to Germany	23.2	40.1	24.8	11.9
Netherlands	Born in the Netherlands	8.9	25.4	45.2	20.5
	Immigrated to the Netherlands	27.4	30.8	30.0	11.8
Sweden	Born in Sweden	4.3	18.0	40.3	37.3
	Immigrated to Sweden	24.7	27.3	30.8	17.2
Switzerland (French)	Born in Switzerland	10.2	29.3	42.6	18.0
	Immigrated to Switzerland	31.5	28.1	29.4	11.0
Switzerland (German)	Born in Switzerland	8.7	31.3	41.9	18.1
	Immigrated to Switzerland	56.6	20.7	14.5	8.2
United States	Born in the United States	17.5	27.4	34.0	21.2
	Immigrated to the United States	54.2	19.7	19.1	6.9

For example, 29.3% of those in Switzerland (French) who are born in Switzerland are at Level 2 on this scale.

Table B-12c

Proportion of those who are immigrants and of those who are native born at each literacy level, quantitative scale

		Level 1	Level 2	Level 3	Level 4/5
		Percentage			
Canada	Born in Canada	13.8	28.2	37.4	20.6
	Immigrated to Canada	28.9	18.2	24.9	28.0
Germany	Born in Germany	5.8	25.4	44.7	24.2
	Immigrated to Germany	17.2	40.9	26.0	15.8
Netherlands	Born in the Netherlands	8.9	25.3	45.5	20.4
	Immigrated to the Netherlands	29.5	29.3	27.8	13.4
Sweden	Born in Sweden	4.8	17.9	39.9	37.4
	Immigrated to Sweden	24.5	25.4	29.7	20.4
Switzerland (French)	Born in Switzerland	6.4	24.5	45.9	23.3
	Immigrated to Switzerland	29.3	24.7	32.9	13.0
Switzerland (German)	Born in Switzerland	5.8	27.0	46.1	21.1
	Immigrated to Switzerland	47.7	23.3	18.6	10.5
United States	Born in the United States	14.9	26.7	33.4	24.9
	Immigrated to the United States	53.5	15.2	21.8	9.5

For example, 18.6% of those in Switzerland (German) who are immigrants are at Level 3 on this scale.

Table B-13a

Proportion of each sex at each literacy level, prose scale

		Level 1	Level 2	Level 3	Level 4/5
		Percentage			
Canada	Male	19.0	26.6	37.0	17.4
	Female	14.3	24.7	33.2	27.8
Germany	Male	15.4	31.8	37.9	55.4
	Female	13.3	36.7	38.0	12.0
Netherlands	Male	10.5	31.3	43.6	14.6
	Female	10.5	28.8	44.6	16.0
Poland	Male	43.3	35.4	18.7	2.6
	Female	42.0	33.7	20.8	3.5
Sweden	Male	7.9	20.9	39.9	31.3
	Female	7.1	19.8	39.5	33.6
Switzerland (French)	Male	17.1	31.2	40.9	10.8
	Female	18.2	36.2	36.4	9.2
Switzerland (German)	Male	17.9	32.9	40.0	9.2
	Female	20.7	38.4	32.1	8.7
United States	Male	22.2	28.0	29.8	20.0
	Female	19.3	23.9	34.7	22.1

For example, 7.9% of the males in Sweden are at Level 1 on this scale.

Table B-13b

Proportion of each sex at each literacy level, document scale

		Level 1	Level 2	Level 3	Level 4/5
		Percentage			
Canada	Male	17.0	25.7	31.8	25.0
	Female	19.3	23.8	32.3	24.7
Germany	Male	7.8	31.0	38.7	22.4
	Female	10.1	34.4	40.2	15.3
Netherlands	Male	8.5	23.9	45.0	22.7
	Female	11.9	27.7	43.3	17.1
Poland	Male	43.7	31.1	18.7	6.4
	Female	47.0	30.4	17.4	5.2
Sweden	Male	5.0	16.8	39.6	38.6
	Female	7.3	21.0	39.3	32.4
Switzerland (French)	Male	14.0	27.0	40.3	18.7
	Female	18.5	30.6	37.5	13.4
Switzerland (German)	Male	15.2	26.7	39.7	18.4
	Female	21.1	31.4	33.6	13.9
United States	Male	25.2	24.9	30.4	19.5
	Female	22.4	26.7	32.3	18.5

For example, 43.7% of the males in Poland are at Level 1 on this scale.

Table B-13c

Proportion of each sex at each literacy level, quantitative scale

		Level 1	Level 2	Level 3	Level 4/5
		Percentage			
Canada	Male	17.2	24.9	33.8	24.1
	Female	16.6	27.2	35.9	20.2
Germany	Male	5.7	22.7	42.9	28.7
	Female	7.6	30.5	43.5	18.4
Netherlands	Male	8.2	20.8	46.4	24.6
	Female	12.4	30.4	42.1	15.1
Poland	Male	36.2	29.7	26.1	8.0
	Female	42.0	30.6	21.7	5.7
Sweden	Male	5.2	15.3	37.6	41.9
	Female	8.0	21.8	40.4	29.8
Switzerland (French)	Male	11.0	19.8	43.8	25.4
	Female	14.8	29.1	40.7	15.5
Switzerland (German)	Male	12.2	22.2	41.9	23.7
	Female	16.1	30.2	39.6	14.2
United States	Male	20.9	22.2	29.9	27.1
	Female	21.0	28.1	32.5	18.4

For example, 20.2% of the females in Canada are at Level 4/5 on this scale.

Appendix C

Tables: the practice(s) of literacy

Table C-1a

Proportion of respondents within a level who reported engaging in each of several reading activities at work at least once a week, prose scale

		Directions	Bills	Diagrams	Manuals	Reports	Letters
		Percentage					
Canada	Level 1	16.8	24.8	18.3	23.0	25.5	35.0
	Level 2	28.5	52.8	27.3	40.1	46.1	62.3
	Level 3	32.6	49.8	37.5	54.2	59.8	76.3
	Level 4/5	35.6	52.2	36.5	62.7	71.5	84.9
Germany	Level 1	26.8	52.6	37.5	48.6	46.9	63.7
	Level 2	37.2	59.8	51.6	61.1	65.4	76.0
	Level 3	28.5	66.6	54.4	64.0	70.8	85.9
	Level 4/5	33.7	62.1	53.1	61.6	74.7	87.8
Netherlands	Level 1	17.0	22.2	26.2	29.1	30.5	37.1
	Level 2	24.7	42.5	37.2	44.9	54.3	58.1
	Level 3	25.7	44.2	41.0	55.3	65.4	71.6
	Level 4/5	20.3	49.5	45.8	62.5	73.7	77.7
Poland	Level 1	16.6	18.5	13.4	14.4	15.7	21.0
	Level 2	24.9	33.8	24.6	29.7	34.8	37.9
	Level 3	32.5	34.4	25.6	41.3	43.8	46.6
	Level 4/5	53.4	44.2	43.1	59.8	61.7	58.3
Sweden	Level 1	N/A	41.0	47.1	53.5	61.9	52.9
	Level 2	N/A	48.8	56.1	64.8	71.1	69.0
	Level 3	N/A	59.7	63.1	74.2	82.4	81.4
	Level 4/5	N/A	62.2	69.5	76.1	84.9	84.2
Switzerland (French)	Level 1	19.2	42.1	16.5	48.4	53.7	57.0
	Level 2	17.7	54.3	32.2	45.9	65.7	66.0
	Level 3	21.3	61.7	43.7	52.3	79.8	79.8
	Level 4/5	15.1	65.7	64.9	58.6	88.4	88.7
Switzerland (German)	Level 1	20.2	45.8	11.8	35.7	40.5	49.8
	Level 2	17.4	59.5	23.9	52.4	66.2	79.1
	Level 3	15.7	67.5	43.3	63.2	81.8	90.5
	Level 4/5	16.6	64.5	44.8	70.1	83.5	95.3
United States	Level 1	20.9	26.7	20.9	32.8	29.0	40.6
	Level 2	36.7	45.0	32.9	57.0	51.6	64.7
	Level 3	35.8	53.3	41.1	66.7	66.3	79.7
	Level 4/5	36.2	55.3	47.9	77.0	78.0	86.4

For example, 33.8% of those at Level 2 on this scale in Poland read bills.

Table C-1b

Proportion of respondents within a level who reported engaging in each of several reading activities at work at least once a week, document scale

		Directions	Bills	Diagrams	Manuals	Reports	Letters
				Percentage			
Canada	Level 1	23.5	24.1	14.1	21.5	24.4	34.2
	Level 2	23.4	45.0	28.0	41.0	50.1	67.0
	Level 3	31.1	50.8	33.7	51.2	58.4	73.7
	Level 4/5	38.5	57.5	42.4	65.5	69.1	83.8
Germany	Level 1	23.9	46.1	32.3	39.7	41.9	62.7
	Level 2	34.2	60.8	47.8	57.4	62.2	75.2
	Level 3	31.6	62.9	54.1	65.5	70.9	82.6
	Level 4/5	31.8	66.2	55.8	62.3	72.2	88.1
Netherlands	Level 1	13.2	24.4	18.3	22.6	27.9	34.4
	Level 2	24.9	38.8	37.9	44.0	55.9	57.7
	Level 3	25.2	44.4	39.4	54.5	63.3	69.3
	Level 4/5	22.9	49.3	48.1	61.7	71.4	77.4
Poland	Level 1	17.9	18.4	15.2	17.7	18.4	23.5
	Level 2	22.9	32.6	22.1	25.2	29.9	35.3
	Level 3	31.9	35.9	25.9	41.4	46.1	45.7
	Level 4/5	45.8	44.9	36.9	49.3	52.6	52.5
Sweden	Level 1	N/A	31.2	48.5	51.4	61.4	55.1
	Level 2	N/A	49.0	52.7	63.8	73.3	67.6
	Level 3	N/A	58.6	61.8	70.7	79.8	78.9
	Level 4/5	N/A	63.4	71.1	79.6	85.6	85.6
Switzerland (French)	Level 1	18.5	38.7	19.5	42.2	47.0	55.4
	Level 2	21.7	56.8	29.7	48.4	68.5	68.3
	Level 3	19.3	60.0	40.9	50.7	77.3	76.4
	Level 4/5	14.8	61.7	59.3	57.9	84.3	84.2
Switzerland (German)	Level 1	18.9	36.1	10.1	32.6	35.7	45.1
	Level 2	16.3	59.2	24.9	51.9	68.7	78.2
	Level 3	17.5	66.3	37.8	63.0	81.1	91.1
	Level 4/5	15.9	73.4	47.6	66.1	76.7	91.6
United States	Level 1	25.1	27.1	24.7	34.6	30.4	43.3
	Level 2	31.6	42.5	32.0	56.3	54.7	68.4
	Level 3	40.9	54.5	41.3	68.7	66.5	79.2
	Level 4/5	32.5	59.1	48.5	78.0	78.3	85.8

For example, 62.2% of those at Level 2 on this scale in Germany read reports.

Table C-1c

Proportion of respondents within a level who reported engaging in each of several reading activities at work at least once a week, quantitative scale

		Directions	Bills	Diagrams	Manuals	Reports	Letters
					Percentage		
Canada	Level 1	19.4	21.3	14.3	17.4	22.8	42.8
	Level 2	30.5	43.2	25.0	44.0	53.2	68.5
	Level 3	32.4	55.3	37.7	51.5	54.2	69.0
	Level 4/5	32.8	54.8	40.3	65.6	73.8	85.8
Germany	Level 1	23.1	52.5	27.8	53.5	48.2	70.4
	Level 2	35.6	59.9	49.4	62.1	62.3	77.5
	Level 3	29.9	61.7	51.6	60.2	68.3	79.0
	Level 4/5	33.5	65.8	56.5	61.9	71.6	86.6
Netherlands	Level 1	15.7	19.1	19.3	26.5	25.3	32.1
	Level 2	24.4	35.8	30.6	39.4	52.1	56.2
	Level 3	24.9	45.0	41.5	55.1	64.5	70.1
	Level 4/5	23.5	52.3	50.5	63.9	73.5	78.3
Poland	Level 1	15.6	16.4	12.5	14.0	15.0	21.5
	Level 2	23.9	29.8	22.5	26.7	28.8	33.3
	Level 3	28.0	34.7	24.8	35.0	43.0	42.3
	Level 4/5	47.6	50.6	37.9	55.2	54.9	57.8
Sweden	Level 1	N/A	31.0	49.3	48.7	47.7	54.6
	Level 2	N/A	49.8	52.2	63.7	57.8	69.7
	Level 3	N/A	58.6	61.3	71.3	66.7	78.9
	Level 4/5	N/A	63.1	71.9	79.3	72.5	84.9
Switzerland (French)	Level 1	16.4	33.5	14.0	43.9	46.3	55.9
	Level 2	23.1	52.0	30.8	48.5	63.4	66.9
	Level 3	20.1	58.5	39.0	48.4	76.0	74.9
	Level 4/5	13.7	68.5	54.9	58.7	85.3	82.5
Switzerland (German)	Level 1	16.1	39.6	10.1	33.1	31.3	39.2
	Level 2	15.5	57.0	20.1	49.5	66.6	75.7
	Level 3	17.5	65.1	37.4	59.1	77.0	88.5
	Level 4/5	18.6	68.9	45.8	69.0	80.7	92.6
United States	Level 1	22.9	23.1	18.7	31.7	28.5	40.8
	Level 2	34.7	42.0	28.1	55.6	50.8	66.2
	Level 3	38.4	51.2	39.0	65.7	65.5	76.8
	Level 4/5	34.1	63.4	56.1	80.1	79.9	88.7

For example, 38.4% of those at Level 3 on this scale in the United States read directions.

Table C-2a

Proportion of respondents within a level who reported engaging in each of several writing activities at work at least once a week, prose scale

		Reports	Forms	Letters	Specifications
		Percentage			
Canada	Level 1	20.9	25.9	24.7	18.2
	Level 2	35.2	49.8	48.7	20.5
	Level 3	44.8	50.9	58.4	30.7
	Level 4/5	44.4	49.5	65.2	30.3
Germany	Level 1	32.5	39.2	49.3	18.3
	Level 2	45.7	57.9	68.7	26.2
	Level 3	53.0	62.7	77.1	29.9
	Level 4/5	54.2	59.7	85.5	27.8
Netherlands	Level 1	16.7	12.3	22.3	25.7
	Level 2	32.6	31.2	42.7	34.2
	Level 3	37.7	26.0	59.2	29.2
	Level 4/5	44.7	25.9	65.7	32.0
Poland	Level 1	12.1	17.9	18.6	4.4
	Level 2	19.4	32.7	33.1	8.3
	Level 3	24.0	40.3	40.5	13.7
	Level 4/5	29.5	45.5	60.9	24.0
Sweden	Level 1	40.5	36.7	40.4	26.3
	Level 2	46.1	37.9	63.6	26.7
	Level 3	56.3	49.4	76.3	31.2
	Level 4/5	59.6	53.0	82.2	31.5
Switzerland (French)	Level 1	24.2	33.7	40.8	17.1
	Level 2	44.1	43.5	51.2	21.5
	Level 3	51.7	52.5	70.9	29.4
	Level 4/5	59.3	54.7	77.3	23.5
Switzerland (German)	Level 1	18.2	33.4	50.5	11.9
	Level 2	39.8	56.6	75.1	27.1
	Level 3	51.4	64.2	89.1	27.9
	Level 4/5	55.4	67.4	94.4	27.5
United States	Level 1	23.4	29.1	28.8	17.4
	Level 2	36.1	51.1	50.8	27.3
	Level 3	51.3	58.0	66.4	32.7
	Level 4/5	55.2	58.1	74.3	33.7

For example, 49.5% of those at Level 4/5 on this scale in Canada fill out forms.

Table C-2b

Proportion of respondents within a level who reported engaging in each of several writing activities at work at least once a week, document scale

		Reports	Forms	Letters	Specifications
		Percentage			
Canada	Level 1	18.3	24.0	28.4	17.7
	Level 2	35.3	50.1	45.8	21.4
	Level 3	43.1	47.9	55.3	26.8
	Level 4/5	47.7	54.1	69.2	34.9
Germany	Level 1	33.0	40.5	47.3	18.1
	Level 2	42.1	57.1	67.3	24.7
	Level 3	52.2	59.9	74.8	28.7
	Level 4/5	53.9	59.8	81.7	29.5
Netherlands	Level 1	17.9	15.8	18.4	24.5
	Level 2	29.2	23.9	41.7	29.3
	Level 3	38.2	28.4	58.8	30.0
	Level 4/5	42.5	27.1	61.7	35.3
Poland	Level 1	12.7	17.6	19.2	4.9
	Level 2	19.0	32.4	31.7	8.2
	Level 3	21.7	38.7	41.7	10.2
	Level 4/5	30.8	52.0	49.7	25.1
Sweden	Level 1	36.8	27.5	49.1	19.3
	Level 2	48.1	38.4	63.6	26.5
	Level 3	54.3	47.3	73.6	29.9
	Level 4/5	60.0	55.0	82.2	33.5
Switzerland (French)	Level 1	23.0	30.8	38.3	19.7
	Level 2	44.7	45.5	52.6	17.2
	Level 3	50.3	51.7	67.7	28.2
	Level 4/5	53.9	49.6	73.7	30.8
Switzerland (German)	Level 1	16.8	28.7	48.6	9.9
	Level 2	42.8	52.8	75.2	26.7
	Level 3	48.3	65.6	87.2	28.9
	Level 4/5	51.1	69.2	91.2	27.2
United States	Level 1	23.7	29.7	32.4	15.2
	Level 2	39.5	48.0	53.6	29.3
	Level 3	49.9	59.9	66.2	32.1
	Level 4/5	56.7	61.3	73.5	35.8

For example, 17.9% of those at Level 1 on this scale in the Netherlands write reports.

Table C-2c

Proportion of respondents within a level who reported engaging in each of several writing activities at work at least once a week, quantitative scale

		Reports	Forms	Letters	Specifications
		Percentage			
Canada	Level 1	23.6	25.3	24.1	14.6
	Level 2	33.9	46.7	48.9	20.1
	Level 3	42.1	52.8	57.1	27.7
	Level 4/5	48.4	50.1	67.2	37.0
Germany	Level 1	33.0	41.9	51.0	16.9
	Level 2	42.3	57.9	66.0	24.6
	Level 3	48.9	58.9	71.6	27.4
	Level 4/5	55.0	59.1	82.6	30.2
Netherlands	Level 1	17.1	12.9	21.7	20.8
	Level 2	27.8	24.6	40.7	25.7
	Level 3	38.2	29.1	58.4	30.4
	Level 4/5	44.3	26.0	63.1	38.7
Poland	Level 1	11.3	16.9	17.8	4.1
	Level 2	16.9	28.7	30.8	7.3
	Level 3	22.6	37.8	39.1	10.0
	Level 4/5	31.7	49.5	46.2	24.2
Sweden	Level 1	33.7	21.4	49.9	16.5
	Level 2	46.7	38.9	64.9	23.4
	Level 3	55.2	46.9	74.4	29.2
	Level 4/5	60.2	55.9	80.8	36.1
Switzerland (French)	Level 1	21.6	25.7	37.9	10.6
	Level 2	39.5	39.6	48.2	20.3
	Level 3	48.7	51.0	65.5	25.6
	Level 4/5	58.0	55.9	74.5	31.9
Switzerland (German)	Level 1	15.8	30.5	47.1	8.5
	Level 2	37.8	50.3	67.4	21.4
	Level 3	48.1	64.5	86.7	30.5
	Level 4/5	51.2	64.5	93.3	27.6
United States	Level 1	21.7	27.3	30.3	13.3
	Level 2	36.1	46.7	52.3	22.7
	Level 3	47.4	57.2	61.7	31.1
	Level 4/5	61.2	64.8	78.0	42.6

For example, 23.4% of those at Level 2 on this scale in Sweden write specifications.

Table C-3a

Proportion of respondents within a level who reported engaging in each of two numeracy activities at work at least once a week, prose scale

		Measurements	Prices
		Percentage	
Canada	Level 1	22.6	38.8
	Level 2	43.8	45.1
	Level 3	53.6	49.4
	Level 4/5	58.8	49.7
Germany	Level 1	31.0	28.3
	Level 2	41.7	28.3
	Level 3	48.6	27.6
	Level 4/5	42.4	29.1
Netherlands	Level 1	30.5	39.5
	Level 2	48.5	50.5
	Level 3	47.1	45.8
	Level 4/5	52.0	36.2
Poland	Level 1	19.2	39.1
	Level 2	31.0	55.4
	Level 3	32.2	51.1
	Level 4/5	37.2	57.3
Sweden	Level 1	34.5	48.9
	Level 2	41.0	56.8
	Level 3	51.0	54.6
	Level 4/5	52.3	50.1
Switzerland (French)	Level 1	34.5	36.6
	Level 2	43.6	37.1
	Level 3	51.7	38.4
	Level 4/5	54.1	33.9
Switzerland (German)	Level 1	23.5	39.1
	Level 2	36.1	51.3
	Level 3	42.9	43.1
	Level 4/5	40.2	38.6
United States	Level 1	29.1	43.1
	Level 2	50.0	51.1
	Level 3	57.2	47.5
	Level 4/5	62.3	48.1

For example, 43.6% of those at Level 2 on this scale in Switzerland (French) calculate measurements.

Table C-3b

Proportion of respondents within a level who reported engaging in each of two numeracy activities at work at least once a week, document scale

		Measurements	Prices
		Percentage	
Canada	Level 1	29.7	40.1
	Level 2	42.1	48.2
	Level 3	48.0	44.7
	Level 4/5	63.5	52.2
Germany	Level 1	26.4	20.4
	Level 2	40.5	27.8
	Level 3	47.5	29.4
	Level 4/5	43.7	28.6
Netherlands	Level 1	32.3	37.5
	Level 2	42.0	47.2
	Level 3	48.1	45.6
	Level 4/5	53.6	43.3
Poland	Level 1	19.0	41.2
	Level 2	29.5	50.4
	Level 3	34.1	55.1
	Level 4/5	41.2	60.0
Sweden	Level 1	26.9	45.9
	Level 2	39.0	52.5
	Level 3	50.2	53.6
	Level 4/5	54.1	53.9
Switzerland (French)	Level 1	28.7	33.8
	Level 2	43.4	40.3
	Level 3	52.2	35.1
	Level 4/5	51.8	39.0
Switzerland (German)	Level 1	19.2	33.9
	Level 2	34.8	44.8
	Level 3	43.2	48.3
	Level 4/5	43.0	48.0
United States	Level 1	29.6	42.3
	Level 2	49.1	50.3
	Level 3	57.3	51.1
	Level 4/5	66.1	44.6

For example, 28.6% of those at Level 4/5 on this scale in Germany calculate prices.

Table C-3c

Proportion of respondents within a level who reported engaging in each of two numeracy activities at work at least once a week, quantitative scale

		Measurements	Prices
		Percentage	
Canada	Level 1	23.2	39.3
	Level 2	44.1	45.0
	Level 3	52.4	48.7
	Level 4/5	60.0	50.8
Germany	Level 1	26.7	23.8
	Level 2	38.2	27.4
	Level 3	44.3	27.4
	Level 4/5	48.7	30.9
Netherlands	Level 1	27.4	34.5
	Level 2	39.7	42.1
	Level 3	50.1	48.9
	Level 4/5	53.4	42.0
Poland	Level 1	17.3	38.2
	Level 2	28.7	51.7
	Level 3	32.1	53.0
	Level 4/5	42.6	61.2
Sweden	Level 1	21.9	40.9
	Level 2	39.7	48.8
	Level 3	49.7	54.0
	Level 4/5	55.2	55.7
Switzerland (French)	Level 1	23.6	33.9
	Level 2	39.3	33.1
	Level 3	51.6	39.5
	Level 4/5	54.6	38.2
Switzerland (German)	Level 1	19.3	27.8
	Level 2	31.8	43.1
	Level 3	42.3	47.2
	Level 4/5	43.4	51.8
United States	Level 1	28.5	38.4
	Level 2	47.1	48.3
	Level 3	55.6	49.7
	Level 4/5	67.4	51.1

For example, 27.8% of those at Level 1 on this scale in Switzerland (German) calculate prices.

Table C-4a

Proportion of each level who gave a particular self-assessment of their reading skills for their main job, prose scale

		Level 1	Level 2	Level 3	Level 4/5
			Percentage		
Canada	Excellent	20.3	47.3	62.3	79.9
	Good	25.6	40.9	30.1	18.9
	Moderate	17.3	10.1	5.0	0.7
	Poor	16.7	0.1	0.5	0.0
	No opinion	20.0	1.6	2.2	0.4
Germany	Excellent	24.7	45.3	55.7	68.1
	Good	52.9	47.8	39.6	31.3
	Moderate	12.0	3.8	4.1	0.6
	Poor	7.0	0.3	0.0	0.0
	No opinion	3.4	2.8	0.7	0.0
Netherlands	Excellent	7.1	11.0	20.7	34.0
	Good	40.3	55.7	61.7	57.1
	Moderate	42.6	29.6	15.2	6.7
	Poor	3.5	1.6	0.3	0.5
	No opinion	6.6	2.1	2.1	1.7
Poland*	Excellent	8.4	21.2	33.6	51.6
	Good	67.4	69.6	63.1	48.4
	Moderate	21.6	9.1	2.5	0.0
	Poor	2.6	0.0	0.8	0.0
Switzerland (French)	Excellent	14.8	40.5	61.9	82.9
	Good	49.1	44.1	30.6	14.3
	Moderate	19.3	12.2	7.1	2.8
	Poor	12.6	1.0	0.0	0.0
	No opinion	4.2	2.2	0.5	0.0
Switzerland (German)	Excellent	38.2	68.1	74.9	83.7
	Good	26.0	28.9	24.8	16.3
	Moderate	18.7	2.5	0.4	0.0
	Poor	14.9	0.2	0.0	0.0
	No opinion	2.4	0.4	0.0	0.0
United States	Excellent	23.1	46.6	67.3	78.0
	Good	37.3	44.4	28.0	20.0
	Moderate	15.6	7.5	3.7	1.4
	Poor	20.2	0.6	0.3	0.0
	No opinion	3.7	1.0	0.6	0.5

*   The no opinion category was not an option on the Polish questionnaire.

For example, 47.3% of those at Level 2 on this scale in Canada said they had excellent reading skills for their main job.

Table C-4b

Proportion of each level who gave a particular self-assessment of their reading skills for their main job, document scale

		Level 1	Level 2	Level 3	Level 4/5
			Percentage		
Canada	Excellent	22.4	45.4	65.1	75.9
	Good	26.4	42.5	26.6	22.3
	Moderate	15.3	9.4	6.4	0.8
	Poor	15.9	0.7	0.5	0.0
	No opinion	19.9	2.1	1.5	1.0
Germany	Excellent	24.0	40.8	53.2	68.1
	Good	50.3	49.6	42.8	29.7
	Moderate	13.8	5.1	3.4	2.0
	Poor	6.8	1.4	0.1	0.0
	No opinion	5.0	3.1	0.5	0.2
Netherlands	Excellent	8.9	10.8	20.2	28.9
	Good	44.5	54.3	61.1	57.4
	Moderate	32.3	31.2	16.6	11.1
	Poor	6.5	0.8	0.7	0.0
	No opinion	7.8	3.0	1.3	2.6
Poland*	Excellent	11.2	20.2	29.9	39.1
	Good	68.0	68.1	65.2	57.0
	Moderate	18.4	11.5	4.6	3.3
	Poor	2.5	0.2	0.3	0.7
Switzerland (French)	Excellent	19.0	36.2	60.8	71.0
	Good	46.9	44.7	32.2	22.5
	Moderate	15.9	15.2	6.6	5.5
	Poor	13.1	1.6	0.4	0.0
	No opinion	5.1	2.5	0.0	1.1
Switzerland (German)	Excellent	36.3	64.4	76.1	81.4
	Good	32.4	31.3	22.3	18.2
	Moderate	14.1	3.4	1.7	0.3
	Poor	15.2	0.2	0.0	0.0
	No opinion	2.0	0.6	0.0	0.0
United States	Excellent	23.1	53.9	66.2	77.2
	Good	40.2	37.7	29.1	22.1
	Moderate	16.0	7.0	3.6	0.3
	Poor	17.0	1.0	0.0	0.3
	No opinion	3.7	0.4	1.1	0.1

*   The no opinion category was not an option on the Polish questionnaire.

For example, 40.2% of those at Level 1 on this scale in the United States said they had good reading skills for their main job.

Table C-4c

Proportion of each level who gave a particular self-assessment of their reading skills for their main job, quantitative scale

		Level 1	Level 2	Level 3	Level 4/5
			Percentage		
Canada	Excellent	28.5	44.9	61.5	80.0
	Good	27.2	38.3	31.2	18.5
	Moderate	14.5	11.9	4.1	1.4
	Poor	13.1	2.1	0.5	0.0
	No opinion	16.7	2.8	2.8	0.2
Germany	Excellent	22.4	43.9	50.3	61.4
	Good	50.2	46.4	44.6	35.0
	Moderate	14.9	4.7	3.8	3.2
	Poor	7.7	1.3	0.5	0.2
	No opinion	4.7	3.8	0.8	0.2
Netherlands	Excellent	9.6	11.0	18.6	31.8
	Good	37.8	58.1	60.8	56.6
	Moderate	40.1	26.7	18.6	9.0
	Poor	3.9	1.3	0.8	0.0
	No opinion	8.6	2.8	1.2	2.6
Poland*	Excellent	9.3	19.1	28.3	37.2
	Good	68.1	68.5	65.0	59.8
	Moderate	19.9	11.8	6.7	1.7
	Poor	2.6	0.5	0.0	1.3
Switzerland (French)	Excellent	17.4	36.6	55.0	69.4
	Good	37.9	41.7	37.1	26.5
	Moderate	21.1	16.4	7.8	3.2
	Poor	17.0	2.5	0.0	0.0
	No opinion	6.6	2.9	0.1	0.9
Switzerland (German)	Excellent	30.3	62.2	76.8	75.3
	Good	28.8	33	21.1	24.4
	Moderate	17.3	4.3	1.7	0.3
	Poor	20.9	0.0	0.2	0.0
	No opinion	2.7	0.4	0.2	0.0
United States	Excellent	21.0	52.3	65.5	76.1
	Good	40.7	39.8	28.6	22.6
	Moderate	16.4	6.2	4.3	1.3
	Poor	18.1	1.1	0.5	0.0
	No opinion	3.8	0.6	1.2	0.1

*   The no opinion category was not an option on the Polish questionnaire.

For example, 62.2% of those at Level 2 on this scale in Switzerland (German) said they had excellent reading skills for their main job.

Table C-5a

Proportion of each level who gave a particular self-assessment of their writing skills for their main job, prose scale

		Level 1	Level 2	Level 3	Level 4/5
			Percentage		
Canada	Excellent	16.9	42.1	51.6	63.4
	Good	27.1	39.0	34.8	33.2
	Moderate	17.3	12.1	9.0	2.6
	Poor	24.0	4.1	0.8	0.1
	No opinion	14.7	2.8	3.8	0.7
Germany	Excellent	22.0	39.8	51.0	64.6
	Good	49.5	51.3	44.3	34.1
	Moderate	16.1	5.7	3.6	1.3
	Poor	8.0	0.7	0.0	0.0
	No opinion	4.3	2.5	1.1	0.0
Netherlands	Excellent	1.5	9.4	14.1	26.4
	Good	38.6	46.4	58.1	58.1
	Moderate	44.5	34.4	24.4	12.0
	Poor	8.2	7.3	1.4	0.9
	No opinion	7.2	2.5	2.0	2.6
Poland*	Excellent	6.1	17.2	27.1	40.9
	Good	66.6	69.8	66.3	57.7
	Moderate	24.3	12.6	6.0	1.4
	Poor	2.9	0.4	0.6	0.0
Switzerland (French)	Excellent	8.0	27.8	47.0	63.0
	Good	35.6	36.0	37.4	28.8
	Moderate	24.7	25.1	14.3	6.8
	Poor	26.5	9.7	1.3	1.4
	No opinion	5.2	1.4	0.0	0.0
Switzerland (German)	Excellent	34.3	56.7	62.5	73.5
	Good	21.2	32.5	33.2	25.6
	Moderate	20.2	9.2	3.2	0.9
	Poor	18.2	0.9	1.1	0.0
	No opinion	6.1	0.7	0.0	0.0
United States	Excellent	17.2	33.5	52.5	64.9
	Good	35.4	51.2	37.4	29.7
	Moderate	20.0	11.8	7.4	4.6
	Poor	23.9	2.3	1.5	0.0
	No opinion	3.6	1.2	1.3	0.7

* The no opinion category was not an option on the Polish questionnaire.

For example, 22.0% of those at Level 1 on this scale in Germany said they had excellent writing skills for their main job.

Table C-5b

Proportion of each level who gave a particular self-assessment of their writing skills for their main job, document scale

		Level 1	Level 2	Level 3	Level 4/5
			Percentage		
Canada	Excellent	19.7	36.8	56.3	60.1
	Good	26.6	41.3	32.1	34.9
	Moderate	15.9	15.2	7.0	3.6
	Poor	24.3	1.0	2.8	0.2
	No opinion	13.6	5.6	1.9	1.3
Germany	Excellent	24.6	35.7	48.6	62.3
	Good	42.3	54.9	45.2	34.5
	Moderate	15.9	5.6	5.2	2.6
	Poor	10.8	1.1	0.2	0.0
	No opinion	6.5	2.8	0.7	0.7
Netherlands	Excellent	3.7	8.3	14.0	22.7
	Good	36.1	44.4	58.3	57.0
	Moderate	43.6	36.9	23.9	16.8
	Poor	9.7	6.9	2.3	0.5
	No opinion	6.8	3.6	1.4	3.1
Poland*	Excellent	8.4	17.1	23.8	28.6
	Good	66.6	68.8	67.3	66.9
	Moderate	22.3	13.6	8.6	3.7
	Poor	2.7	0.6	0.3	0.7
Switzerland (French)	Excellent	13.4	24.8	46.2	50.8
	Good	28.5	38.2	34.8	38.4
	Moderate	24.0	27.3	14.7	9.2
	Poor	27.7	8.2	4.3	1.6
	No opinion	6.4	1.6	0.0	0.0
Switzerland (German)	Excellent	34.0	50.9	64.0	72.7
	Good	22.9	36.7	31.0	24.7
	Moderate	18.7	10.1	3.9	2.6
	Poor	18.6	1.9	0.6	0.0
	No opinion	5.8	0.4	0.5	0.0
United States	Excellent	17.2	40.4	51.8	62.9
	Good	38.6	45.7	38.6	31.4
	Moderate	19.6	11.2	6.7	5.2
	Poor	21.1	1.8	1.3	0.3
	No opinion	3.6	0.8	1.6	0.2

*   The no opinion category was not an option on the Polish questionnaire.

For example, 28.6% of those at Level 4/5 on this scale in Poland said they had excellent writing skills for their main job.

Table C-5c

Proportion of each level who gave a particular self-assessment of their writing skills for their main job, quantitative scale

		Level 1	Level 2	Level 3	Level 4/5
		Percentage			
Canada	Excellent	25.0	39.2	54.3	58.8
	Good	26.9	35.7	34.0	37.2
	Moderate	14.6	14.3	7.7	3.4
	Poor	22.9	4.6	1.0	0.1
	No opinion	10.6	6.2	3.1	0.5
Germany	Excellent	21.1	39.0	46.3	55.4
	Good	43.4	47.8	48.1	41.2
	Moderate	18.6	7.3	4.6	2.6
	Poor	11.7	2.0	0.2	0.1
	No opinion	5.2	3.9	0.8	0.6
Netherlands	Excellent	4.7	8.6	13.6	23.1
	Good	31.2	46.4	58.8	55.7
	Moderate	47.4	35.8	24.2	16.1
	Poor	9.0	5.9	2.2	1.9
	No opinion	7.8	3.3	1.3	3.2
Poland*	Excellent	7.0	16.0	22.4	28.4
	Good	65.5	68.7	68.2	68.2
	Moderate	24.6	14.1	9.4	2.8
	Poor	2.9	1.2	0.0	0.5
Switzerland (French)	Excellent	8.0	23.3	42.6	51.5
	Good	26.5	35.9	35.7	39.5
	Moderate	27.6	27.5	16.9	8.6
	Poor	29.8	11.5	4.8	0.4
	No opinion	8.2	1.8	0.1	0.0
Switzerland (German)	Excellent	26.6	53.3	61.9	68.2
	Good	21.7	33.8	32.0	27.7
	Moderate	17.9	12.1	4.4	3.5
	Poor	25.8	0.7	1.1	0.7
	No opinion	8.0	0.2	0.6	0.0
United States	Excellent	17.5	37.6	51.2	61.9
	Good	37.8	46.7	38.9	32.0
	Moderate	18.6	12.2	7.0	5.6
	Poor	22.1	3.1	0.8	0.5
	No opinion	4.0	0.4	2.0	0.1

For example, 0.7% of those at Level 2 on this scale in Switzerland (German) said they had poor writing skills for their main job.

*   The no opinion category was not an option on the Polish questionnaire.

Table C-6a

Proportion of each level who gave a particular self-assessment of their numeracy skills for their main job, prose scale

		Level 1	Level 2	Level 3	Level 4/5
			Percentage		
Canada	Excellent	27.6	37.9	51.6	52.9
	Good	33.0	47.7	35.3	36.7
	Moderate	18.0	8.3	5.6	8.9
	Poor	8.2	2.2	1.4	0.1
	No opinion	13.3	4.0	6.2	1.3
Germany	Excellent	17.7	28.0	38.8	49.3
	Good	56.4	58.3	52.0	47.3
	Moderate	16.5	9.3	6.8	2.7
	Poor	4.7	1.1	0.5	0.0
	No opinion	4.7	3.4	1.8	0.7
Netherlands	Excellent	9.0	14.2	18.7	27.4
	Good	46.3	57.0	58.4	54.4
	Moderate	34.6	23.1	18.0	14.2
	Poor	5.1	1.6	1.2	0.2
	No opinion	4.9	4.2	3.7	3.7
Poland*	Excellent	5.7	16.1	22.1	48.4
	Good	63.4	69.4	65.8	50.3
	Moderate	25.0	12.8	11.9	1.4
	Poor	5.9	1.7	0.3	0.0
Switzerland (French)	Excellent	23.3	33.0	50.7	61.4
	Good	43.1	41.9	39.3	26.6
	Moderate	23.4	19.9	7.8	8.5
	Poor	5.0	2.6	1.3	1.7
	No opinion	5.1	2.6	1.0	1.8
Switzerland (German)	Excellent	38.2	57.5	63.1	71.8
	Good	39.8	35.1	29.9	24.0
	Moderate	8.0	5.4	5.0	4.2
	Poor	1.1	0.8	0.4	0.0
	No opinion	12.8	1.1	1.5	0.0
United States	Excellent	19.1	34.8	52.9	61.9
	Good	48.1	52.4	38.3	33.1
	Moderate	15.0	9.4	6.7	2.9
	Poor	12.8	1.3	0.7	0.7
	No opinion	5.0	2.2	1.5	1.3

*   The no opinion category was not an option on the Polish questionnaire.

For example, 2.9% of those at Level 4/5 on this scale in the United States said they had moderate numeracy skills for their main job.

Table C-6b

Proportion of each level who gave a particular self-assessment of their numeracy skills for their main job, document scale

		Level 1	Level 2	Level 3	Level 4/5
			Percentage		
Canada	Excellent	27.4	28.2	52.3	60.3
	Good	33.7	50.8	33.4	35.8
	Moderate	16.6	10.4	9.9	2.2
	Poor	10.6	2.4	0.4	0.3
	No opinion	11.8	8.1	4.1	1.4
Germany	Excellent	18.6	24.2	37.2	48.8
	Good	48.3	60.1	54.1	46.7
	Moderate	21.0	10.6	6.4	3.5
	Poor	4.6	1.8	0.6	0.0
	No opinion	7.5	3.4	1.7	1.0
Netherlands	Excellent	5.4	11.5	17.9	29.0
	Good	40.9	55.1	60.3	53.8
	Moderate	42.8	25.7	17.8	12.8
	Poor	6.3	2.1	0.8	0.7
	No opinion	4.6	5.6	3.2	3.7
Poland*	Excellent	7.1	14.3	21.4	36.7
	Good	63.2	70.0	66.7	57.5
	Moderate	24.0	14.1	11.1	5.8
	Poor	5.6	1.6	0.8	0.0
Switzerland (French)	Excellent	25.0	32.9	46.5	58.9
	Good	44.0	41.1	38.8	34.3
	Moderate	19.4	20.0	12.2	5.0
	Poor	5.4	2.8	1.7	0.8
	No opinion	6.3	3.2	0.8	0.9
Switzerland (German)	Excellent	36.8	55.5	64.3	67.0
	Good	39.5	34.4	30.4	29.6
	Moderate	8.0	7.9	3.8	3.4
	Poor	1.5	1.3	0.0	0.0
	No opinion	14.1	0.9	1.6	0.0
United States	Excellent	17.1	42.2	51.4	61.8
	Good	50.9	47.3	39.6	33.2
	Moderate	15.6	8.6	6.4	2.6
	Poor	11.3	0.6	0.8	1.2
	No opinion	5.1	1.3	1.9	1.2

*   The no opinion category was not an option on the Polish questionnaire.

For example, 20.0% of those at Level 2 on this scale in Switzerland (French) said they had moderate numeracy skills for their main job.

Table C-6c

Proportion of each level who gave a particular self-assessment of their numeracy skills for their main job, quantitative scale

		Level 1	Level 2	Level 3	Level 4/5
			Percentage		
Canada	Excellent	26.2	32.3	51.2	59.9
	Good	33.9	46.4	39.7	30.7
	Moderate	17.3	11.6	4.4	7.6
	Poor	10.0	2.8	0.4	0.1
	No opinion	12.6	6.9	4.2	1.6
Germany	Excellent	16.4	25.9	33.7	46.3
	Good	48.6	55.4	56.5	50.0
	Moderate	21.5	11.7	7.9	2.5
	Poor	7.3	2.6	0.1	0.0
	No opinion	6.2	4.5	1.7	1.1
Netherlands	Excellent	5.1	10.2	16.1	33.8
	Good	37.7	52.0	63.1	52.1
	Moderate	43.4	29.5	17.0	10.6
	Poor	9.5	2.5	0.6	0.0
	No opinion	4.3	5.8	3.2	3.4
Poland*	Excellent	6.2	13.0	20.6	32.0
	Good	60.1	70.4	68.0	64.8
	Moderate	27.2	14.6	11.0	3.2
	Poor	6.6	2.0	0.4	0.0
Switzerland (French)	Excellent	21.9	29.8	43.0	62.3
	Good	38.3	42.4	41.5	31.6
	Moderate	24.7	21.5	12.7	4.5
	Poor	7.0	3.1	1.9	0.3
	No opinion	8.1	3.2	0.9	1.3
Switzerland (German)	Excellent	26.6	50.8	63.6	72.4
	Good	46.5	38.7	29.9	24.3
	Moderate	7.0	9.2	4.3	2.6
	Poor	1.3	0.3	0.9	0.0
	No opinion	18.6	1.1	1.3	0.7
United States	Excellent	16.1	35.1	49.9	66.8
	Good	49.0	53.1	40.3	30.1
	Moderate	17.1	8.7	7.1	1.8
	Poor	12.1	1.4	1.1	0.2
	No opinion	5.6	1.7	1.6	1.1

For example, 16.1% of those at Level 3 on this scale in the Netherlands said they had excellent numeracy skills for their main job.

*   The no opinion category was not an option on the Polish questionnaire.

Table C-7a

Proportion of respondents in each literacy level who reported whether their reading skills limited their job opportunities, prose scale

		Level 1	Level 2	Level 3	Level 4/5
		Percentage			
Canada	Greatly limiting	12.9	2.7	2.3	0.0
	Somewhat limiting	29.5	13.3	4.9	0.9
	Not at all limiting	57.6	84.0	92.8	99.1
Germany	Greatly limiting	15.2	16.8	2.2	0.0
	Somewhat limiting	44.2	28.5	11.5	0.0
	Not at all limiting	40.6	54.6	86.3	100.0
Netherlands	Greatly limiting	6.3	1.1	1.3	1.6
	Somewhat limiting	11.8	11.6	5.6	4.4
	Not at all limiting	81.9	87.2	93.2	93.9
Poland	Greatly limiting	2.1	0.7	0.5	0.0
	Somewhat limiting	10.5	7.4	3.8	1.7
	Not at all limiting	87.4	91.9	95.7	98.3
Switzerland (French)	Greatly limiting	6.6	1.8	1.4	2.2
	Somewhat limiting	16.8	18.1	7.1	4.9
	Not at all limiting	76.6	80.1	91.5	92.9
Switzerland (German)	Greatly limiting	7.6	1.3	1.3	0.0
	Somewhat limiting	10.7	3.9	1.9	0.7
	Not at all limiting	81.8	94.8	96.8	99.3
United States	Greatly limiting	17.4	1.7	0.4	0.6
	Somewhat limiting	21.9	8.7	4.7	2.8
	Not at all limiting	60.7	89.7	94.9	96.6

For example, 44.2% of those at Level 1 on this scale in Germany said that their reading skills were somewhat limiting their job opportunities.

Table C-7b

Proportion of respondents in each literacy level who reported whether their reading skills limited their job opportunities, document scale

		Level 1	Level 2	Level 3	Level 4/5
		Percentage			
Canada	Greatly limiting	13.3	4.1	1.2	0.1
	Somewhat limiting	27.2	12.3	6.5	1.1
	Not at all limiting	59.5	83.6	92.3	98.8
Germany	Greatly limiting	22.5	9.3	2.7	0.0
	Somewhat limiting	38.1	35.6	14.8	22.8
	Not at all limiting	39.3	55.1	82.5	77.2
Netherlands	Greatly limiting	7.4	1.0	1.5	1.2
	Somewhat limiting	11.4	9.1	7.4	4.9
	Not at all limiting	81.2	89.9	91.1	94.0
Poland	Greatly limiting	2.0	1.0	0.3	0.0
	Somewhat limiting	11.4	7.5	2.1	2.8
	Not at all limiting	86.6	91.5	97.6	97.2
Switzerland (French)	Greatly limiting	8.0	0.8	1.8	2.6
	Somewhat limiting	16.2	16.5	11.3	2.6
	Not at all limiting	75.7	82.7	86.9	94.8
Switzerland (German)	Greatly limiting	8.8	0.9	1.5	0.0
	Somewhat limiting	8.9	5.5	2.2	0.0
	Not at all limiting	82.2	93.6	96.3	100.0
United States	Greatly limiting	15.5	1.3	0.2	1.0
	Somewhat limiting	18.6	9.6	4.6	2.5
	Not at all limiting	65.9	89.2	95.2	96.5

For example, 2.0% of those at Level 1 on this scale in Poland said that their reading skills were greatly limiting their job opportunities.

Table C-7c

Proportion of respondents in each literacy level who reported whether their reading skills limited their job opportunities, quantitative scale

		Level 1	Level 2	Level 3	Level 4/5
		Percentage			
Canada	Greatly limiting	10.6	6.1	0.6	0.2
	Somewhat limiting	28.4	15.5	3.7	0.8
	Not at all limiting	61.1	78.4	95.7	99.1
Germany	Greatly limiting	20.8	12.7	9.3	0.0
	Somewhat limiting	35.1	43.4	24.4	19.0
	Not at all limiting	44.1	44.0	66.4	81.0
Netherlands	Greatly limiting	6.5	0.7	1.3	1.9
	Somewhat limiting	8.2	10.0	7.4	4.9
	Not at all limiting	85.3	89.2	91.3	93.2
Poland	Greatly limiting	2.2	1.4	0.0	0.0
	Somewhat limiting	12.4	7.7	3.2	2.8
	Not at all limiting	85.5	90.9	96.8	97.2
Switzerland (French)	Greatly limiting	7.7	2.5	1.7	1.4
	Somewhat limiting	14.4	20.6	10.2	5.1
	Not at all limiting	77.9	77.0	88.2	93.5
Switzerland (German)	Greatly limiting	10.3	1.8	1.4	0.0
	Somewhat limiting	5.5	7.5	2.1	1.3
	Not at all limiting	84.2	90.8	96.5	98.7
United States	Greatly limiting	17.1	0.9	0.3	1.0
	Somewhat limiting	18.1	12.5	3.8	2.4
	Not at all limiting	64.8	86.5	95.9	96.6

For example, 84.2% of those at Level 1 on this scale in Switzerland (German) said that their reading skills were not at all limiting their job opportunities.

Table C-8a

Proportion of respondents in each literacy level who reported whether their writing skills limited their job opportunities, prose scale

		Level 1	Level 2	Level 3	Level 4/5
		Percentage			
Canada	Greatly limiting	16.5	5.4	0.8	0.0
	Somewhat limiting	19.6	13.4	8.3	2.6
	Not at all limiting	63.9	81.1	90.9	97.4
Germany	Greatly limiting	14.2	9.2	3.0	0.0
	Somewhat limiting	33.6	26.2	19.2	0.0
	Not at all limiting	52.2	64.6	77.8	100.0
Netherlands	Greatly limiting	7.2	3.6	1.3	2.1
	Somewhat limiting	13.8	10.2	5.6	4.8
	Not at all limiting	79.0	86.2	93.1	93.1
Poland	Greatly limiting	1.6	0.8	0.5	0.0
	Somewhat limiting	11.2	6.3	5.3	5.0
	Not at all limiting	87.2	92.9	94.3	95.0
Switzerland (French)	Greatly limiting	12.0	3.5	2.2	2.5
	Somewhat limiting	19.7	28.4	11.2	7.1
	Not at all limiting	68.3	68.1	86.6	90.4
Switzerland (German)	Greatly limiting	8.5	1.9	1.2	0.0
	Somewhat limiting	14.4	7.1	3.2	2.7
	Not at all limiting	77.0	91.0	95.6	97.3
United States	Greatly limiting	20.3	2.2	0.9	0.5
	Somewhat limiting	18.7	8.9	5.1	4.6
	Not at all limiting	61.1	88.9	94.0	94.9

For example, 8.3% of those at Level 3 on this scale in Canada said that their writing skills were somewhat limiting their job opportunities.

Table C-8b

Proportion of respondents in each literacy level who reported whether their writing skills limited their job opportunities, document scale

		Level 1	Level 2	Level 3	Level 4/5
			Percentage		
Canada	Greatly limiting	16.9	2.5	2.5	0.2
	Somewhat limiting	18.4	15.4	7.2	3.1
	Not at all limiting	64.7	82.0	90.2	96.6
Germany	Greatly limiting	15.5	16.0	0.0	0.0
	Somewhat limiting	42.6	29.7	12.6	7.5
	Not at all limiting	41.9	54.3	87.4	92.5
Netherlands	Greatly limiting	7.1	3.1	2.3	1.2
	Somewhat limiting	12.8	10.0	6.7	4.5
	Not at all limiting	80.0	86.9	91.0	94.3
Poland	Greatly limiting	1.3	1.4	0.2	0.0
	Somewhat limiting	11.9	6.6	3.9	2.3
	Not at all limiting	86.9	92.0	95.8	97.7
Switzerland (French)	Greatly limiting	13.8	2.2	3.5	2.0
	Somewhat limiting	22.0	26.1	13.9	9.6
	Not at all limiting	64.2	71.7	82.6	88.4
Switzerland (German)	Greatly limiting	7.9	1.3	2.2	0.0
	Somewhat limiting	15.5	7.4	3.7	2.2
	Not at all limiting	76.6	91.3	94.1	97.8
United States	Greatly limiting	18.0	1.9	0.6	0.9
	Somewhat limiting	17.9	9.0	4.4	4.6
	Not at all limiting	64.1	89.1	94.9	94.5

For example, 1.2% of those at Level 4/5 on this scale in the Netherlands said that their writing skills were greatly limiting their job opportunities.

Table C-8c

Proportion of respondents in each literacy level who reported whether their writing skills limited their job opportunities, quantitative scale

		Level 1	Level 2	Level 3	Level 4/5
			Percentage		
Canada	Greatly limiting	14.3	6.5	0.8	0.0
	Somewhat limiting	19.0	15.5	6.8	2.8
	Not at all limiting	66.7	78.1	92.4	97.2
Germany	Greatly limiting	15.2	16.7	0.0	0.0
	Somewhat limiting	37.5	33.1	20.7	0.0
	Not at all limiting	47.3	50.2	79.3	100.0
Netherlands	Greatly limiting	9.4	1.3	2.2	2.4
	Somewhat limiting	8.1	11.4	6.4	4.9
	Not at all limiting	82.5	87.3	91.4	92.7
Poland	Greatly limiting	1.4	1.3	0.5	0.0
	Somewhat limiting	13.5	6.9	3.4	3.0
	Not at all limiting	85.1	91.7	96.2	97.0
Switzerland (French)	Greatly limiting	13.8	4.4	3.1	1.4
	Somewhat limiting	20.4	31.5	14.9	7.4
	Not at all limiting	65.8	64.1	82.0	91.2
Switzerland (German)	Greatly limiting	11.0	3.2	1.0	0.0
	Somewhat limiting	11.2	9.1	4.4	3.5
	Not at all limiting	77.8	87.6	94.6	96.5
United States	Greatly limiting	19.6	2.2	0.6	0.7
	Somewhat limiting	17.9	9.3	5.4	4.1
	Not at all limiting	62.5	88.5	94.0	95.1

For example, 14.9% of those at Level 3 on this scale in Switzerland (French) said that their writing skills were somewhat limiting their job opportunities.

Table C-9a

Proportion of respondents in each literacy level who reported whether their numeracy skills limited their job opportunities, prose scale

		Level 1	Level 2	Level 3	Level 4/5
			Percentage		
Canada	Greatly limiting	13.3	1.4	0.6	0.2
	Somewhat limiting	19.3	16.9	9.5	3.7
	Not at all limiting	67.4	81.7	89.9	96.2
Germany	Greatly limiting	7.7	2.3	1.3	0.0
	Somewhat limiting	32.8	10.7	29.1	0.0
	Not at all limiting	59.5	87.0	69.6	100.0
Netherlands	Greatly limiting	5.4	2.5	1.6	1.0
	Somewhat limiting	11.5	7.2	4.9	3.3
	Not at all limiting	83.1	90.3	93.5	95.7
Poland	Greatly limiting	3.5	1.4	1.2	0.0
	Somewhat limiting	13.8	8.1	7.7	5.0
	Not at all limiting	82.7	90.6	91.1	95.0
Switzerland (French)	Greatly limiting	6.5	1.6	1.2	2.2
	Somewhat limiting	23.5	22.5	7.7	8.1
	Not at all limiting	70.1	75.9	91.1	89.7
Switzerland (German)	Greatly limiting	1.2	0.5	1.7	0.0
	Somewhat limiting	12.8	3.9	1.8	0.0
	Not at all limiting	86.1	95.6	96.5	100.0
United States	Greatly limiting	11.1	2.1	0.9	0.0
	Somewhat limiting	17.8	8.4	5.6	4.6
	Not at all limiting	71.2	89.5	93.5	95.4

For example, 89.5% of those at Level 2 on this scale in the United States said that their numeracy skills were not at all limiting their job opportunities.

Table C-9b

Proportion of respondents in each literacy level who reported whether their numeracy skills limited their job opportunities, document scale

		Level 1	Level 2	Level 3	Level 4/5
			Percentage		
Canada	Greatly limiting	14.1	0.7	0.8	0.2
	Somewhat limiting	22.2	15.5	8.6	5.1
	Not at all limiting	63.7	83.8	90.6	94.6
Germany	Greatly limiting	11.8	1.3	0.9	0.0
	Somewhat limiting	34.5	24.3	13.7	0.0
	Not at all limiting	53.6	74.4	85.4	100.0
Netherlands	Greatly limiting	4.8	2.0	2.1	1.2
	Somewhat limiting	16.2	5.8	4.9	4.5
	Not at all limiting	79.0	92.2	93.0	94.3
Poland	Greatly limiting	3.4	1.8	0.7	0.0
	Somewhat limiting	14.3	8.3	7.0	2.6
	Not at all limiting	82.3	89.9	92.4	97.4
Switzerland (French)	Greatly limiting	7.1	1.8	0.9	2.6
	Somewhat limiting	24.8	23.3	10.6	4.2
	Not at all limiting	68.1	75.0	88.5	93.2
Switzerland (German)	Greatly limiting	1.2	0.7	1.5	0.5
	Somewhat limiting	12.6	3.5	2.7	0.6
	Not at all limiting	86.2	95.9	95.8	99.0
United States	Greatly limiting	10.0	2.0	0.7	0.0
	Somewhat limiting	17.6	8.9	3.9	5.3
	Not at all limiting	72.5	89.1	95.3	94.7

For example, 14.1% of those at Level 1 on this scale in Canada said that their numeracy skills were greatly limiting their job opportunities.

Table C-9c

Proportion of respondents in each literacy level who reported whether their numeracy skills limited their job opportunities, quantitative scale

		Level 1	Level 2	Level 3	Level 4/5
			Percentage		
Canada	Greatly limiting	12.0	2.1	0.7	0.2
	Somewhat limiting	22.6	17.8	8.3	2.7
	Not at all limiting	65.4	80.1	91.1	97.1
Germany	Greatly limiting	11.8	3.1	0.0	0.0
	Somewhat limiting	32.6	20.7	21.2	0.0
	Not at all limiting	55.6	76.1	78.8	100.0
Netherlands	Greatly limiting	5.7	1.5	2.3	0.9
	Somewhat limiting	12.3	7.2	5.0	3.8
	Not at all limiting	82.0	91.3	92.6	95.3
Poland	Greatly limiting	4.2	1.3	1.1	0.0
	Somewhat limiting	15.6	9.6	5.5	4.2
	Not at all limiting	80.2	89.2	93.5	95.8
Switzerland (French)	Greatly limiting	8.3	2.7	0.9	1.9
	Somewhat limiting	20.0	23.7	14.1	4.9
	Not at all limiting	71.7	73.6	85.1	93.3
Switzerland (German)	Greatly limiting	1.7	1.0	1.1	0.7
	Somewhat limiting	13.9	5.1	2.1	1.5
	Not at all limiting	84.4	93.9	96.8	97.8
United States	Greatly limiting	11.1	2.3	0.5	0.0
	Somewhat limiting	19.5	10.0	4.7	3.1
	Not at all limiting	69.4	87.7	94.8	96.9

For example, 1.1% of those at Level 3 on this scale in Poland said that their numeracy skills were greatly limiting their job opportunities.

Table C-10a

Proportion of respondents within a level who reported engaging in each of several literacy activities in their daily lives, prose scale

		Read newspapers at least once a week	Read books at least once a week	Write letters at least once a week	Visit a library at least once a month
		Percentage			
Canada	Level 1	68.7	28.5	10.5	12.8
	Level 2	92.4	40.5	15.6	17.1
	Level 3	91.1	54.3	18.4	27.3
	Level 4/5	92.1	74.9	24.8	40.2
Germany	Level 1	90.5	34.7	12.6	12.5
	Level 2	97.2	41.5	17.3	15.4
	Level 3	97.7	50.0	26.0	22.9
	Level 4/5	97.4	64.0	26.9	36.3
Netherlands	Level 1	87.5	25.2	9.4	15.4
	Level 2	93.7	36.6	14.1	27.2
	Level 3	97.0	49.0	20.7	42.0
	Level 4/5	95.7	60.0	26.4	46.4
Poland	Level 1	83.4	24.8	5.6	10.6
	Level 2	94.4	41.3	15.2	22.4
	Level 3	97.4	56.4	23.1	31.5
	Level 4/5	97.5	78.7	40.0	45.8
Sweden	Level 1	94.5	34.9	9.8	20.1
	Level 2	98.0	41.9	9.5	23.1
	Level 3	99.2	51.1	11.7	32.4
	Level 4/5	99.1	63.5	18.9	44.1
Switzerland (French)	Level 1	94.6	40.0	13.6	13.1
	Level 2	94.2	49.2	20.4	14.0
	Level 3	98.1	62.1	33.4	20.3
	Level 4/5	99.5	65.6	39.6	31.5
Switzerland (German)	Level 1	91.9	36.6	15.8	4.5
	Level 2	97.4	46.3	20.9	11.3
	Level 3	97.4	62.1	28.2	20.4
	Level 4/5	97.4	82.5	36.7	31.7
United States	Level 1	67.0	33.7	15.4	12.8
	Level 2	89.3	45.5	17.2	17.9
	Level 3	92.0	57.4	21.8	28.8
	Level 4/5	97.0	59.6	23.5	35.3

For example, 46.4% of those at Level 4/5 on this scale in the Netherlands visit a library at least once a month.

Table C-10b

Proportion of respondents within a level who reported engaging in each of several literacy activities in their daily lives, document scale

		Read newspapers at least once a week	Read books at least once a week	Write letters at least once a week	Visit a library at least once a month
			Percentage		
Canada	Level 1	71.8	36.4	10.8	15.9
	Level 2	89.8	44.7	19.1	21.3
	Level 3	91.5	57.1	18.1	27.0
	Level 4/5	93.1	60.6	21.4	33.7
Germany	Level 1	88.7	36.2	11.0	8.4
	Level 2	95.9	37.6	14.1	13.9
	Level 3	97.8	51.1	25.6	21.7
	Level 4/5	98.4	58.4	29.1	35.8
Netherlands	Level 1	87.2	27.6	8.2	15.1
	Level 2	94.1	42.3	14.1	30.9
	Level 3	95.9	46.1	20.9	40.4
	Level 4/5	97.3	51.9	23.4	40.4
Poland	Level 1	84.8	26.8	7.0	13.1
	Level 2	93.9	42.7	14.2	21.4
	Level 3	96.9	52.8	23.0	28.2
	Level 4/5	96.4	61.0	30.2	38.7
Sweden	Level 1	92.7	33.4	6.8	19.6
	Level 2	98.4	47.7	12.5	27.3
	Level 3	98.9	50.6	11.6	32.5
	Level 4/5	99.2	59.3	17.1	40.0
Switzerland (French)	Level 1	95.9	43.2	12.6	12.8
	Level 2	96.4	49.0	22.2	14.0
	Level 3	96.4	59.5	32.6	19.2
	Level 4/5	96.8	62.5	31.3	27.9
Switzerland (German)	Level 1	91.1	37.0	14.9	4.9
	Level 2	96.8	51.4	24.8	11.5
	Level 3	97.8	56.1	25.0	18.5
	Level 4/5	97.6	68.4	29.5	25.0
United States	Level 1	71.2	36.0	12.7	15.5
	Level 2	88.7	47.6	19.6	20.0
	Level 3	93.7	57.5	22.6	28.7
	Level 4/5	94.2	57.9	23.4	32.5

For example, 71.2% of those at Level 1 on this scale in the United States read a newspaper at least once a week.

Table C-10c

Proportion of respondents within a level who reported engaging in each of several literacy activities in their daily lives, quantitative scale

		Read newspapers at least once a week	Read books at least once a week	Write letters at least once a week	Visit a library at least once a month
		Percentage			
Canada	Level 1	70.7	35.4	10.4	12.3
	Level 2	89.1	46.9	18.2	20.8
	Level 3	92.5	52.5	18.2	28.3
	Level 4/5	92.5	66.4	22.6	35.6
Germany	Level 1	89.2	32.0	15.2	11.7
	Level 2	95.2	44.2	17.1	16.7
	Level 3	97.3	47.1	23.4	19.7
	Level 4/5	98.4	52.9	23.5	29.1
Netherlands	Level 1	87.0	30.8	8.4	19.9
	Level 2	92.8	41.3	14.7	31.7
	Level 3	96.5	46.7	21.2	39.7
	Level 4/5	97.7	50.2	22.1	38.3
Poland	Level 1	84.6	24.9	6.0	12.3
	Level 2	92.0	39.9	14.5	21.7
	Level 3	96.2	51.8	21.1	26.7
	Level 4/5	97.0	61.5	24.1	32.0
Sweden	Level 1	93.1	36.1	8.5	19.2
	Level 2	98.2	47.2	11.9	28.1
	Level 3	98.8	52.0	13.9	33.9
	Level 4/5	99.5	57.5	14.6	38.2
Switzerland (French)	Level 1	94.3	45.3	11.6	14.5
	Level 2	96.4	49.6	20.1	15.1
	Level 3	95.8	56.8	30.5	19.2
	Level 4/5	98.7	60.7	33.2	21.5
Switzerland (German)	Level 1	91.3	38.1	14.0	5.2
	Level 2	96.8	47.0	23.5	12.7
	Level 3	97.0	59.5	26.1	17.6
	Level 4/5	97.9	60.3	26.8	20.2
United States	Level 1	68.4	36.7	15.6	13.4
	Level 2	87.0	48.9	17.9	20.9
	Level 3	94.6	56.4	20.7	28.0
	Level 4/5	95.0	54.9	24.1	32.3

For example, 36.1% of those at Level 1 on this scale in Sweden read a book at least once a week.

Table C-11a

Proportion of each level who reported various frequencies for watching television each day, prose scale

		Level 1	Level 2	Level 3	Level 4/5
		Percentage			
Canada	Not on a daily basis	6.1	6.4	8.1	18.6
	1 hour or less per day	11.2	19.0	23.5	28.6
	1 to 2 hours per day	28.2	23.7	30.5	32.2
	More than 2 hours but less than 5	37.0	40.7	33.8	19.3
	5 or more hours per day	16.6	8.1	4.1	1.0
	Do not have a television	0.8	2.1	0.1	0.3
Germany	Not on a daily basis	2.5	1.6	3.0	1.6
	1 hour or less per day	11.2	14.3	20.0	19.6
	1 to 2 hours per day	21.8	32	29.9	36.2
	More than 2 hours but less than 5	51.9	40.9	38.0	31.0
	5 or more hours per day	12.2	11.1	8.8	9.1
	Do not have a television	0.4	0.1	0.3	2.6
Netherlands	Not on a daily basis	2.1	3.5	4.7	10.5
	1 hour or less per day	5.7	13.3	17.1	20.0
	1 to 2 hours per day	22.3	29.8	37.8	37.1
	More than 2 hours but less than 5	53.4	44.5	35.6	30.5
	5 or more hours per day	15.4	7.8	3.4	0.6
	Do not have a television	1.1	1.1	1.4	1.2
Poland	Not on a daily basis	7.0	8.4	11.3	14.2
	1 hour or less per day	10.4	12.4	14.6	13.0
	1 to 2 hours per day	38.8	41.7	44.4	49.5
	More than 2 hours but less than 5	35.7	33.3	27.2	20.8
	5 or more hours per day	7.6	4.0	1.9	2.5
	Do not have a television	0.4	0.1	0.6	0.0
Switzerland (French)	Not on a daily basis	7.1	7.9	15.6	27.3
	1 hour or less per day	15.3	12.6	21.5	12.5
	1 to 2 hours per day	40.3	39.2	34.6	38.9
	More than 2 hours but less than 5	31.5	32.0	19.1	13.4
	5 or more hours per day	2.9	2.9	3.4	0.8
	Do not have a television	2.9	5.4	5.7	7.2
Switzerland (German)	Not on a daily basis	11.3	16.1	27.2	40.3
	1 hour or less per day	22.9	27.0	24.0	26.0
	1 to 2 hours per day	31.2	32.7	29.5	12.7
	More than 2 hours but less than 5	30.2	19.7	12.6	6.8
	5 or more hours per day	2.7	1.5	0.4	0.0
	Do not have a television	1.6	3.0	6.4	14.2
United States	Not on a daily basis	1.9	3.4	3.5	6.3
	1 hour or less per day	18.6	18.7	25.1	34.1
	1 to 2 hours per day	27.2	31.3	32.1	32.5
	More than 2 hours but less than 5	32.4	30.8	30.3	24.9
	5 or more hours per day	17.9	14.8	7.9	2.2
	Do not have a television	2.0	1.0	1.1	0.0

For example, 49.5% of those at Level 4/5 on this scale in Poland watch television 1 to 2 hours per day.

Table C-11b

Proportion of each level who reported various frequencies for watching television each day, document scale

		Level 1	Level 2	Level 3	Level 4/5
				Percentage	
Canada	Not on a daily basis	6.1	7.8	9.3	14.7
	1 hour or less per day	12.4	19.4	27.6	22.2
	1 to 2 hours per day	23.6	29.5	24.5	37.2
	More than 2 hours but less than 5	38.6	35.1	34.3	24.5
	5 or more hours per day	17.4	7.5	3.6	1.3
	Do not have a television	2.0	0.7	0.7	0.1
Germany	Not on a daily basis	1.7	1.9	2.2	3.2
	1 hour or less per day	12.2	13.9	18.1	20.8
	1 to 2 hours per day	25.0	27.3	31.1	36.3
	More than 2 hours but less than 5	45.1	44.3	39.1	32.2
	5 or more hours per day	15.2	12.4	8.8	6.4
	Do not have a television	0.9	0.1	0.6	1.0
Netherlands	Not on a daily basis	3.2	3.3	5.3	7.2
	1 hour or less per day	5.1	12.5	16.3	21.6
	1 to 2 hours per day	22.0	31.1	36.9	35.7
	More than 2 hours but less than 5	52.3	43.4	36.9	32.9
	5 or more hours per day	16.7	7.9	3.6	1.3
	Do not have a television	0.8	1.8	1.0	1.1
Poland	Not on a daily basis	7.8	7.8	11.0	10.9
	1 hour or less per day	11.3	12.5	13.0	11.9
	1 to 2 hours per day	38.8	41.9	45.8	42.4
	More than 2 hours but less than 5	34.9	33.1	26.8	32.3
	5 or more hours per day	6.7	4.6	3.2	1.2
	Do not have a television	0.4	0.1	0.2	1.3
Switzerland (French)	Not on a daily basis	7.2	7.2	15.5	21.3
	1 hour or less per day	17.6	17.1	16.5	14.9
	1 to 2 hours per day	35.9	39.0	38.2	34.5
	More than 2 hours but less than 5	33.4	30.5	20.7	17.8
	5 or more hours per day	4.5	2.4	3.3	1.4
	Do not have a television	1.4	3.9	5.8	10.2
Switzerland (German)	Not on a daily basis	15.1	18.2	24.6	27.3
	1 hour or less per day	20.3	24.6	25.0	30.4
	1 to 2 hours per day	30.7	34.8	30.0	17.2
	More than 2 hours but less than 5	30.1	18.5	14.1	12.5
	5 or more hours per day	2.7	1.2	0.6	0.9
	Do not have a television	1.0	2.7	5.7	11.7
United States	Not on a daily basis	2.2	3.9	4.2	4.7
	1 hour or less per day	18.7	19.1	25.8	34.5
	1 to 2 hours per day	28.0	29.8	32.6	33.5
	More than 2 hours but less than 5	30.9	33.0	30.1	22.8
	5 or more hours per day	18.5	12.9	6.8	3.7
	Do not have a television	1.7	1.3	0.5	0.9

For example, 5.8% of those at Level 3 on this scale in Switzerland (French) do not have a television.

Table C-11c

Proportion of each level who reported various frequencies for watching television each day, quantitative scale

		Level 1	Level 2	Level 3	Level 4/5
			Percentage		
Canada	Not on a daily basis	6.1	7.1	9.8	15.5
	1 hour or less per day	11.8	20.6	23.4	26.8
	1 to 2 hours per day	24.2	26.9	28.2	35.2
	More than 2 hours but less than 5	37.3	38.0	34.0	21.4
	5 or more hours per day	18.9	6.7	3.9	0.8
	Do not have a television	1.6	0.7	0.7	0.3
Germany	Not on a daily basis	1.8	1.5	2.1	3.5
	1 hour or less per day	8.6	13.6	18.0	20.2
	1 to 2 hours per day	27.7	29.5	27.9	36.2
	More than 2 hours but less than 5	43.9	42.4	41.9	33.0
	5 or more hours per day	17.0	12.9	9.7	5.8
	Do not have a television	0.9	0.1	0.4	1.3
Netherlands	Not on a daily basis	2.7	4.7	5.1	6.1
	1 hour or less per day	4.4	13.1	15.1	23.9
	1 to 2 hours per day	21.9	29.2	37.7	36.4
	More than 2 hours but less than 5	52.3	45.5	37.1	29.9
	5 or more hours per day	18.0	5.5	4.2	2.3
	Do not have a television	0.8	2.0	0.8	1.4
Poland	Not on a daily basis	8.5	8.6	9.1	7.0
	1 hour or less per day	10.9	13.1	11.8	14.1
	1 to 2 hours per day	38.3	41.3	44.8	45.8
	More than 2 hours but less than 5	35.2	31.7	31.0	29.5
	5 or more hours per day	6.7	5.2	3.2	2.5
	Do not have a television	0.4	0.1	0.2	1.1
Switzerland (French)	Not on a daily basis	7.1	9.1	14.0	17.8
	1 hour or less per day	14.2	15.9	16.9	17.6
	1 to 2 hours per day	36.1	37.8	36.8	39.3
	More than 2 hours but less than 5	37.0	28.2	24.1	16.5
	5 or more hours per day	3.5	4.4	2.4	1.8
	Do not have a television	1.9	4.6	5.7	7.0
Switzerland (German)	Not on a daily basis	17.5	14.0	24.3	29.1
	1 hour or less per day	22.8	25.5	25.8	24.3
	1 to 2 hours per day	24.5	32.5	29.8	27.3
	More than 2 hours but less than 5	27.5	23.3	14.3	11.0
	5 or more hours per day	4.7	1.4	0.6	0.0
	Do not have a television	3.2	3.4	5.2	8.3
United States	Not on a daily basis	2.1	2.8	3.9	6.3
	1 hour or less per day	18.2	18.1	23.3	37.1
	1 to 2 hours per day	28.8	32.2	31.3	31.2
	More than 2 hours but less than 5	31.4	31.7	31.9	22.7
	5 or more hours per day	17.6	13.5	8.9	2.7
	Do not have a television	1.9	1.7	0.7	0.1

For example, 1.5% of those at Level 2 on this scale in Germany do not watch television on a daily basis.

Table C-12

Proportion of each level who reported participating in community or volunteer activities at least once a month for each scale

		Prose	Document	Quantitative
			Percentage	
Canada	Level 1	10.6	9.0	7.0
	Level 2	15.9	19.7	18.2
	Level 3	24.1	30.5	27.8
	Level 4/5	39.6	28.0	34.7
Germany	Level 1	17.7	19.7	22.4
	Level 2	25.8	23.5	23.7
	Level 3	28.5	27.6	27.6
	Level 4/5	25.2	27.5	24.9
Netherlands	Level 1	24.1	22.3	18.3
	Level 2	28.9	30.9	30.2
	Level 3	33.1	31.1	31.4
	Level 4/5	37.1	38.0	40.3
Poland	Level 1	6.9	6.7	5.6
	Level 2	10.3	10.9	10.8
	Level 3	11.1	9.7	10.9
	Level 4/5	7.4	12.4	11.5
Sweden	Level 1	34.1	28.3	30.3
	Level 2	42.1	43.5	40.7
	Level 3	46.7	46.9	47.6
	Level 4/5	54.3	52.9	53.4
Switzerland (French)	Level 1	10.3	9.4	3.8
	Level 2	21.0	20.6	18.5
	Level 3	22.2	22.3	22.8
	Level 4/5	24.2	23.5	24.8
Switzerland (German)	Level 1	11.6	9.8	6.1
	Level 2	21.9	19.7	20.6
	Level 3	25.9	25.3	24.7
	Level 4/5	36.8	36.1	32.5
United States	Level 1	18.5	20.1	17.2
	Level 2	29.9	27.3	27.6
	Level 3	37.7	42.2	40.1
	Level 4/5	44.4	42.8	44.6

For example, 52.9% of those at Level 4/5 on the document scale in Sweden participate in community or volunteer activities at least once a month.

Table C-13a

Proportion of each level who gave a particular self-assessment of their reading skills in their daily life, prose scale

		Level 1	Level 2	Level 3	Level 4/5
			Percentage		
Canada	Excellent	13.2	47.1	67.2	83.9
	Good	28.3	43.6	29.5	15.8
	Moderate	28.1	7.2	3.1	0.3
	Poor	23.8	2.0	0.1	0.0
	No opinion	6.5	0.1	0.0	0.0
Germany	Excellent	31.6	46.2	61.3	72.5
	Good	49.7	48.9	34.9	26.7
	Moderate	12.2	2.8	3.8	0.8
	Poor	5.0	0.3	0.0	0.0
	No opinion	1.4	1.9	0.0	0.0
Netherlands	Excellent	4.6	13.1	21.5	38.0
	Good	47.8	58.3	64.9	53.2
	Moderate	38.8	27.1	13.2	8.3
	Poor	7.3	1.1	0.1	0.2
	No opinion	1.4	0.4	0.2	0.3
Poland*	Excellent	9.9	22.3	34.3	50.2
	Good	63.9	70.0	61.3	49.8
	Moderate	21.9	7.7	4.4	0.0
	Poor	4.3	0.0	0.0	0.0
Sweden**	Excellent	24.9	33.8	50.7	66.2
	Good	56.3	62.4	48.4	33.7
	Poor	18.8	3.7	0.9	0.1
Switzerland (French)	Excellent	15.8	37.2	60.2	74.8
	Good	44.7	47.1	33.9	21.8
	Moderate	24.1	14.1	5.3	3.4
	Poor	13.5	1.0	0.4	0.0
	No opinion	1.9	0.6	0.2	0.0
Switzerland (German)	Excellent	40.1	71.1	79.7	86.6
	Good	27.2	26.5	19.5	13.4
	Moderate	21.0	2.4	0.8	0.0
	Poor	8.8	0.0	0.0	0.0
	No opinion	2.9	0.0	0.0	0.0
United States	Excellent	14.4	45.6	66.7	79.3
	Good	38.1	46.4	29.9	19.7
	Moderate	18.9	7.1	3.2	1.0
	Poor	26.5	0.6	0.2	0.0
	No opinion	2.1	0.2	0.0	0.0

For example, 2.0% of those at Level 2 on this scale in Canada said they had poor reading skills in their daily life.

*   The no opinion category was not an option on the Polish questionnaire.

**   The no opinion or moderate categories were not options on the Swedish questionnaire.

Table C-13b

Proportion of each level who gave a particular self-assessment of their reading skills in their daily life, document scale

		Level 1	Level 2	Level 3	Level 4/5
			Percentage		
Canada	Excellent	21.9	42.9	68.3	81.5
	Good	26.5	46.2	28.4	17.9
	Moderate	23.9	8.7	3.1	0.6
	Poor	22.0	1.9	0.2	0.0
	No opinion	5.7	0.3	0.0	0.0
Germany	Excellent	33.9	44.5	56.1	72.4
	Good	43.0	49.0	40.6	25.6
	Moderate	13.4	4.3	3.1	2.1
	Poor	6.7	0.5	0.1	0.0
	No opinion	3.0	1.8	0.0	0.0
Netherlands	Excellent	3.9	13.5	21.4	32.2
	Good	49.6	58.2	63.0	57.5
	Moderate	37.1	26.9	15.2	9.8
	Poor	8.0	1.1	0.2	0.1
	No opinion	1.5	0.4	0.2	0.2
Poland*	Excellent	11.9	23.4	30.9	35.6
	Good	64.5	67.4	63.8	60.6
	Moderate	19.6	9.1	5.3	3.7
	Poor	4.0	0.1	0.0	0.0
Sweden**	Excellent	16.3	39.7	49.7	62.7
	Good	65.2	55.5	49.3	36.9
	Poor	18.5	4.7	1.0	0.4
Switzerland (French)	Excellent	19.0	35.2	56.0	69.3
	Good	46.7	46.3	36.0	26.3
	Moderate	19.0	16.4	7.0	4.4
	Poor	14.0	1.2	0.8	0.0
	No opinion	1.4	1.0	0.2	0.0
Switzerland (German)	Excellent	42.8	68.5	78.7	81.7
	Good	25.6	27.1	20.2	18.3
	Moderate	18.8	4.4	1.2	0.0
	Poor	9.6	0.0	0.0	0.0
	No opinion	3.2	0.0	0.0	0.0
United States	Excellent	18.2	50.6	65.7	79.3
	Good	39.7	40.6	32.0	19.5
	Moderate	18.1	7.2	2.0	1.2
	Poor	22.1	1.5	0.2	0.0
	No opinion	1.9	0.1	0.1	0.0

For example, 81.7% of those at Level 4/5 on this scale in Switzerland (German) said they had excellent reading skills in their daily life.

* The no opinion category was not an option on the Polish questionnaire.

** The no opinion or moderate categories were not options on the Swedish questionnaire.

Table C-13c

Proportion of each level who gave a particular self-assessment of their reading skills in their daily life, quantitative scale

		Level 1	Level 2	Level 3	Level 4/5
			Percentage		
Canada	Excellent	22.9	44.4	65.1	84.8
	Good	26.9	45.3	29.7	14.1
	Moderate	22.4	8.7	3.8	1.2
	Poor	21.8	1.3	1.4	0.0
	No opinion	6.0	0.3	0.0	0.0
Germany	Excellent	30.4	45.9	54.4	66.4
	Good	45.4	45.8	42.0	31.2
	Moderate	14.4	5.1	3.3	2.2
	Poor	7.2	0.9	0.1	0.2
	No opinion	2.6	2.3	0.1	0.0
Netherlands	Excellent	4.6	11.1	21.0	35.7
	Good	47.9	60.3	63.4	55.0
	Moderate	36.8	27.5	15.4	8.7
	Poor	8.5	0.7	0.2	0.3
	No opinion	2.2	0.3	0.1	0.2
Poland*	Excellent	11.1	20.7	30.6	34.5
	Good	64.1	68.7	63.1	61.0
	Moderate	20.5	10.1	6.2	4.6
	Poor	4.3	0.5	0.0	0.0
Sweden**	Excellent	23.5	40.0	50.3	60.7
	Good	60.4	55.9	48.4	38.6
	Poor	16.1	4.1	1.3	0.6
Switzerland (French)	Excellent	18.1	35.6	50.8	66.5
	Good	35.4	46.1	40.0	30.0
	Moderate	25.7	15.7	8.8	2.7
	Poor	19.0	1.5	0.3	0.5
	No opinion	1.9	1.2	0.0	0.3
Switzerland (German)	Excellent	37.5	68.2	78.0	76.9
	Good	21.0	27.7	19.8	23.1
	Moderate	23.4	4.2	2.2	0.0
	Poor	13.6	0.0	0.0	0.0
	No opinion	4.5	0.0	0.0	0.0
United States	Excellent	17.1	47.3	65.1	77.5
	Good	38.4	44.7	31.0	20.8
	Moderate	18.5	6.4	3.4	1.8
	Poor	24.0	1.4	0.6	0.0
	No opinion	2.0	0.3	0.0	0.0

For example, 38.4% of those at Level 1 on this scale in the United States said they had good reading skills in their daily life.

*   The no opinion category was not an option on the Polish questionnaire.

**   The no opinion or moderate categories were not options on the Swedish questionnaire.

Table C-14a

Proportion of each level who gave a particular self-assessment of their writing skills in their daily life, prose scale

		Level 1	Level 2	Level 3	Level 4/5
			Percentage		
Canada	Excellent	8.0	35.1	51.7	71.8
	Good	27.0	45.0	38.8	26.1
	Moderate	25.8	12.7	8.5	2.0
	Poor	32.1	7.1	0.9	0.1
	No opinion	7.1	0.1	0.0	0.0
Germany	Excellent	24.7	40.8	54.8	68.9
	Good	50.6	51.5	39.8	28.8
	Moderate	15.2	5.4	5.0	1.9
	Poor	7.4	0.5	0.0	0.0
	No opinion	2.1	1.8	0.4	0.4
Netherlands	Excellent	1.8	10.6	16.4	31.0
	Good	41.8	49.6	61.3	57.9
	Moderate	38.2	33.9	21.2	10.3
	Poor	18.2	5.6	1.0	0.5
	No opinion	0.0	0.2	0.2	0.3
Poland	Excellent	8.2	16.1	26.3	34.0
	Good	60.6	72.2	66.5	63.8
	Moderate	26.2	11.3	7.2	2.3
	Poor	5.0	0.4	0.0	0.0
Sweden	Excellent	18.4	27.1	42.7	56.6
	Good	52.8	63.3	53.5	42.1
	Poor	28.7	9.6	3.9	1.2
Switzerland (French)	Excellent	9.5	25.6	42.3	59.6
	Good	26.2	42.2	43.9	31.2
	Moderate	31.9	22.9	11.1	9.3
	Poor	31.2	9.1	2.5	0.0
	No opinion	1.3	0.3	0.2	0.0
Switzerland (German)	Excellent	35.1	62.6	70.2	78.7
	Good	24.7	28.8	26.6	20.9
	Moderate	21.3	7.8	2.4	0.4
	Poor	16.5	0.8	0.9	0.0
	No opinion	2.5	0.0	0.0	0.0
United States	Excellent	14.4	45.6	66.7	79.3
	Good	38.1	46.4	29.9	19.7
	Moderate	18.9	7.1	3.2	1.0
	Poor	26.5	0.6	0.2	0.0
	No opinion	2.1	0.2	0.0	0.0

*   The no opinion category was not an option on the Polish questionnaire.

**   The no opinion or moderate categories were not options on the Swedish questionnaire.

For example, 72.2% of those at Level 2 on this scale in Poland said they had good writing skills in their daily life.

Table C-14b

Proportion of each level who gave a particular self-assessment of their writing skills in their daily life, document scale

		Level 1	Level 2	Level 3	Level 4/5
		Percentage			
Canada	Excellent	12.8	32.5	54.1	67.9
	Good	30.1	45.7	35.8	29.1
	Moderate	21.6	16.0	7.7	2.6
	Poor	28.8	5.8	2.3	0.4
	No opinion	6.6	0.0	0.0	0.0
Germany	Excellent	31.7	36.8	51.5	65.6
	Good	40.0	53.7	42.6	31.4
	Moderate	16.3	6.4	5.4	2.6
	Poor	8.7	1.2	0.1	0.0
	No opinion	3.2	1.9	0.3	0.4
Netherlands	Excellent	2.2	10.8	16.7	25.0
	Good	41.7	51.0	58.9	59.3
	Moderate	39.2	32.3	22.5	14.5
	Poor	16.8	5.8	1.6	1.0
	No opinion	0.0	0.1	0.3	0.2
Poland*	Excellent	9.7	17.2	23.1	24.7
	Good	62.0	69.6	68.7	68.2
	Moderate	23.7	12.8	8.2	7.1
	Poor	4.7	0.4	0.0	0.0
Sweden**	Excellent	13.8	30.4	42.0	53.6
	Good	56.9	60.2	52.9	45.0
	Poor	29.3	9.5	5.0	1.4
Switzerland (French)	Excellent	13.6	22.9	39.5	53.2
	Good	27.6	41.1	42.9	37.2
	Moderate	26.8	27.6	12.3	8.2
	Poor	30.6	8.1	5.1	1.4
	No opinion	1.4	0.4	0.2	0.0
Switzerland (German)	Excellent	37.6	60.5	68.7	74.3
	Good	23.4	29.3	26.5	24.3
	Moderate	18.3	9.0	4.1	1.4
	Poor	17.9	1.2	0.7	0.0
	No opinion	2.7	0.0	0.0	0.0
United States	Excellent	18.2	50.6	65.7	79.3
	Good	39.7	40.6	32.0	19.5
	Moderate	18.1	7.2	2.0	1.2
	Poor	22.1	1.5	0.2	0.0
	No opinion	1.9	0.1	0.1	0.0

For example, 0.4% of those at Level 4/5 on this scale in Canada said they had poor writing skills in their daily life.

* The no opinion category was not an option on the Polish questionnaire.

** The no opinion or moderate categories were not options on the Swedish questionnaire.

Table C-14c

Proportion of each level who gave a particular self-assessment of their writing skills in their daily life, quantitative scale

		Level 1	Level 2	Level 3	Level 4/5
			Percentage		
Canada	Excellent	11.0	35.0	51.4	71.5
	Good	32.3	43.0	38.3	24.9
	Moderate	20.5	15.0	8.2	3.4
	Poor	29.2	6.9	2.0	0.2
	No opinion	7.0	0.1	0.0	0.0
Germany	Excellent	25.5	41.0	47.4	61.6
	Good	43.3	47.0	46.9	34.8
	Moderate	19.5	7.6	4.9	3.1
	Poor	10.1	1.6	0.3	0.1
	No opinion	1.6	2.8	0.4	0.3
Netherlands	Excellent	2.4	8.8	16.5	27.9
	Good	39.8	52.6	59.8	56.2
	Moderate	41.3	33.2	21.7	14.0
	Poor	16.5	5.0	1.9	1.5
	No opinion	0.0	0.3	0.0	0.5
Poland*	Excellent	8.9	15.5	23.1	23.7
	Good	61.2	69.2	68.3	69.4
	Moderate	24.8	14.6	8.4	6.9
	Poor	5.0	0.7	0.3	0.0
Sweden**	Excellent	19.6	32.3	41.9	51.8
	Good	53.6	59.5	53.5	45.4
	Poor	26.8	8.2	4.6	2.8
Switzerland (French)	Excellent	12.0	23.4	35.9	50.0
	Good	20.3	37.7	44.4	40.1
	Moderate	30.8	27.3	14.6	8.6
	Poor	35.0	11.2	5.1	1.0
	No opinion	1.9	0.4	0.0	0.3
Switzerland (German)	Excellent	30.9	59.4	69.6	68.9
	Good	24.2	30.7	24.4	26.5
	Moderate	17.0	8.8	5.2	3.9
	Poor	24.0	1.0	0.8	0.8
	No opinion	3.9	0.0	0.0	0.0
United States	Excellent	17.1	47.3	65.1	77.5
	Good	38.4	44.7	31.0	20.8
	Moderate	18.5	6.4	3.4	1.8
	Poor	24.0	1.4	0.6	0.0
	No opinion	2.0	0.3	0.0	0.0

* The no opinion category was not an option on the Polish questionnaire.

** The no opinion or moderate categories were not options on the Swedish questionnaire.

For example, 41.3% of those at Level 1 on this scale in the Netherlands said they had moderate writing skills in their daily life.

Table C-15a

Proportion of each level who gave a particular self-assessment of their numeracy skills in their daily life, prose scale

		Level 1	Level 2	Level 3	Level 4/5
			Percentage		
Canada	Excellent	18.9	38.0	51.2	59.8
	Good	37.7	44.1	38.6	31.3
	Moderate	23.1	12.7	9.3	8.7
	Poor	13.5	5.2	0.9	0.2
	No opinion	6.7	0.1	0.0	0.0
Germany	Excellent	25.8	31.1	46.5	58.8
	Good	51.8	59.3	48.7	37.7
	Moderate	18.6	8.9	4.7	3.5
	Poor	3.8	0.7	0.1	0.0
Netherlands	Excellent	3.8	13.3	18.6	29.6
	Good	49.0	57.6	59.3	57.4
	Moderate	34.4	25.7	20.1	12.0
	Poor	12.9	3.3	2.0	0.8
	No opinion	0.0	0.1	0.0	0.3
Poland*	Excellent	8.4	19.2	26.5	43.3
	Good	63.1	69.8	65.6	56.7
	Moderate	23.6	10.1	7.8	0.0
	Poor	4.8	0.9	0.2	0.0
Sweden**	Excellent	27.6	32.8	49.4	60.6
	Good	60.4	62.5	48.2	38.1
	Poor	12.0	4.7	2.4	1.3
Switzerland (French)	Excellent	19.6	32.6	49.1	64.1
	Good	40.0	47.0	44.0	26.1
	Moderate	33.0	17.9	6.0	8.2
	Poor	6.1	2.5	0.9	1.6
	No opinion	1.3	0.0	0.0	0.0
Switzerland (German)	Excellent	43.2	59.6	70.8	81.3
	Good	34.1	33.6	24.5	14.2
	Moderate	16.0	6.2	4.2	4.5
	Poor	3.9	0.2	0.5	0.0
	No opinion	2.7	0.3	0.0	0.0
United States	Excellent	14.4	45.7	66.7	79.3
	Good	38.1	46.3	29.9	19.7
	Moderate	18.9	7.1	3.2	1.0
	Poor	26.5	0.6	0.2	0.0
	No opinion	2.1	0.2	0.0	0.0

For example, 59.3% of those at Level 2 on this scale in Germany said they had good numeracy skills in their daily life.

*   The no opinion category was not an option on the Polish questionnaire.

**   The no opinion or moderate categories were not options on the Swedish questionnaire.

Table C-15b

Proportion of each level who gave a particular self-assessment of their numeracy skills in their daily life, document scale

		Level 1	Level 2	Level 3	Level 4/5
			Percentage		
Canada	Excellent	17.3	33.7	52.4	64.3
	Good	40.1	48.1	34.2	32.2
	Moderate	21.4	13.7	13.0	3.4
	Poor	14.9	4.4	0.4	0.0
	No opinion	6.3	0.0	0.0	0.0
Germany	Excellent	26.7	30.1	43.4	56.0
	Good	45.2	58.9	51.2	41.0
	Moderate	21.7	10.5	5.3	2.8
	Poor	6.4	0.5	0.2	0.2
Netherlands	Excellent	3.0	11.4	18.2	29.4
	Good	44.7	57.1	60.0	58.6
	Moderate	40.3	27.3	19.7	11.1
	Poor	12.0	4.2	2.0	0.8
	No opinion	0.0	0.0	0.1	0.2
Poland*	Excellent	9.7	18.0	25.5	38.5
	Good	63.6	69.9	66.6	57.4
	Moderate	22.1	11.4	7.7	3.0
	Poor	4.6	0.8	0.1	1.1
Sweden**	Excellent	17.7	32.9	46.8	62.6
	Good	67.8	62.9	50.1	36.4
	Poor	14.5	4.2	3.1	1.0
Switzerland (French)	Excellent	19.9	31.5	46.6	58.5
	Good	41.8	45.3	43.6	35.9
	Moderate	30.8	20.2	8.9	4.3
	Poor	6.1	3.0	1.0	1.3
	No opinion	1.4	0.0	0.0	0.0
Switzerland (German)	Excellent	43.3	57.5	71.1	73.1
	Good	30.1	35.0	24.9	23.1
	Moderate	19.2	6.7	3.6	3.8
	Poor	3.5	0.7	0.4	0.0
	No opinion	3.8	0.0	0.0	0.0
United States	Excellent	18.2	50.6	65.8	79.3
	Good	39.7	40.6	31.9	19.5
	Moderate	18.1	7.2	2.0	1.2
	Poor	22.1	1.5	0.2	0.0
	No opinion	1.9	0.1	0.1	0.0

For example, 8.9% of those at Level 3 on this scale in Switzerland (French) said they had moderate numeracy skills in their daily life.

*   The no opinion category was not an option on the Polish questionnaire.

**   The no opinion or moderate categories were not options on the Swedish questionnaire.

Table C-15c

Proportion of each level who gave a particular self-assessment of their numeracy skills in their daily life, quantitative scale

		Level 1	Level 2	Level 3	Level 4/5
			Percentage		
Canada	Excellent	17.9	31.2	52.9	66.9
	Good	38.1	46.6	39.5	26.4
	Moderate	21.7	18.0	7.1	6.7
	Poor	15.7	4.2	0.6	0.0
	No opinion	6.6	0.0	0.0	0.0
Germany	Excellent	20.1	31.5	39.7	55.7
	Good	47.3	55.0	54.8	41.5
	Moderate	24.7	13.2	5.1	2.7
	Poor	7.9	0.3	0.4	0.1
Netherlands	Excellent	3.3	7.7	18.4	33.5
	Good	37.9	57.4	61.2	59.0
	Moderate	43.3	30.2	19.0	7.3
	Poor	15.5	4.7	1.3	0.0
	No opinion	0.0	0.0	0.1	0.2
Poland*	Excellent	8.5	17.0	24.1	37.5
	Good	62.3	70.1	67.9	58.3
	Moderate	24.1	11.9	7.6	3.7
	Poor	5.1	1.0	0.4	0.5
Sweden**	Excellent	18.7	32.5	46.5	63.1
	Good	65.1	61.7	51.5	36.1
	Poor	16.2	5.8	2.1	0.8
Switzerland (French)	Excellent	18.1	27.6	44.7	57.7
	Good	31.5	47.6	43.9	39.3
	Moderate	39.5	21.9	10.0	2.7
	Poor	9.0	2.9	1.4	0.2
	No opinion	1.9	0.0	0.0	0.0
Switzerland (German)	Excellent	39.2	53.5	68.8	77.7
	Good	34.4	36.1	25.8	20.4
	Moderate	18.6	9.4	4.9	1.2
	Poor	3.6	0.6	0.5	0.7
	No opinion	4.2	0.4	0.0	0.0
United States	Excellent	17.1	47.3	65.2	77.5
	Good	38.4	44.7	30.9	20.8
	Moderate	18.5	6.4	3.4	1.8
	Poor	24.0	1.4	0.6	0.0
	No opinion	2.0	0.3	0.0	0.0

*   The no opinion category was not an option on the Polish questionnaire.

**   The no opinion or moderate categories were not options on the Swedish questionnaire.

For example, 20.8% of those at Level 4/5 on this scale in the United States said they had good numeracy skills in their daily life.

MAIN SALES OUTLETS OF OECD PUBLICATIONS
PRINCIPAUX POINTS DE VENTE DES PUBLICATIONS DE L'OCDE

ARGENTINA – ARGENTINE
Carlos Hirsch S.R.L.
Galería Güemes, Florida 165, 4° Piso
1333 Buenos Aires   Tel. (1) 331.1787 y 331.2391
Telefax: (1) 331.1787

AUSTRALIA – AUSTRALIE
D.A. Information Services
648 Whitehorse Road, P.O.B 163
Mitcham, Victoria 3132   Tel. (03) 9873.4411
Telefax: (03) 9873.5679

AUSTRIA – AUTRICHE
Gerold & Co.
Graben 31
Wien I   Tel. (0222) 533.50.14
Telefax: (0222) 512.47.31.29

BELGIUM – BELGIQUE
Jean De Lannoy
Avenue du Roi 202 Koningslaan
B-1060 Bruxelles   Tel. (02) 538.51.69/538.08.41
Telefax: (02) 538.08.41

CANADA
Renouf Publishing Company Ltd.
1294 Algoma Road
Ottawa, ON K1B 3W8   Tel. (613) 741.4333
Telefax: (613) 741.5439
Stores:
61 Sparks Street
Ottawa, ON K1P 5R1   Tel. (613) 238.8985
211 Yonge Street
Toronto, ON M5B 1M4   Tel. (416) 363.3171
Telefax: (416)363.59.63

Les Éditions La Liberté Inc.
3020 Chemin Sainte-Foy
Sainte-Foy, PQ G1X 3V6   Tel. (418) 658.3763
Telefax: (418) 658.3763

Federal Publications Inc.
165 University Avenue, Suite 701
Toronto, ON M5H 3B8   Tel. (416) 860.1611
Telefax: (416) 860.1608

Les Publications Fédérales
1185 Université
Montréal, QC H3B 3A7   Tel. (514) 954.1633
Telefax: (514) 954.1635

CHINA – CHINE
China National Publications Import
Export Corporation (CNPIEC)
16 Gongti E. Road, Chaoyang District
P.O. Box 88 or 50
Beijing 100704 PR   Tel. (01) 506.6688
Telefax: (01) 506.3101

CHINESE TAIPEI – TAIPEI CHINOIS
Good Faith Worldwide Int'l. Co. Ltd.
9th Floor, No. 118, Sec. 2
Chung Hsiao E. Road
Taipei   Tel. (02) 391.7396/391.7397
Telefax: (02) 394.9176

CZECH REPUBLIC – RÉPUBLIQUE TCHÈQUE
Artia Pegas Press Ltd.
Narodni Trida 25
POB 825
111 21 Praha 1   Tel. (2) 2 46 04
Telefax: (2) 2 78 72

DENMARK – DANEMARK
Munksgaard Book and Subscription Service
35, Nørre Søgade, P.O. Box 2148
DK-1016 København K   Tel. (33) 12.85.70
Telefax: (33) 12.93.87

EGYPT – ÉGYPTE
Middle East Observer
41 Sherif Street
Cairo   Tel. 392.6919
Telefax: 360-6804

FINLAND – FINLANDE
Akateeminen Kirjakauppa
Keskuskatu 1, P.O. Box 128
00100 Helsinki
Subscription Services/Agence d'abonnements :
P.O. Box 23
00371 Helsinki   Tel. (358 0) 121 4416
Telefax: (358 0) 121.4450

FRANCE
OECD/OCDE
Mail Orders/Commandes par correspondance:
2, rue André-Pascal
75775 Paris Cedex 16   Tel. (33-1) 45.24.82.00
Telefax: (33-1) 49.10.42.76
Telex: 640048 OCDE
Internet: Compte.PUBSINQ @ oecd.org

Orders via Minitel, France only/
Commandes par Minitel, France exclusivement :
36 15 OCDE

OECD Bookshop/Librairie de l'OCDE :
33, rue Octave-Feuillet
75016 Paris   Tel. (33-1) 45.24.81.81
(33-1) 45.24.81.67
Dawson
B.P. 40
91121 Palaiseau Cedex   Tel. 69.10.47.00
Telefax : 64.54.83.26

Documentation Française
29, quai Voltaire
75007 Paris   Tel. 40.15.70.00

Economica
49 rue Héricart
75015 Paris   Tel. 45.78.12.92
Telefax : 40.58.15.70

Gibert Jeune (Droit-Économie)
6, place Saint-Michel
75006 Paris   Tel. 43.25.91.19

Librairie du Commerce International
10, avenue d'Iéna
75016 Paris   Tel. 40.73.34.60

Librairie Dunod
Université Paris-Dauphine
Place du Maréchal de Lattre de Tassigny
75016 Paris   Tel. 44.05.40.13

Librairie Lavoisier
11, rue Lavoisier
75008 Paris   Tel. 42.65.39.95

Librairie des Sciences Politiques
30, rue Saint-Guillaume
75007 Paris   Tel. 45.48.36.02

P.U.F.
49, boulevard Saint-Michel
75005 Paris   Tel. 43.25.83.40

Librairie de l'Université
12a, rue Nazareth
13100 Aix-en-Provence   Tel. (16) 42.26.18.08

Documentation Française
165, rue Garibaldi
69003 Lyon   Tel. (16) 78.63.32.23

Librairie Decitre
29, place Bellecour
69002 Lyon   Tel. (16) 72.40.54.54

Librairie Sauramps
Le Triangle
34967 Montpellier Cedex 2   Tel. (16) 67.58.85.15
Tekefax: (16) 67.58.27.36

A la Sorbonne Actual
23 rue de l'Hôtel des Postes
06000 Nice   Tel. (16) 93.13.77.75
Telefax: (16) 93.80.75.69

GERMANY – ALLEMAGNE
OECD Publications and Information Centre
August-Bebel-Allee 6
D-53175 Bonn   Tel. (0228) 959.120
Telefax: (0228) 959.12.17

GREECE – GRÈCE
Librairie Kauffmann
Mavrokordatou 9
106 78 Athens   Tel. (01) 32.55.321
Telefax: (01) 32.30.320

HONG-KONG
Swindon Book Co. Ltd.
Astoria Bldg. 3F
34 Ashley Road, Tsimshatsui
Kowloon, Hong Kong   Tel. 2376.2062
Telefax: 2376.0685

HUNGARY – HONGRIE
Euro Info Service
Margitsziget, Európa Ház
1138 Budapest   Tel. (1) 111.62.16
Telefax: (1) 111.60.61

ICELAND – ISLANDE
Mál Mog Menning
Laugavegi 18, Pósthólf 392
121 Reykjavik   Tel. (1) 552.4240
Telefax: (1) 562.3523

INDIA – INDE
Oxford Book and Stationery Co.
Scindia House
New Delhi 110001   Tel. (11) 331.5896/5308
Telefax: (11) 332.5993
17 Park Street
Calcutta 700016   Tel. 240832

INDONESIA – INDONÉSIE
Pdii-Lipi
P.O. Box 4298
Jakarta 12042   Tel. (21) 573.34.67
Telefax: (21) 573.34.67

IRELAND – IRLANDE
Government Supplies Agency
Publications Section
4/5 Harcourt Road
Dublin 2   Tel. 661.31.11
Telefax: 475.27.60

ISRAEL
Praedicta
5 Shatner Street
P.O. Box 34030
Jerusalem 91430   Tel. (2) 52.84.90/1/2
Telefax: (2) 52.84.93

R.O.Y. International
P.O. Box 13056
Tel Aviv 61130   Tel. (3) 546 1423
Telefax: (3) 546 1442

Palestinian Authority/Middle East:
INDEX Information Services
P.O.B. 19502
Jerusalem   Tel. (2) 27.12.19
Telefax: (2) 27.16.34

ITALY – ITALIE
Libreria Commissionaria Sansoni
Via Duca di Calabria 1/1
50125 Firenze   Tel. (055) 64.54.15
Telefax: (055) 64.12.57
Via Bartolini 29
20155 Milano   Tel. (02) 36.50.83

Editrice e Libreria Herder
Piazza Montecitorio 120
00186 Roma   Tel. 679.46.28
Telefax: 678.47.51

Libreria Hoepli
Via Hoepli 5
20121 Milano   Tel. (02) 86.54.46
                      Telefax: (02) 805.28.86

Libreria Scientifica
Dott. Lucio de Biasio 'Aeiou'
Via Coronelli, 6
20146 Milano   Tel. (02) 48.95.45.52
                      Telefax: (02) 48.95.45.48

JAPAN – JAPON
OECD Publications and Information Centre
Landic Akasaka Building
2-3-4 Akasaka, Minato-ku
Tokyo 107   Tel. (81.3) 3586.2016
                      Telefax: (81.3) 3584.7929

KOREA – CORÉE
Kyobo Book Centre Co. Ltd.
P.O. Box 1658, Kwang Hwa Moon
Seoul   Tel. 730.78.91
                      Telefax: 735.00.30

MALAYSIA – MALAISIE
University of Malaya Bookshop
University of Malaya
P.O. Box 1127, Jalan Pantai Baru
59700 Kuala Lumpur
Malaysia   Tel. 756.5000/756.5425
                      Telefax: 756.3246

MEXICO – MEXIQUE
OECD Publications and Information Centre
Edificio INFOTEC
Av. San Fernando no. 37
Col. Toriello Guerra
Tlalpan C.P. 14050
Mexico D.F.
          Tel. (525) 606 00 11 Extension 100
                      Fax : (525) 606 13 07

Revistas y Periodicos Internacionales S.A. de C.V.
Florencia 57 - 1004
Mexico, D.F. 06600   Tel. 207.81.00
                      Telefax: 208.39.79

NETHERLANDS – PAYS-BAS
SDU Uitgeverij Plantijnstraat
Externe Fondsen
Postbus 20014
2500 EA's-Gravenhage Tel. (070) 37.89.880
Voor bestellingen: Telefax: (070) 34.75.778

NEW ZEALAND
NOUVELLE-ZÉLANDE
GPLegislation Services
P.O. Box 12418
Thorndon, Wellington Tel. (04) 496.5655
                      Telefax: (04) 496.5698

NORWAY – NORVÈGE
Narvesen Info Center – NIC
Bertrand Narvesens vei 2
P.O. Box 6125 Etterstad
0602 Oslo 6   Tel. (022) 57.33.00
                      Telefax: (022) 68.19.01

PAKISTAN
Mirza Book Agency
65 Shahrah Quaid-E-Azam
Lahore 54000   Tel. (42) 353.601
                      Telefax: (42) 231.730

PHILIPPINE – PHILIPPINES
International Booksource Center Inc.
Rm 179/920 Cityland 10 Condo Tower 2
HV dela Costa Ext cor Valero St.
Makati Metro Manila   Tel. (632) 817 9676
                      Telefax : (632) 817 1741

POLAND – POLOGNE
Ars Polona
00-950 Warszawa
Krakowskie Przedmieácie 7   Tel. (22) 264760
                      Telefax : (22) 268673

PORTUGAL
Livraria Portugal
Rua do Carmo 70-74
Apart. 2681
1200 Lisboa   Tel. (01) 347.49.82/5
                      Telefax: (01) 347.02.64

SINGAPORE – SINGAPOUR
Gower Asia Pacific Pte Ltd.
Golden Wheel Building
41, Kallang Pudding Road, No. 04-03
Singapore 1334   Tel. 741.5166
                      Telefax: 742.9356

SPAIN – ESPAGNE
Mundi-Prensa Libros S.A.
Castelló 37, Apartado 1223
Madrid 28001   Tel. (91) 431.33.99
                      Telefax: (91) 575.39.98

Mundi-Prensa Barcelona
Consell de Cent No. 391
08009 – Barcelona   Tel. (93) 488.34.92
                      Telefax: (93) 487.76.59

Llibreria de la Generalitat
Palau Moja
Rambla dels Estudis, 118
08002 – Barcelona
          (Subscripcions) Tel. (93) 318.80.12
          (Publicacions) Tel. (93) 302.67.23
                      Telefax: (93) 412.18.54

SRI LANKA
Centre for Policy Research
c/o Colombo Agencies Ltd.
No. 300-304, Galle Road
Colombo 3   Tel. (1) 574240, 573551-2
                      Telefax: (1) 575394, 510711

SWEDEN – SUÈDE
CE Fritzes AB
S–106 47 Stockholm   Tel. (08) 690.90.90
                      Telefax: (08) 20.50.21

Subscription Agency/Agence d'abonnements :
Wennergren-Williams Info AB
P.O. Box 1305
171 25 Solna   Tel. (08) 705.97.50
                      Telefax: (08) 27.00.71

SWITZERLAND – SUISSE
Maditec S.A. (Books and Periodicals - Livres
et périodiques)
Chemin des Palettes 4
Case postale 266
1020 Renens VD 1   Tel. (021) 635.08.65
                      Telefax: (021) 635.07.80

Librairie Payot S.A.
4, place Pépinet
CP 3212
1002 Lausanne   Tel. (021) 320.25.11
                      Telefax: (021) 320.25.14

Librairie Unilivres
6, rue de Candolle
1205 Genève   Tel. (022) 320.26.23
                      Telefax: (022) 329.73.18

Subscription Agency/Agence d'abonnements :
Dynapresse Marketing S.A.
38 avenue Vibert
1227 Carouge   Tel. (022) 308.07.89
                      Telefax: (022) 308.07.99

See also – Voir aussi :
OECD Publications and Information Centre
August-Bebel-Allee 6
D-53175 Bonn (Germany)   Tel. (0228) 959.120
                      Telefax: (0228) 959.12.17

THAILAND – THAÏLANDE
Suksit Siam Co. Ltd.
113, 115 Fuang Nakhon Rd.
Opp. Wat Rajbopith
Bangkok 10200   Tel. (662) 225.9531/2
                      Telefax: (662) 222.5188

TURKEY – TURQUIE
Kültür Yayinlari Is-Türk Ltd. Sti.
Atatürk Bulvari No. 191/Kat 13
Kavaklidere/Ankara   Tel. 428.11.40 Ext. 2458
Dolmabahce Cad. No. 29
Besiktas/Istanbul   Tel. (312) 260 7188
                      Telex: (312) 418 29 46

UNITED KINGDOM – ROYAUME-UNI
HMSO
Gen. enquiries   Tel. (171) 873 8496
Postal orders only:
P.O. Box 276, London SW8 5DT
Personal Callers HMSO Bookshop
49 High Holborn, London WC1V 6HB
                      Telefax: (171) 873 8416
Branches at: Belfast, Birmingham, Bristol,
Edinburgh, Manchester

UNITED STATES – ÉTATS-UNIS
OECD Publications and Information Center
2001 L Street N.W., Suite 650
Washington, D.C. 20036-4910 Tel. (202) 785.6323
                      Telefax: (202) 785.0350

VENEZUELA
Libreria del Este
Avda F. Miranda 52, Aptdo. 60337
Edificio Galipán
Caracas 106   Tel. 951.1705/951.2307/951.1297
                      Telegram: Libreste Caracas

Subscriptions to OECD periodicals may also be
placed through main subscription agencies.

Les abonnements aux publications périodiques de
l'OCDE peuvent être souscrits auprès des
principales agences d'abonnement.

Orders and inquiries from countries where Distribu-
tors have not yet been appointed should be sent to:
OECD Publications Service, 2 rue André-Pascal,
75775 Paris Cedex 16, France.

Les commandes provenant de pays où l'OCDE n'a
pas encore désigné de distributeur peuvent être
adressées à : OCDE, Service des Publications,
2, rue André-Pascal, 75775 Paris Cedex 16, France.

10-1995

STATISTICS CANADA

Data in many forms...

Statistics Canada disseminates data in a variety of forms. In addition to publications, both standard and special tabulations are offered. Data are available on compact disc, diskette, computer print-out, magnetic tape, microfiche and microfilm. Maps and other geographic reference materials are available for some types of data. Direct online access to aggregated information is possible through CANSIM, Statistics Canada's machine-readable database and retrieval system.

How to obtain more information

Inquiries about this publication and related statistics or services should be directed to:

Special Surveys Division
Statistics Canada
Ottawa, K1A 0T6
Telephone: 1-613-951-9476

Or to the Statistics Canada Regional Reference Centre in:

Halifax	1-902-426-5331	Regina	1-306-780-5405
Montréal	1-514-283-5725	Edmonton	1-403-495-3027
Ottawa	1-613-951-8116	Calgary	1-403-292-6717
Toronto	1-416-973-6586	Vancouver	1-604-666-3691
Winnipeg	1-204-983-4020		

Toll-free access is provided in all provinces and territories, **for users who reside outside the local dialing area** of any of the Regional Reference Centres.

National enquiries line	1-800-263-1136
National telecommunications device for the hearing impaired	1-800-363-7629
National toll-free, order-only line (Canada and United States)	1-800-267-6677

How to order publications

This and other Statistics Canada publications may be purchased from local authorized agents and other community bookstores, through local Statistics Canada offices, or by mail order to Statistics Canada, Operations and Integration Division, Circulation Management, 120 Parkdale Ave., Ottawa, Ontario, K1A 0T6.

Telephone: 1-613-951-7277
Facsimile: 1-613-951-1584
Toronto, credit card only: 1-416-973-8018

Standards of service to the public

To maintain quality service to the public, Statistics Canada follows established standards covering statistical products and services, delivery of statistical information, cost-recovered services and services to respondents. To obtain a copy of these service standards, please contact your nearest Statistics Canada Regional Reference Centre.

Statistics Canada
PRINTED IN CANADA
Catalogue 89-545E
ISBN 92-64-14655-5